The Little Russians:

An Ailing Father's Letters to his Children

The Little Russians:

An Ailing Father's Letters to his Children

William F. Jack

ISBN 978-0-557-44579-0

This book is dedicated to all those friends, relatives, and colleagues who helped bring you three children to the United States and to your new lives, filled with opportunity.

Preface

To the Kids

This is your story and my story, our story. To protect the privacy of you children, I changed your names. I bet you will have no trouble figuring out who is who. To protect the privacy of your Mother, my former wife, I changed her name to 'Rose,' and I have deleted as many references to her and her family as possible, for legal reasons not of my choosing. This I regret. I could have written some truly wonderful things about them, but I don't like people yelling at me or suing me.

Your Mother does not want me to publish this. Her motives are good ones. She wants things to 'unfold' for you, naturally, on their own, at their chosen speed. You would learn about your adoption, your early lives, your adoptive Father and his life – All of this in bits and pieces, over the years, with your Mother and your Father answering your questions, as they arise – a natural flow of things.

Fine.

But when I look into the mirror, I see a frail man, sixty-four years old, who's had six major surgeries, a mended heart, and who had to retire on disability two years ago because of a breathing problem that will not go away.

One of my sisters and three of my younger brothers have died, all of them under fifty years of age.

So I can hang around and answer your questions, bit-by-bit?

Not a good bet. "Don't buy any green bananas," is what my Grandfather would have said.

I want you to learn about me, about yourselves, when I am gone, by reading <u>my</u> own words, unfiltered.

Your Mother and I come from completely different backgrounds, from different layers of society. I want you to know about my background, my layer. I would not work to get this published if I thought it would do you harm.

I recall when Anna started kindergarten, barely a month after she came to this country. The local paper did a full-page spread, with big photos, on her first day at school. Anna basked in her glory and so did her Brother and Sister.

You three have watched me sitting in my trailer kitchen and typing and typing and typing and editing and editing and editing. You have read parts of the manuscript, and you, without exception, have been extremely interested in all this. "Would other people really want to read about us?"

Yes. "You betcha," as they often say in Minnesota

I may be gone, dearest Alex, by the time you finish college. Please follow though on the plans you have now, and become a police officer and a firefighter and an astronaut and a builder and general helper of people. I would be in my late eighties then, if I was still around, and probably would have forgotten even my own name.

Anna and Katya – You excel in all that you try, and you conceal your planned careers. Do well, and be well and succeed in all things.

All of you. Remember some of the things your Father told you.

How long will I hang around to answer your questions, 'as they arise?' For how many years will I be lucid? How much will I remember?

Memory disintegrates in old age. One day, you just sit slumped in your wheelchair all drugged up in the hallway of the Veterans' Home, your head hanging sideways, stains on your moth-eaten cardigan sweater, and you wonder who has chunks of food all over their pajama bottoms, and it's you.

Please catch what you can from these letters. Thank you.

Love,

Your Papa

Notes

You already know that I have changed your names and the name of your Mother, my former wife. A good idea. I have also changed the names of most of the other characters in this book too. Some people don't like to be talked about or written about. I know that if someone was writing bad things about me, I would be glad if they changed my name. But the people remain who they are or who they were, just wearing different name tags.

I have been extra-careful with the identities of Russians. Perhaps this is a hold-over from Cold War days. I have been especially vague about my Russian fiancee. Not having seen her for forty years, I wonder where she is and what she is doing, and I fear that my mentioning her by name could bring harm to her. Forget about the wide pendulum swings of Russian-American relations, for a moment. What if she lives with her husband and their two children? Perhaps she's a grandmother and a widow and she lives with a son or daughter. Maybe it wouldn't be good for others to know that she, in her youth, was once engaged to a weird American exchange student.

To conceal her identity further, I have changed her profession. Yes, she worked as an artist in an art-related endeavor, and she was highly regarded. Revealing her profession and place would make it easy to identify her. So I have changed her profession. She, who, as far as I know, never played the violin, is now a violinist in the Leningrad Civic Orchestra, an organization that I made up.

Writers of memoirs are sometimes criticized for creating "composite" characters, meaning that their characters aren't 'real' in any 'real' sense, but that they are somehow typical anyway, combining the traits of many to form a perfectly typical individual.

With me, what you read is what you get. The characters are or were all real, albeit with different name tags. I admit not to creating a composite character, but to distilling several meetings with one character into two meetings. This 'non-composite' character is the Russian literature professor at Leningrad State University.

I stand by my words. I describe things as I *remember* them (hence, I suppose, the word 'memoir').

Be forewarned. This is not an historical text. I didn't spend years locked up in a library microfiche room, zipping through dim white-on-black slides containing pagers of primary and secondary sources, and then interviewing hundreds of witnesses. I am writing what I remember.

I hope that my memory, and my memoir, will hurt no one or distort anything.

You will learn later, children, about my hidden agenda.

Dearest Alex, Katya, Anna:

Your lives are unusual; there's no doubt about that. Adopting three children all at once rarely happens.

Further, your new Father is twice as old as your Mother

I hope I can give you a sense of what your Father was all about, and how and why, decades before you were born, he had become so enchanted by Sankt Peterburg, your native city.

You have asked often about my childhood, sometimes out of real curiosity, sometimes just to see if I adhered to the same standards to which I hold you. (Answer: Hardly ever.)

This may be my only chance to tell you.

Dear Alex, Anna, and Katya:

Why did you come to us, to me?

It had taken me a lifetime, but I had finally reached some goals that others often reach in their twenties. I was happily married. We had a beautiful home. I had a profession and a job that I loved. I had a car that ran. It was now time for the biggest and best job of all – raising children.

I found out in 2003 that I couldn't have children of my own. The specialist, whom I didn't really like very much, said that there was a problem with my 'software.' He made that awful, overly-used two-handed 'quotation mark' gesture when he leaned back in his chair and said 'software.' What did he mean? Was it my age (fifty-eight or so then)? Was it because of a certain unmentionable surgery I had in 2000? (Oh, alright. It was prostate surgery. Who cares?). Or, did I just lack a sufficient number of competently-swimming microscopic critters?

We decided to adopt, and one thing was certain for me: There was no question that the adopted kids would come from Sankt Peterburg. This desire was too strong to ignore, despite all the rumors and reports about how polluted the city was – ground, air, and water, everything else being alright. Read on, and you will find out why it had to be Sankt Peterburg.

That city has served as a perfect backdrop for the novels that Dostoevsky wrote in the late 1870s. Take the city out of his novels, and they would have been less because of it.

The same goes for Nikolai Gogol, whose stories were filled with references to cold, smog, smoke, and other unhealthy conditions. Move the setting of his works to a different place, and his stories would be less funny and less believable and less valued.

Not to mention poetry. Peterburg was a central theme running through the poems of Mandelstam and Akhmatova and Zabolotsky.

Sometimes it feels like the city is a major character in a work, and sometimes it is. Your native city has been a major character in my life.

So, then, I, who had been a literary specialist at one time, insisted on Sankt Peterburg. I wanted my children to come from that eerie, captivating place. Luckily, your adoptive Mother did not object.

But, how many problems had there been with other Americans trying to adopt from Russia? And how many times did the adopted children exhibit extreme behavioral problems later, after their adoptions? The Russian press invariably reports each incident when a Russian orphan adopted in America has been murdered or put into child slavery, or dumped onto a plane for an unescorted trip back to Russia.

It is truly disgusting, and Russia has the right to publish it. Some Americans have gotten defensive. They claim that Russia was 'dumping' its 'inferior' children in the adoption market, keeping the good ones to itself. (You proved them wrong.) China or Guatemala would have been easier choices for adopting, but neither of those countries has a Sankt Peterburg.

I hunted around for a local agency that had connections with any orphanage in Sankt Peterburg, and I found one. Your adoption took barely ten months. It was a record, I think, for wading through those oceans of Russian and American paperwork.

A few weeks after we signed up, the adoption lady mailed us a few photos of available orphans. I recall some cute young girls, but nothing 'clicked' in me, or, I suspect, in Rose.

Then the adoption lady sent us a VHS tape, a short video of three captivating kids, with the devil in their eyes, in a Sankt Peterburg orphanage. Watching you three in action, moving around, I knew you had to be the ones.

We were lucky, with that VHS tape. Receiving it was a surprise because, generally, because I had read that prospective adoptive parents don't get to see even a photograph of the targeted orphans until <u>after</u> they have signed up for their adoptions.

On that particular tape, one child was a toddler – a little boy barely able to walk. The thick diaper wrapped between his legs didn't help. His lower lip showed that he was pouting, probably because he was being deprived of the breakfast that the other kids in the background seemed to be enjoying so much.

Next came a round-faced little girl with a high forehead and a wide smile. As the camera approached, she was busy eating her bowl of kasha with a spoon that was bigger than her mouth – a spoon bigger than what we call a 'table spoon' here in the United States. With her free hand, she tried to shoo away the camera person and the person holding the 9,000-watt floodlights that no doubt were used for the filming.

Last on the film came an attractive young lady, about four years old, with an utterly dour expression. She was sitting at the breakfast table, glaring at the camera, and tapping impatiently on the edge of a piece of toast that she held, while the other children talked and ate their breakfasts happily. The tables were long and low, the chairs tiny.

Then there was a splice in the film and in the next segment, this toast-tapping young lady was shown standing alone in a different room and holding a "Sesame Street" Elmo. The girl then was almost smiling, or trying to smile, perhaps after being ordered to look pleasant, or else.

I was absolutely intrigued by all of you. Each of you appeared so different, and yet, like siblings, you seemed alike too. I watched that video so many times, and discussed and analyzed it so often – After a while, it was like watching old friends.

To me, there was something very un-child-like about you three.

I wanted to meet you, citizens of Peterburg. I wanted your personalities and characters and spirit to unfold before me. They were already there, for sure. It was just a matter of discerning them as they unfolded. I wanted to visit you and your city. The days and months passed slowly.

Dear Kids:

In the spring of 2004, we planned a brunch where people could come and donate money for the expenses connected with your adoption. I don't recall the exact count of either the money collected or the number of attendees, but both were formidable.

And the money was much-needed. There were adoption fees and agency fees and barely-concealed bribes to the right people, and two trips to Russia. Rose and I needed to stay in Peterburg for a couple weeks, considering both trips. We had to do all this while we were not working, of course, and not collecting our salaries.

Your maternal grandparents helped in numberless ways.

Bless bless bless all of those who contributed. Bless Reverend John Snider and his wife, Polly, who had been my office mate in a law firm for years. John gave us use of his church's spacious hall for our brunch. Bless all who helped with money. We owe them much gratitude.

Kids, there is a great number of people who helped you come to America.

Be grateful.

Perhaps the best gift you can give them in return is for all three of you to turn out well.

Dear Anna, Katya, Alex:

June came.

I prepared for the trip. What would Sankt Peterburg be like, I wondered. What kind of damage or what degree of progress had it made in the four years since I had been there?

My previous trip there, in 2000, had not left me with a good image of your city. I thought I was done with it, but it was not done with me.

Peterburg was not the same city as Leningrad, and yet the two somehow remained the same. I had been to Leningrad about twenty times, and some bad things had happened to me there. But I never lost that queer combination of love and loathing for that city, no matter what it was called. There is no other place like it. Sometimes I think that it is the one place in the world most unlike any other place.

At times, it seemed to have less to do with Russia than with the West. Read on.

Dear Kids/Young Adults:

Good for you that you don't recall all the hours that we spent together in the orphanage play areas. Never mind the weather – whether raining or sunny, warm or cold, we were relegated to the outdoors. For some reason, the orphanage building itself was out of bounds during the first visit and for most of the second visit. Did they have something to hide?

The first time I saw you three was, of course, outside, in one of the play areas. After a long wait on a cold and windy day, Olga, the adoption assistant, steered you three timid little kids around the corner of the building and over to Rose and me. Three cute puppets, dressed in so many layers of clothing that you had trouble walking. We were standing under a wooden canopy. Strange, I felt that I knew you-- It was as if you were wearing disguises, posing as small children.

Those first moments were awkward for all of us, I think. This might have been the first time you had seen anyone who was not on the orphanage staff. I didn't know how much you three knew about adoptions, about leaving the orphanage. I found out later that the orphans are frequently told about adoptions. They all seem to know what it is, and they all want it. Other kids looked on with envy whenever we played with you three.

I tried speaking with you, Anna, in Russian. You seemed to understand me, but I had a very hard time understanding you. You had a few linguistic idiosyncrasies that confounded me, and others. None of those idiosyncrasies carried over into your English, which is perfect, with just the slightest, gentle touch of a Russian, Peterburg, accent.

I tried to get a sense of your personalities, but couldn't. I made some guesses; some were right, it seems, and some were way off the mark. Alex seemed entirely timid. Maybe that was because he was just getting used to knowing his sisters, having just been moved to their part of the orphanage, and now he was looking at two odd people wearing extremely strange clothes. One of them spoke Russian with a funny accent and wore a weird, tangled thing around his neck that was called a 'bow-tie' In English, a 'butterfly' in Russian.

Dear Anna:

Of the three children, you perhaps present the most challenge. You are ten years old now. One moment you are a young lady; the next, an infant. Other parents say this is common. I give Katya a turn sitting on my lap, then Alex wants his turn, and then you want yours too. The next moment you are on the cell phone, gossiping like any American pre-teen.

Part of the reason for your complexity, I think, is that you took care of your Brother and Sister in the orphanage, and in the horrible year or so before the orphanage. You took such good care of Katya, in fact, that her Russian health records indicated she was deaf. She was not; she merely had no reason to speak. You were her voice.

So you were the care-giver, and coming to America, you were relegated to the position of eldest child. This was a big change for you.

You didn't have the same effect on Alex as you did on Katya, and that is probably because you barely knew him when I first met you. He lived in a separate part of the orphanage that was reserved for infants. When the orphanage people found out that he might be adopted along with his Sisters, he was moved up to your pod.

Anna, you are sometimes jealous and always protective. I recall my visits to the orphanage. Any time I struck up a conversation with any other orphan, you were quick to grab my hand and lead me back to Katya and Alex. There could be no doubt – we were yours, and you were ours.

The orphanage was housed in a stand-alone two-story building, all of it painted a clean and glistening white, in a part of the city that wore drab colors and carried much soot. We were allowed inside your white building briefly, only once during our first stay in the city. I had guessed that they were ashamed of the interior, but I was way off the mark. Inside, the wooden floors were so well-polished that I feared falling. The place was jammed with caregivers bearing various titles. Having spent many years in restaurants while working on my various graduate degrees, I learned to know what a professional kitchen should look like, and what equipment it should contain. The orphanage kitchen was among the best I'd seen anywhere.

There was no way these people could be ashamed of their institution. It was truly a showcase. Why, then, were we relegated to the yard, without regard to the weather? I never found out why.

Was this particular place vastly different from other Russian orphanages? I don't know. Maybe it was the iron hand of the kindly Doctor Ivanova, who ran the place, that made it so clean and well-supplied, and perhaps different from other orphanages, or perhaps not. Was it that she had the 'right connections,' which can be quite important in Russia.

But this was not a showcase for foreigners; there were far too few foreign adoptions coming out of Peterburg, and a showplace for foreigners would not have been located so far from the city center, in such an unappealing, industrial section.

The orphanage grounds were well-kept and wrapped the building on three sides with well-equipped playgrounds. There was no way I could claim that any person working there did not like her job – they all seemed so connected with the kids and concerned about them. The fourth side of the building was blocked off by a fence about eight feet tall. A few times I was able to peer through gaps in the fence slats. The parking lot contained Mercedes-Benz cars and BMWs and Volvos. No Moskvitch or old Volga sedan junkers there. Hmm, so that's where part of the 'valiuta,' foreign currency, went.

We got to know the other three sides of the orphanage grounds very well. Even the meeting with the local Child Welfare Deputy Director was held on an outside picnic bench, on a cold and rainy day. Most of the meetings with you kids occurred outside too, where we played with you on the playground equipment for whatever hours were granted. It got old after the first week, but this was my only chance to see you, so I did it without complaint. So did Rose.

A nice, no-nonsense man driving a decrepit Volga auto that reeked of gasoline shuttled us back-and-forth to the orphanage from our rented apartments in the center of the city. The trip to your place took over an hour, when traffic was good, which was hardly ever.

To save money, I had decided we would not stay in the incredibly pricey Russian hotels that always gouge tourists, no matter what the city is named. Three hundred and fifty dollars a night for a plain room was about average.

14

Instead, I found an online organization that rented out Peterburg apartments. The photos on their website were gorgeous. The reality was a bit different, but who cared? The locations were good. We stayed across the street from Saint Isaac's Cathedral, for example. Imagine! But to reach our flat, we had to walk through a trash-strewn courtyard, and up an incredibly filthy set of stairs – I mean puddles of urine and feces from various creatures, including humans, I am sure. The stairs were littered with cigarettes and cigarette packages and empty vodka bottles.

But once inside the rented apartment, things were not bad, the difference between hallways and apartments being a standard Russian mode of living. We had four rooms that were about fifteen feet high. The furniture was sparse, with unmatched pieces of Ikea, Danish Modern, and gaudy German stuff. Each room had windows nearly from floor to ceiling. These were great for the hot days. Sadly, Russia has yet to invent screens, and the city's notoriously aggressive mosquitoes had an easy entry and exit.

When we returned to Peterburg on our second visit, we stayed in a cozy apartment across the street from an open market and not far from Haymarket Square, made famous by Dostoevsky's <u>Crime and Punishment</u>. The stairway and halls of this apartment building were clean and freshly painted. I don't recall ever seeing hallways and stairs like that anywhere in Russia.

The rental agency called and told me that the apartment's owner, a widow, was returning early from her summer cottage, so we moved to an unbelievably awful place on Nevsky Prospekt, not far from the train station. This street is the 'Fifth Avenue' of the city, so I expected elegant accommodations, just like the pictures on the rental agency's website. But that was a dream, far from reality. To get to the apartment entrance, you literally had to peel open a tin billboard that was fastened to the front of the building. The first time, it took about forty-five minutes to locate the entrance. Our crabby 'Gracious Hostess,' who was the guide for our Peterburg stays, finally got on her cell phone and contacted the rental company. They told us about the tin billboard and how best to pry it open, as if it was perfectly normal and expected, to have an apartment hidden behind a bent, tin billboard and up a dark and dirty stairway.

The 'Gracious Hostess' was a curt, stern-looking woman in her mid-fifties. Her salary must have been good, because she wore gaudy but expensive clothes, and she appeared to go through about one can of hair spray per day. She was the one who would steer us through the bureaucratic mazes, and that she did, but she was blunt and rude. I am sure she didn't like it that I spoke some Russian. Sometimes she slipped, I know, and said things she would have said only when people assigned to her couldn't understand her. Also, she didn't like it that I was an attorney.

I know her name but will not give it. She is 'Gracious Hostess' in these letters, a fright in real life. Strangely, at the very end of things, she wished us well with as much cordiality as she could mine out of her stone heart.

Weird, the transformation. But I had seen such changes in the USSR and in Russia many times. Back in the 1970's, when I first started going to Russia, Soviet university professors railed for hours in class against the evils of capitalism and of the United States, and then, after the lecture, they would linger in the hallway and try to buy books and American cigarettes and jeans and, in fact, anything American from us.

Gracious Hostess and Driver were assigned to us by an agency that represented many American adoptions institutions. Some American agencies boast that they 'have an office in Peterburg' or some other Russian city. Not true, usually. The local American adoption agencies affiliate themselves with an American-Russian joint venture agency.

I could tell you about that joint venture company, but I don't like people yelling at me or suing me.

Gracious Hostess thought I was nuts. How could I stay in such dismal apartments? She just had to get out of the first one – The atmosphere was 'stifling,' she said. What was the matter with us? Did we have no money? Why was I so old?

We were also 'serviced' by a younger Russian woman, whose name I will not mention. I will call her 'Olga.' She was like a two-sided coin – one moment completely contemptuous of us, and the next moment amiable. She was the poor woman who had to race home every afternoon and translate and type up all the documents necessary for the next day, the next step in this long and convoluted process.

She did not hesitate to tell us how much she was shocked at our 'stinginess' in buying in a Peterburg corner store such lousy candy for the other orphan kids. No one had warned us that we should bring sacks of American candy with us, for the 'ceremony' held when orphans leave the orphanage.

She was utterly speechless over the appearance of the apartments we rented. I am sure she ran home and took a bath as soon as possible, after spending just a few moments in such hovels.

I saw her studying hard the photos of our own house in America. Russian ministry officials required such photos, and they became part of the official record. It was clear that we were losers. Other Americans brought enlarged photos of bedrooms done up all in pink and loaded with stuffed animals and dolls and such, just waiting for their lucky occupant. Our pictures were plain, our house old. To make matters even worse for us, there were two big dogs in one of the photos. That really threw her.

Olga and Gracious Hostess apparently changed their opinion of us towards the end of our Peterburg visit, perhaps after they discovered that we had given a small gift to the lady notary whose hands worked faster than any I had ever seen, and who had to sign and seal (with wax and a stamp – the old-fashioned way) about twenty-five documents for us, in the space of about four minutes.

Of course, before leaving the United States, I had been given a list of those Russian officials who needed to receive 'gifts,' if I wanted the adoption process to run smoothly, or to run at all: The ladies in the citizenship office, the Deputy Director of the Children's Ministry, the workers in the ZAGS office (Vital Statistics), court officials (some Russians had to wait up to a year or more to get heard in a court of law, whereas we got right in). Gracious Hostess ordered us to bring impressive gifts on the second trip, and nothing made in Japan, China, or Korea, please.

This was part of the bribe or semi-bribe process that kept the wheels turning. I don't know why that poor notary was not included on the list for gifts. She did a lot for your adoption. Of course, others too worked behind the scenes.

Without them, Rose and I might have been relegated to sitting on a wooden bench for a day or two, waiting to be seen while the clerks did their nails and gossiped and twiddled their ballpoint pens that never worked.

The city? It was Putin's hometown, and it was in remarkably good shape, at least on the surface. The beggars were all gone. Had the economy improved that much, or had the beggars lost the permits that allowed them to stay in the city? I suspect it was the latter.

The real wealth lay out in the countryside, I heard, in mansions and estates that hid themselves behind locked gates. Everyone had body guards. Mornings, the roads coming in from Karelia were jammed with BMW's and Mercedes.

I didn't like it that many of the buildings, particularly the ornate ones along Nevsky Prospekt, were covered with billboards that were two or three stories high and that obscured the beautiful, old facades behind them. I feared for the condition of some of those concealed facades. I had seen a cornice or two fall off buildings during my 2000 visit.

There is earnest talk now of building a skyscraper right on the Neva River for GazProm, the giant Russian gas company. A skyscraper within view of the Winter Palace? Lord! Peter the Great had decreed, around the year 1713, that no building should rise higher than the angel atop the church in the Peter and Paul Fortress. His wishes had been honored for centuries. Around 1905, for example, the Singer Sewing Machine Company tried to put up a tall building on Nevsky. It was not allowed, but the architects designed the building so that the trademark spinning 'Singer' Ball at the top was just one meter lower than the fortress church angel.

I have seen many parts of the world 'cleaned up' during my relatively long lifetime, and I am not always pleased with the results. Take New York, my favorite American city, as an example. Times Square used to be a litter-strewn, a grimy and gritty part of the city. Now, it looks like something from Disney World, not a real place where real people live. In the process of getting cleaned up, it lost its distinctiveness and character. The same goes for all of Greenwich Village too; it used to be the place where composers and writers and poets lived, then it got cleaned up and now few artists of any media can afford to live there. The once-famous Greenwich Village is now home for lawyers and accountants.

The same can be said for much of Peterburg. Parts of it have lost their character. Take the Evropeisky Hotel, for instance. It used to be an incredible structure shrouded in a dirty gray. Now, the Kampinsky Hotel Company re-did everything and runs it. The hotel is now dazzling, but it looks pretty much like luxury hotels in any city.

My children, why would your Father find such 'improvements' undesirable? Read on, and you shall discover the answer.

Dear Anna, Katya, and Alex:

Do not bemoan the fact that you know little about your native city. Believe me, if I am around for several years yet, I will have taught you much or else bored you a lot.

It is surprising to me sometimes how little Peterburg natives know about their city. Here is an example that I hope can make things clear without taking up too many pages or making me seem boastful.

Late one morning on our second visit, we finished up our business in the family court building, a block or so from the Neva River. We had barely made our court appearance on time because we had driven through the center of the city on a day when Putin was in town and was opening a giant G-8 or Y-9 or some other kind of summit meeting. It looked as if dignitaries from many countries had ordered their chauffeurs to give them a tour of the city. Traffic was gridlocked all over the place.

Time was tight, and the lovely and charming Gracious Hostess needed to stop off at her apartment to get documents that she had to send to Moscow by overnight mail. There was a deadline for drop-off, and we had to hurry; every second counted.

Okay. Picture this. We are a block from the Neva River. Directly across the river is Vasilievsky Island, where the university is located. Gracious Hostess lived, it turned out, just about directly across the river from where we were. 'As the crow flies,' from the court building, she was about two miles from her apartment, which was in the center of the island, halfway between the university and the 'kapitalist' dorm I had stayed in while studying in the city in 1970.

We had the same driver that we always had, a very gracious, down-to-earth kind of guy who made a living as a private driver, and earlier as a city cab driver. The only thing wrong with him was that his car stunk. "I hope we can make it in time," he said, hunkering down over the steering wheel.

What? He was heading back into the gridlocked mess around the Admiralty and Decembrist Square and the Winter Palace? There, he'd eventually manage to cross the Palace Bridge and drive halfway up Vasilievsky Island, to the apartment of the Most Gracious Hostess, but it might take all afternoon and evening.

"Excuse me," I said very politely. "But isn't the Lieutenant Schmidt Bridge just a few short blocks in the opposite direction? It would take us right into the middle of Vasilievsky Island, and we'd avoid all the downtown traffic."

Gracious Hostess laughed. Contemptible Americans, speaking a little bit of Russian and thinking they know it all! "The Lieutenant Schmidt Bridge, you say? Hah! That is about five bridges in the opposite direction! We would end up crossing the river after the Alexander Nevsky Monastery, for God's sake – absolutely the opposite direction from where we need to be. Sit back in your seat and let us do the driving!"

Admittedly, she was hot under the collar. It was a scorching summer day and we had spent hours sitting in a car that reeked of gasoline fumes while stuck in the middle of a city-wide gridlock. Air-conditioning – what is that? I knew she didn't like me. More than once she had referred to me as 'Ded' – 'Gramps.'

The driver agreed with her about the bridges, but he was much more polite. "I am afraid she is correct. There is no escaping the fact that we must drive through all that traffic."

It took hours. My back brace was cutting into my ribs, and a river of sweat trickled down my spine.

Back in our rented room, behind the tin billboard and up the stairway littered with pee and poop stains and cigarette butts and empty vodka bottles, I looked at my map of Peterburg.

Damn! I was correct! When we left the Family Court building, we were just two short blocks from the Lieutenant Schmidt Bridge, for crying out loud! From the other end of that bridge, Gracious Hostess' apartment was about a half mile, and traffic there had been light. We would have been there in just a few minutes, I am sure.

I did not bring up the subject with Driver or with Gracious Hostess, but I was totally intrigued. Here were two natives of the city. One was a professional driver, and the other, Gracious Hostess, was always chasing about town. Why didn't they know the location of one of the main bridges of their city?

There is one other reason why middle-aged and older Peterburg natives might have challenges navigating their city. So many street names have changed since 1990. My 1970 map of the city is good only as a souvenir.

One day in 2000 I was walking back from the central post office and I was waiting for the 'Walk' sign to come on so I could get across Nevsky. ('Walk' signs in that country merely mean that you stand a little bit less a chance of being run over by cars and trucks that seem to be aiming directly at you.) A bearded gentleman with a briefcase was waiting with me. "Why did they have to change the name of this street?" he wanted to know.

It used to be 'Gogol Street,' Gogol being one of Russia's greatest writers of the mid nineteenth century or of any time, although his humor is darker than any dark book you might choose to read.

"Gogol was no communist, for heaven's sake!" said the man. "And now they named the street 'Morskaya' ('Naval'). What were those idiots thinking of? How many 'Morskaya Streets' do we have already? Morskoi Prospekt. Morskoi Avenue. Little Morskaya, Big Morskaya, Central Morskaya, Morskaya Highway!"

The poor man had a legitimate gripe. But at least some of the more ludicrous Communist names had disappeared. 'Victories of October Twenty-Fifth Avenue,' or 'Mighty Proletarian Heroes of the 1905 Revolution Street,' or some such.

Dear Alex, Katya, and Sonya:

We were getting ready for our court appearance. Gracious Hostess had said it was a mere formality, nothing to worry about, but as the stinky car was taking us back to the city center from your orphanage, Gracious Hostess said, "There will be problems in Moscow."

I was not surprised. For one thing, Muscovites don't think much of Peterburg people and vice-versa, and for another thing, this was Russia, world headquarters for bureaucratic barricades and hurdles. "I suppose there will be some problems," I said politely in Russian.

"No. One big, big problem!" Gracious Hostess said.

"What?"

Gracious Hostess shifted in her seat, thus showing off how much room she had, and probably wanting to face us at the moment of her declaration. "A very high personage in Moscow is opposed to this adoption. He wrote across one of your application forms, 'Since when do we allow our children to leave the country with old grandfathers?'"

"Bullshit!" I said to myself. "Just another way to delay things, to make them more difficult and to perhaps provide new avenues for payment of bribes."

I snapped, something I always try to avoid when in that country. If you lose your temper, you lose the thing that you wanted, and you lose your power, as well as their respect.

"So, in other words, you are telling me that all our efforts and all the time and all the money has been for naught!" I said, nearly shouting. "And why? There are a number of men who have fathered children when they were in their eighties! Besides, I am good for at least twenty years! That is more than three times the average duration of a Russian marriage, for Christ's sake. In twenty years, the youngest child will be – let's see – yes, he will have finished college."

Gracious Hostess waved her arm gallantly. "It is nothing to worry about. It is something that I am capable of overcoming."

My cynicism grew. I had encountered similar scenes before, usually in Russia but sometimes in America too. Read on, and I will tell you how in America I used my bus pass as a diploma from

Leningrad State University.

"And since I am doing you such a large favor, Mister Jack,' Gracious Hostess continued. "I can expect one favor from you. You will find me an American husband, someone like yourself."

I don't have any male enemies bad enough to merit such a spouse.

There, again, was that queer conjunction of cruelty and kindness that I had seen before.

Dear Alex, Katya, and Anna:

When we were staying at the apartment behind the tin billboard on Nevsky, I heard noise out the window one morning. I think it was a Sunday.

Weird. There was no traffic on a street that was usually choking with cars, busses, and trucks. Instead, a lone priest wearing a jeweled robe walked solemnly down the middle of the empty street. What was up? Behind that priest came a double row of priests. And then came a priest walking all alone, holding up high a rather large icon.

Ah, I remembered reading "The Moscow Times" on the web a few months earlier. For the Russian Orthodox Church, this was a big moment! The Tikhvin Virgin icon was being returned to its village after decades in hiding from wars and from communism in general. It was one of the most worshipped Russian Orthodox icons, along with the icons of the Virgins of Vladimir, Smolensk, Iversk and Kazan. The Orthodox believe that four icons protect Russia from invasions from any of the four corners of the world. The problem was that this 'Northern-Eastern' icon had been missing for a long time.

This was its glorious return. Where had it been? During World War Two, it was moved to Chicago for safekeeping. The U.S. Russian Orthodox Church, some fifty years later, finally agreed to allow its return.

Interesting stuff? Legend has it that the apostle Luke painted that icon; it disappeared from Constantinople in 1383. Legend has it too that the icon floated in the air over to Lake Ladoga, not far from Peterburg.

Behind the priest came a mass of chanting and bowing lay people, mostly elderly women, but some young males and women, and even a few children, all praying aloud and all crossing themselves constantly. There must have been five hundred old ladies, all wearing long dark dresses and big white scarves. Some of the stragglers limped by, with canes or wheelchairs, an hour or so after the parade had passed.

The city, like that icon, had witnessed much, and both are now ready for a stable, prosperous future. I pray that happens; yet, I fear for a country that has over sixty billionaires but cannot provide a decent life for many of its residents, especially out in the country, away from the cities.

How did those people become millionaires or billionaires? Easy answer. During Communism, most things were owned by the State. With the dissolution of the USSR, many state-owned enterprises were handed over to those well-connected to the leadership.

I should not complain. While those guys were busy becoming billionaires, I enriched myself, as well, and at Russia's expense – I became the Father of three wonderful and intriguing kids.

Finally, all the paperwork in Peterburg was done. We appeared before a judge, and Rose read a document called 'intentions' into the record. The Judge did a pretty thorough grilling of some of the child welfare people present. There was some lamentation on the fact that not enough effort had been put into locating potential relatives The counsel women being grilled explained all the work they had done, but the judge's interrogation was so intense that one of the women was in tears.

But then gifts were distributed, bribes were paid, no doubt, outside the chambers, paperwork was signed and notarized, and later, back at the orphanage, Doctor Ivanova even invited us inside. This place was for real – it was well-cared for through and through, its clean exterior matched by the building's interior.

The doctor liked us, I think, and she wished us the best as we prepared to take on the challenge of three children, all at once. She had been looking at a stack of bills and invoices on her desk and was complaining. Your Mother and I decided to dip into the money we had remaining, and give the doctor a contribution. She refused. "You will need all that money for the three children you are taking with you. I will get through all these bills, and I will accept money from those who are more wealthy than you."

She went through your kids' health records in great detail, and without actually saying so, she managed to let me know which terms were bogus – inserted just so the child in question could be labeled 'defective' and thus able to be adopted by a foreign couple.

It seemed that everyone in the orphanage wished us well, and many, if not most, of them gave little hints or related potentially helpful things about you kids. Anna loves to sing Russian folk songs and will do it for hours. (Well, you lost that, gal, but you can sing all the lyrics to "High School Musical I, II, and III'.) Alex needed to be 'toughened up,' they said. Katya is a middle child, and must not get lost in the shuffle. Oh, and she hasn't urinated for several days. She has artistic talent, whereas her older Sister has musical talent. Their Brother's talents? They couldn't think of any.

On your very last day there, children/young adults, we stood at the curb of the gated parking lot. Clothes that Rose had purchased in America were passed over the fence – It was not allowed for Russian orphans to leave carrying any orphanage property, including clothes, even underwear and diapers. Through the fence, I saw a few tearful farewells. It was a big thing, I am sure, for three children to leave all at the same time, particularly when they were siblings, and particularly when the kids' family had lived just a few blocks away, and when several of the orphanage workers lived in the same apartment building.

Kids:

After we finished up things in Peterburg, it was on to Moscow to finish off the adoption with the Russians and then to take you to the American Embassy, to start on all the papers that the Americans require. Perhaps your ride in the stinky car out to the Peterburg airport was the first time you had been in a car. How nice it would be for you to discover later than not all cars reek of gasoline fumes.

We all had crammed into the stinky sedan – you three kids, Olga, the young assistant, Rose and I – all crammed into the back, while the front seats were occupied by the driver and, of course, Gracious Hostess, who kept telling me she was worried about our financial 'stability.'

We bade farewell to Driver, young assistant, Olga, and Gracious Host, and headed into the airport departure area. Gracious Host and Olga were now crying, as if bidding a final farewell to beloved relatives.

I breathed much easier once we passed through the security check. One security matron actually smiled. "You are adopting three Russian children? My, you are saints!"

Kids, I am quite sure that your plane ride to Moscow was your first time in the air. I peeked out the window and saw the endless rows of tall apartment buildings that circle your city, maybe miles thick. Beyond the apartment blocks, I spotted several gaps in the forest or fields – gated communities, no doubt, for some of those billionaires.

You three seemed nonchalant, as if flying was a regular part of your schedule. You stared blankly ahead, as if important messages were etched into the seatbacks in front of you.

Then I spotted a hole in that wide panorama, directly in the center. Yes, there it was, still valiant and still 'laughing through invisible tears,' as the writer Gogol would have put it. There lay the old part of the city, the heart of the city. The rivers. The arching bridges (over seven hundred of them, it is said). Palaces. Squares. Mansions. All of it surrounded by endless, color-less suburbs with their uniform appearance and ten-story height. I thought of a snake coiling around its prey, watching it die.

I didn't want my last 'official' thought about the city while still there (technically, I was still 'in it' because I was in its air space) to be so grim. But there it was.

Some day, you three children of Peterburg and I will return so that, I hope, my last thoughts on that departure will be more positive.

Dearest Children:

This is your Moscow story that you must remember so you can tell your children some day.

Officially, the trip from Peterburg to Moscow is about 450 miles, but, in essence, it is a trip from one civilization to another. How can two cities, so close to one-another and in the same country, be so different?

I had booked a room in the Rossiya Hotel that stood at the wrong edge of the Kremlin. It was a monstrous 1960s construction. Inturist, the tourism arm of the USSR, used to claim it was the largest hotel in the world. It boasted of something like 1,500 guest rooms, and there were at least 1,500 inconveniences that any guest might expect during a stay.

Halls led nowhere. Nobody on the staff knew where anything was, and so they just made up directions when you asked for help. I saw one couple ask for directions to the café. The 'key lady,' a guard and snitcher left over from Cold War days, gave them precise directions. Soon thereafter another couple asked her for directions to the café, and this time the nice key lady sent them in the opposite direction. Chances are that neither couple found the café to eat the meal that was included in their outrageous room prices.

Oh, whenever you wanted to get anywhere in the hotel, there were glass doors every fifty feet or so, and they were usually locked. To get anywhere, you literally had to go outside and then re-enter the hotel in a different entrance (Definition: An 'entrance' in Russia means a dozen doors, usually two rows of them, with nearly all of them locked. 'For heat control,' they claim, even in the summer.)

And since we are on the subject of hotels and doors, here is a bit of trivia. There was a pretty bad fire in the Rossiya Hotel a couple of decades ago. Counting the number of victims, the Russian firefighters came to an awful conclusion: All the doors to the rooms opened out into the hallways, not into the rooms, so, with a lot of people in a hurry to get out, passage was blocked by so many doors jutting out into the hallway. I have since noticed that most Russian hotels have done a bit of carpentry or metal work and have changed the direction of the room doors. The same went for the Rossiya Hotel too, the cause of it all.

I had booked there because, even though the room prices were outlandish, they were still less than half the price of any other Moscow hotel. And, it was relatively close, although at the wrong end of Red Square. I knew that the Rossiya was scheduled to be torn down, so I expected more than the usual curtness from its employees.

I was not disappointed.

Our room had floor-to-ceiling windows – great for ventilation if you don't have small children in the room who might want to play around the window sills; we were on the sixteenth floor. There were no screens.

I asked several staff members if there was a way we could get a barrier or something so we could open windows without endangering the lives of three beautiful children. No one had ever heard of such a request.

We sweated a lot in our hotel room.

Perhaps to keep busy or to pass time or perhaps out of habit, you three kids grabbed whatever cloths you could find and started polishing the mirrors and the wood paneling. Few words were spoken. I told you when it was time to get up or get dressed or eat or leave. You complied, but usually without comment.

Instead of a stinky old sedan and Gracious Hostess, we were whisked around the various Moscow offices by two young and cool engineering students who were making good summertime money, who spoke English flawlessly, and who drove a new Audi. It was quite a change; for me; not having to translate was a relief. It is hard work, especially for someone not so proficient anymore, and whose voice gives out on him at times.

Our Moscow stay was well-choreographed, down-to-the-minute. So many children and adopting parents had gone before us. You three took it all in stride, as if this happened to you daily and you had become bored with it all.

I wanted to see close-up and in 'real vision' the personalities shining on that VHS tape back home. Sadly, I didn't see personalities then – just robots. I am sure this shutting-down was your way of coping with the unbelievable change your lives would endure.

We stopped at a Russian hospital for a final check of you three departing citizens. I mentioned to the doctor that Katya hadn't peed for about five days now. He took off her he clothes and then held her on high, playfully. She smiled, and then managed to pee about four gallons all over the doctor.

What next?

He laughed. "I guess we do not need to worry about any urination problems!" he said.

I was really surprised by the genuine, I am convinced, laughter of the doctor. I don't know how I'd react if a child peed all over me.

All three of you kids passed the examinations. Rose and I both breathed easier, as we did each time we passed another potential hurdle.

Then it was off to the American Embassy. We sat in a giant reception hall along with about twenty-five adopting parents. Rose noted that, eerily, the parents very often resembled the children they were adopting. Somebody had performed a bit of match-making, Rose thought. I am not sure how it worked, but it had to be more than a coincidence. One extremely tubby couple from Oklahoma, for example, got a very tubby baby. A father with pointy ears got a kid with pointy ears – even though his wife's ears appeared to be normal. Our three kids were light-skinned and had blondish hair – just like Rose.

Into the embassy we went. Out we came, an hour later. No hitches. I couldn't believe our luck, and so I waited for the other proverbial shoe to fall -- You never get out of Russia that easily. Note that in the Russian language, you 'go into' or 'come out of' Russia. You simply 'go' to any other country and you 'leave' it. Why the difference? Give me time and I could write a book about that.

We had a bit of free time, some of which we spent at the Moscow Zoo. A giraffe stretched its head down and licked the top of Anna's head. This seems to be about the only thing that Anna remembers about Russia. Or is it that she remembers not the event, but our talking about it months later, in Wisconsin.

Moscow. How it had changed – A gigantic Ikea building and a lot of glass skyscrapers that clashed with Comrade Stalin's grandiose plans for the city. He had seven gothic 'wedding cake'-design skyscrapers, about forty floors high, and they were supposed to dominate the city's silhouette. One was Moscow University, one was a hotel, another was an apartment building. Now, they were challenged by these 'young ones,' or completely obscured by them.

In the 1970's, if you looked down at Moscow from Sparrow Hills, near the university, you would have seen a rather flat city, with just those 'seven sisters' poking upwards. More about one of those sisters later. Read on.

The lookout on Sparrow Hill was on the standard Inturist tour of the city. I recall one frigid winter afternoon at that lookout when the Inturist guide talked on about how clean Moscow air was, and how it was such a healthy place to live. The problem was, you couldn't see anything of the city from the hill that day. All you saw was a thick layer of coal soot and smoke.

That was the 1970s. Today, you'd have a hard time finding those Stalin 'baroque' wedding cake towers. Too many new buildings cast them into their shadows.

Also on the standard Inturist tour was a visit to the world's largest outdoor swimming pool. There were lots of black-and-white postcards of smiling, healthy Communist Russians enjoying the warm water on a frosty day.

The Inturist guide would not have told you that the world's largest swimming pool was really the basement of another Stalin tower, but Stalin had died and with him, luckily, the plans for another wedding-cake building. The Soviet guide may not have drawn attention to the fact that a very large church used to stand there, before Stalin had it blown up in 1931. But six decades later, Muscovites commenced rebuilding the Cathedral of Christ the Savior. No more giant outdoor swimming pool. The new Church was now completed, looking formidable, as if no one would be able to blow it up again, ever.

Moscow is neither humble nor understated. The streets are wider than anywhere else. Everything is the biggest in the world, it seems. But there are two words that make me tremble: Zurab Tsereteli.

Who? Zurab Tsereteli is a sculptor and a friend of Putin and head of the Moscow Academy of the Arts. He and his works are neither humble nor understated. Smack-dab in the middle of the Moscow River now stands a 315-foot-high sculpture of Peter the Great at the helm of a gigantic ship that looks like the one Captain Hook sailed in the Disney movie. You can do a Google search to find out about all the other Zurab Tsereteli statues, several of which are in the United States.

But why a statue of Peter stuck in the middle of the Moscow River? Peter hated Moscow and couldn't wait to finish his own capitol, Sankt Peterburg, and move out of Moscow. Maybe Putin had done this to irritate those Muscovites who do not like Peterburg (i.e., about ninety percent of the city's population). The statue is all out of proportion; the word 'clunky' comes to mind. It has ruined the views of and from the Krymskaya and Yakimanskaya embankments.

And an old joke has been revived, with only the place changed: Where is the best place to view Moscow? From the Peter Statue, of course. Why? Because it's the only place that when you look out at the city skyline, you don't have to look at the Peter statue.

Some radicals once tried to blow it up, but failed. I was ambivalent about it all.

I never felt the same connection to Moscow that I felt to your city.

Dear Children:

It was in Moscow that you three started to talk a little bit, in Russian, to me. Anna was the biggest talker of all, of course, and she explained things to Katya. Alex could do baby talk, and that was all. Russian baby talk sounds just like American baby talk.

You became curious, Anna. You asked about the house you were going to. You asked about my life in the United States and what your life and the lives of your Brother and Sister would be like. You explained everything to Katya, and you acted as if Alex was too young to grasp things, and perhaps he was.

You, Anna, asked why I was talking more than their new Mother, and I explained that she didn't know Russian. Anna didn't understand. I explained that there were more languages in the world than Russian. I spoke some English to her, and she got the idea. Quick kid, that Anna.

You asked about the last time I had been in Russia and I told you. It was the summer of 2000, and I was attending a writers' seminar at the Herzen Pedagological Institute, off the Moika Canal, just behind Our Lady of Kazan Cathedral which, during Soviet years, was known as "The Museum of Anti-Religion And Atheism" where they showed all sorts of cruelties brought about by Christians over the centuries, an easy collection to gather, for sure.

It is interesting that Herzen University, where I studied, started out as a school for orphans.

My Dear Young Adults:

As we were getting ready to leave Moscow, we signed a stack of papers for the Russians, and then the notary tied up chunks of them with a narrow red thread, and then stuffed into official-looking envelopes, which she were sealed with a big gob of wax into which was pounded the official stamp, just like they did in America a hundred years ago. This was to make things tamper-proof.

Across Moscow, the American Embassy official gave us three sealed envelopes with one paper on top of each. "If you should lose these folders," he said. "You may as well forget about adopting, or at least about bringing those children into the United States."

We held onto those envelopes.

You three didn't act as if flying was anything new for you, although I am sure it was, except for our short jump from Peterburg to Moscow. You seemed to take it all in stride, or was it that you were ambulating in a semi-conscious state, or in shock?

It was a day-long trip, with connections. We landed in Amsterdam late in the evening, and our plane to America was leaving early the next morning. We decided it best to stay at an airport hotel. The shuttle bus took us there. The room was a typical 'Marriot Inn' or 'Holiday' room, decent but not opulent. You three seemed unfazed by it, although it was about twenty times more opulent than the Rossiya Hotel, and the staff members smiled and answered questions correctly and gave good directions even, in English tainted by a clipped Dutch accent.

We showed you, by pantomime, how to take a shower. I recall that Katya got great joy out of the bubbles from the shampoo.

It was a long, long trip for you three children. You held up so well. It had always been a long trip for me, whether I was traveling alone or working as a study tour guide with thirty people to care for. This trip was something completely different. I held hard onto those three embassy envelopes.

Finally, we were there, in the Twin Cities. Customs was fast. It was not unusual anymore for Americans to arrive with foreign adopted children. Our papers were all in order, and they took the three envelopes I'd been clutching since Moscow. And, then we stepped out of the customs area and finally, after a long car-ride, we were home.

The first crisis in your new home? I opened the front door, and out bounded Ruthie and Pasha. Ruthie was a brown lab who weighed about forty-five pounds. Pasha was a shepherd/husky mix who weighed about sixty-five pounds.

You three stood clutching one-another and screaming in bloody terror. You perhaps had never seen a dog before. Perhaps you didn't even know what a dog was – what kind of people would live with wild animals? And the animals were nudging and licking you!

Somehow we got you three calmed down and showed you how to pet the dogs. We showed you the house, pointing out your bedrooms. You all looked noncommittal, neither impressed nor disappointed. You perhaps had never seen a one-family structure before, or a bedroom.

I wondered if you were lonely that first night in your own bedrooms. After all, this was undoubtedly the first time that you slept alone in a room. I peeked in on you the first night. You were all sound asleep, no doubt exhausted by all the travel and the stress of all the change on your young, little bodies and minds. I looked at Katya's bedroom that used to be my study. I looked at Anna's bedroom that used to be my exercise room. No more. I had elected to change my life, and drastically, at an age which many thought was too old.

Soon Pasha learned that if he brushed past Alex in a certain way, the kid would spin around like a toy spinning top. Poor Alex often ended up walking in a direction other than what he intended, and sometimes bumping into a wall.

I had a very hard time understanding your Russian, Anna. You did a funny thing with your vowels. 'Ya' came out something like 'o-ii-ay-ya.' I was sorry that my own Russian had become so weak that I couldn't understand you. But then I brought you around some 'real' Russians, and they couldn't understand you either. I felt a little better about it, as if vindicated.

This quirk did not carry over into your English. New words came to you one-at-a-time. It seemed to take only one hearing for you to remember a word. You helped Katya, and you spoke up for her and for Alex.

Soon, you met the neighborhood kids and started to play with them. At first, the kids would stop by and ask if they could play with 'the Russian kids,' but soon they were asking for Anna or Katya or Alex, by name. And you were responding.

Not long after your arrival, we went to friends John and Polly Snider's house. You were becoming a bit talkative by then. Polly asked Anna to call people to dinner. You understood, Anna, and you walked up to John in the living room and said in a low, gravely, commanding voice, "Sit down, please, John!" Your accent was beautiful.

Katya called Polly 'Loppy' until we corrected her at home.

You kids seemed entirely at ease no matter where we took you or whom you met. Perhaps there had been so much change in your lives that you could take anything in stride. I brought you to a mini-reception at the law school where I worked. You were not uncomfortable or shy. Anna grabbed a tray of cookies and started handing them out. I hoped there were no germophobes in the crowd of guests; Anna picked up each cookie and offered it to someone. I had seen children in the orphanage handing out candy that way during the little mini-ceremonies for kids who were leaving.

Soon you got to know your toys. Katya's favorite seemed to be a ragdoll that she called 'Dean.' Weird. Dean was the name of the handyman who was finishing off a new kitchen.

Alex started toddling around the house, exploring. He stared at any male who was present, including me. I am sure that he had seen very few males in his prior life. He was 'imprinting' himself with them, imitating their postures and movements. Rose noted that he started to stand the way I did, with my hands in at my waist (good support for a bad back).

Slowly, very slowly, you were becoming acclimated. I looked at my stack of Russian kids' books and study materials. You would not forget your Russian, I told myself with great determination.

You forgot it.

I think that for every English word any of you added to your vocabularies, you tossed out a dozen Russian words.

You three spent a lot of time with the neighborhood kids, and a lot of time watching television or DVD movies. I am sure that's how you came to know English so rapidly. Necessity is a great tutor, and young children are adept at learning languages.

Soon, Anna, you couldn't remember the words to any of the Russian songs you used to sing.

Soon, you even forgot the melodies.

Dear Anna:

Maybe it was your first week in the United States, or maybe the second or third. My memory fails here, but I do know that this happened, and that it happened soon after your arrival.

It was evening and your Mother was at work, I think, and all of a sudden you and your Brother and Sister disappeared. I figured that perhaps you had wandered outside, had gotten lost, or else had ended up at one of the neighbors, which would have been a good outcome. A busy county road runs by, not far from your house, and cars take the road's many curves at speeds sometimes double the posted speed limit.

I was nervous – three orphans running around territory they didn't know. I put on my jacket and headed for the front door, but then I heard noises in the bathroom. Quiet noises. So I opened the door and went in.

There you were, with your younger Sister and your Brother. All three of you were huddled around the sink, and it was clear that you, Anna, were calling the shots.

First, you let Katya push down on the wastebasket foot pedal, and then, as the top of the can flew open, you all stared, wide-eyed.

Each of you took a couple of turns, but the wonderment didn't seem to diminish.

What an odd child you were, what odd children your Brother and Sister were. Here you were, in a new country, after taking a number of flights before which you had never been on a plane. You saw houses – separate buildings even, and you saw lawn tractors and all kinds of new and strange things.

But there you were, huddled around a bathroom sink, looking with wonder upon an old, tiny wastebasket that had rust around its edges.

Dear kids:

A few months after you arrived in America, I walked into the living room once and found Alex lying on his back on the floor. Katya was ministering to him. Anna stood over them, with a big wheel from one of Alex's toys. Anna spoke. "Touch the steering wheel! Touch the steering wheel! Touch the steering wheel!"

What was going on?

It took a bit of time for me to puzzle it out.

Walt Disney's "Sleeping Beauty" was your favorite movie then, and you were acting out the scene where the evil princess lures Sleeping Beauty into touching the spinning wheel, thereby fulfilling the prophesy made at her birth (i.e., "At age sixteen you will be pricked by the needle of a spinning wheel and you shall die!")

Alex was the princess, somehow already asleep. Katya was the good spirit, and Anna the bad witch.

"Touch the steering wheel?" You didn't know what a spinning wheel was, and so you thought the movie said 'steering wheel.'

Dearest Kids:

For the first few months in America, you were terrified of being abandoned. Each time I left, I'd see three sets of eyes watching me, following the minivan as it rode the driveway up to the road.

One dark winter evening, I was walking up to the road to get the mail. Soon, I was startled – Anna, you were standing behind me, not at all dressed for the weather.

"What are you doing outside?" I asked.

"Katya told me to come out and check on you to make sure you didn't get lost."

There were numerous times that 'Katya' sent you out to help me, just in case I got lost.

Another time, soon after that first time, I was filling the minivan with gas. For some reason, the 'pay at the pump' mechanism wasn't working, so I had to step inside the filling station for a moment in order to pay. I came back outside to see three absolutely traumatized kids running around the filling station grounds.

From that time on, I made sure that you always knew where I was.

I am happy to report that the three of you gradually overcame these 'abandonment issues.'

You even adjusted to the custody exchanges after the divorce – one day with Papa, the next day with Mama. You cried at first, but soon acclimated. You knew you now had two houses as well as two parents.

I think you have acclimated.

I hope it hasn't left deep scars.

Dear Anna:

Your great leap in acclimation began, I think, once you started kindergarten. Poor girl. You had come over here in July, and just eight weeks later you had to start school. I was terrified the morning that we first put you on the school bus, up by the county road.

In the late afternoon, you stepped out of the bus. Would you be crying? Had you jumped off the morning bus and hidden yourself under a stairwell, as I had once done in first grade? (I later found out that your school has no stairwells – It's a one story building.)

No. You were smiling, and I was much relieved. Later, we talked with your teacher. She said you did just fine. You watched the other kids like a hawk and did exactly what they did. 'Once' was all you needed to learn something.

You cried only one time, your teacher said; you were handed a pair of scissors and you didn't know how to use them. You had probably not seen a pair in your whole life.

The local newspaper did a full-page spread on your first day of school, and so you became a local celebrity, with a great number of fans. You were invited to numerous birthday parties, even those of fifth-graders. You were proud of the article and of the photos. I know that's how all three of you will feel if this book gets passed around.

Dear Anna, your English vocabulary grew by the proverbial leaps and bounds, and you were tutoring your younger Sister and Brother.

Dearest Children:

Memory. Russian psychologist L.S. Vigotsky wrote about cultural mediation and internalization, and the effects of memory on both. In a way, then, we are our memories. They are what make us 'us.' I wonder what happens when we lose partial contents of our memories.

Anna, you spent nearly five years in Russia. Katya, you spent three years, and Alex, you spent two years. Yet, none of you knows a word of Russian now, and you don't have any memories at all about Russia, except for the giraffe licking Anna's head at the Moscow Zoo.

How can this be? Some say that you have blocked out those memories and your Russian language abilities in order to hasten your adaptation to your new life and new country. Maybe so. Others suggest that trauma caused these losses.

Yes, I can only imagine the trauma of the first few years of your life.

Yet, Anna, when you first came to America, you and I spoke Russian for a couple of months, thereby disproving the idea that the trauma of your first years is what erased the memory on the 'hard drive' of your brain. You liked to sit in the back seat of the minivan and sing Russian songs for hours, while rocking yourself gently.

Anna, Katya, Alex. These are not your real names, which are more Americanized names. Three wonderfully-adapted, loveable, capable, loving American kids.

But inside each of you hides a Russian, each of whom you profess, or pretend, no longer exists.

Dear Katya:

You are about the oddest, entirely loveable child ever. I recall your first morning in the United States. You got up and with one grand gesture, you threw the linens into place on the bed. That is how you do anything – dive into it and consider the consequences later.

I have seen you in the summer heat, running along the grass as if you had somewhere to go, but you didn't. I think you just wanted to feel the wind on your face, which got redder and redder as you ran, and this made you happy, and your smile got brighter and brighter. One of the prettiest sights I remember is your round, red face during those rushes. It was like witnessing a colt freed after a long time in a stall – get out of the way or you'll be run over.

You learned how to ride a two-wheeler bike that way, and one time Tom Barrett, a good friend of mine from high school days, let you steer his pontoon boat on the Saint Croix River, not far from our home, but on the other river bank, where they had a summer house. Once behind the wheel, a glint came into your eyes, almost like the look of a mad person. You hunkered down and grabbed the wheel with a look of determination that I hadn't seen before. Thankfully, it was a cumbersome pontoon boat, slow to move, slow to respond or change direction, not a runabout or speed boat.

I have watched you swim in lakes and in pools. You love to swim. You have an odd way of doing it. The whole of your face is above water and parallel to it. There it all is, on the surface of the water -- your giant forehead, your beautiful eyes, your wonderful smile tinged a bit with fear of drowning, I am sure.

Who could not love such a face, such a girl?

Dear Alex:

It's worth waiting almost a whole life span, just to have a three-year-old boy, your boy, look up at you, and with a sideways movement of the head directing attention to what is in your hands, say, "Gook, Papa!"

Those 'gook, Papa' years with you and your Sisters pass us, flash by flash, like the shiny, simmering sides of a passenger train passing at full speed while your train too passes at full speed. And not a chintzy American train either, mind you, nor the reliable but cumbersome groaning of the wide-track Soviet trains, but the too-fast French trains.

As you grow and become more American, I see how you continue to 'imprint' yourself on other males. You and I watched two men saw down a dead forty-foot tamarack across the road. You played with your Tonka Toy cherry-picker truck for weeks after. You and I played tree-choppers together. You were Mark and I was Jim.

And one time, out of the corner of my eye, I saw you out on the deck, first standing, then bending, then going down on one knee while spreading forth a tape measure. You practiced until you had it down perfectly. Yes, this was the exact movement the carpenter made the day before when working on the deck.

Not too long ago, I was cleaning up my trailer house, something I don't do nearly often enough, and I came across a small box filled with little chunks of paper and cardboard. Something told me not to throw this out – the pieces were too closely matched. Then it occurred to me: You and I had watched workers at a construction site not far from your Mother's house – they were putting up a new bank. That little box was your 'roll-off' construction trash container, which every construction site needs – you had a plastic dump truck with a lever on its side that lifted up the container and poured its contents into the truck bed.

And when we were alone at home, before the divorce, I let you open the back door of the minivan, if you promised not to tell Mama, and you stuffed that space with scraps of wood and tools and a dolly and a step-ladder even. This was, I could see, your 'work truck,' crammed from floor to ceiling, just like handyman Dean's truck.

You are probably the only kid in this trailer park who keeps a three-ton hydraulic jack in his bedroom. You never know when it might come in handy. Not to mention police things and fireman things and workers' tools and a soldier's uniform. And any number of swords and rifles. You hide your official FBI badge so bad guys won't know your identity. We watched the "Batman Begins" movie, which is the best of all 'Batman' movies, I think. You slipped out of the room and came back, moments later, wearing your Batman costume, your hands on your hips, ready for action, ready to protect the world.

How fast you grow. I recall when you were first learning English. Each time you were told to do something that you didn't want to do, you got angry and plopped yourself down on the floor. "Alex, come here and pick up your mess!" Plop! "Alex, it's time for bed now." Plop!

I let others see it. For a long while, you were known as 'The Plopper.'

My Dear Children:

I wanted to revive your Russian language skills, just like a doctor performs CPR after the patient is dead. One final effort.

I brought over Russian friends, to see if they could coax you three into speaking Russian. Already by then, none of you spoke it; nor did you apparently understand one word of it. The Russian guests were sorely disappointed, and asked what we had done to 'spoil' the kids' memories of their home country. I answered that one angrily.

One evening I was sitting with Katya on my lap as she held her favorite doll. I was speaking Russian, and I used the Russian word 'kukla' to refer to her doll. Her face turned red – as red as only her face can turn. She grabbed the doll, as if protecting it from some impending evil. "Not kukla!" she insisted. She shoved the doll back at me and said, "Dolly!"

It was clear to me, then, Katya, that you had 'bifurcated' your brain. Part of it was English and part of it was Russian. You were shutting down the Russian side and didn't want me to do anything to prolong it.

I was so sorry to see it dissipate.

Dissipate? Is it gone? Or is it there, under lock and key?

Dear Anna:

You are the oldest child. I may know a little about how it is to be the oldest. I was the second child, and the first male, in a family of ten kids. I was often responsible for them – I had to baby-sit younger brothers or sisters for hours at a time. My summers were usually ruined; I'd end up pushing a stroller for hours on end up and down the streets.

The only escape was for me to push the stroller towards Saint Luke's Convent, about two blocks away. Most of my younger brothers and sisters were terrified of those ladies in black, with white pointy things on their heads and their faces surrounded by white. You could smell the starch a block away, or you could hear their big beads clanking – the super-sized rosaries they wore around their waists, with the joyful or sorrowful mysteries dangling at their sides.

"Doo-doos," they were called by the youngest siblings. One look at the nuns, and the kid in the stroller started screaming. I'd rush home fast so that he or she was still screaming in a genuinely holy terror. "Mom, Timmy doesn't want to ride in the stroller anymore. Listen to that crying."

Little kids are always cute and adorable. They get the attention, while the elder child or children sit alone, hardly noticed.

I have seen that in our family. Each time I come to you for a chat or a walk, Alex or Katya will intervene. It is Katya, often. Our time together is limited because of joint custody schedules. But while you kids are around me, the two youngest demand my attention, and they are not willing to share.

Sometimes older children decide to excel in something (e.g. get all A's in school) just so they get some recognition from their parents. "My, that's nice" the parent will say. "Excuse me, but I must get back to your younger Sister. She painted such a lovely picture! And that Alex – He's so darn cute with his batman costume!"

I recall the greatest compliment I received from my Mother when I came home with a Masters' Degree in Slavic Languages and Literature, and a University of Michigan transcript filled with high marks.

My Mother said, "You're so smart. You must have stolen parts of the brains of some of your brothers and sisters."

Gee, thanks, Mom.

Dear Kids:

Each of you has an odd relationship with things. Katya will ask, "Can I have that salt shaker?"

"To use?" Alex asks.

"No, to keep."

Alex rolls his eyes, but a few hours later he asks if he can have the electric drill. Not to move it to his bedroom. Just to 'keep' it.

Not to be outdone, Anna asks if she can 'have' the lamp on her night stand.

What gives?

You children came from an orphanage, and probably none of the things in there belonged to you, or to anyone.

A student of Russian history could go into a long discourse about the lack of private property before and after the revolution (e.g. the 'mir' or peasant commune before the revolution), but I think it's more an orphan thing. You probably wore different clothes each day, none of which belonged to you, and they could disappear without explanation. It was probably the same with toys and silverware and dinnerware and soap dishes. It all belonged to everybody, and now you live in a two-story house and have your own room and your own things. Even in my trailer, or 'mobile home' as it's more delicately called, you have your separate rooms.

In America, you were becoming your new selves, creating your own domains. You went from a world of communal things, from an orphanage in a country not known for its adoration of private property after decades of fighting the concept of private property, and from there, you went to a country that adores and treasures private property. If having one doll is good, then having two dolls is better.

To all three kids: It didn't take long for you to become Americans.

Dear Children:

Then came the divorce. It's been painful for us all. Hardest for me was leaving you. Next hardest is invariably the day after I've returned you to your Mother. The 'hand-off's' from one parent to the other are hard on you too.

It took you a while to get used to my new home, a 1977 Marshfield 12' x 70' mobile home, complete with 1970s shag carpeting, swag lamps, and orange appliances. Anyone walking in here feels as if they've stepped back into the 1970s, which is just fine by me, because for me, that was a good decade.

The mobile home 'park' is a bit down in the mouth, as they say.

It has worked out very well for us, no? You have lots of places to play, including a playground. There are many kids around the trailer park – Chad and Zach and Raven and others. I am glad that some of your friends here are black or Hispanic or oriental. It doesn't seem to make any difference to you, and I pray that things will remain that way.

We are lucky in that my trailer is at the end of a row, and so we have a pretty good-sized yard. There's a nature center right across the street. We have two storage areas lining the trailer; they are so big that we never need to throw out anything.

I could not afford a 'stick house,' as trailer dwellers like to call 'real' houses. This way, we have money left over for toys and vacations. Last summer we drove to Texas and visited Mary Vernon and Sue Sturgeon (you will read more about them later) and other friends and relatives. We stopped at just about every swimming pool between here and there. This year we went not too far away, to Cold Spring, near the Horseshoe chain of lakes where my parents took the family each year for a vacation at Elmwood Resort.

Dear Anna, Katya, and Alex:

Some have asked why I would choose to publish letters that contain so much personal information.

Good question.

I think of Carl Jung and his followers. They might say that the deeper you delve into an individual's psyche, the closer you get to the universality of all. I agree.

Secondly, I dare to believe this is a work of art, and that art is its own world with its own laws, which are sometimes the mirror opposites of those in the real world. If you have 'a gift' for making art, it means that you are obligated to share that 'gift.' After all, it is not you, but the Gift that does the creating. You are merely an instrument; you are life's long telephone wire.

And so I believe that a mediocre writer will say, "Hot Damn, I'm good! I'll make a million dollars over this." But a 'real' writer will lean back in awe, grateful for what the Gift, through him or her, has brought to the world of Art and to the other world as well.

Lastly, I believe that memoirs get a bad rap and are often not considered as art. I believe that this is because there are too many awful memoirs on bookstore shelves or on amazon.com or at Wal-Mart or in airports. Imagine the possibilities for bad memoirs:

I Am A Loving And Caring Person Who Deserves Much, But My Ex-Husband Is A Bastard

Look At All The Wondrous Things I Have Done In My Life; Too Bad You Weren't As Lucky As Me.

My Bosses Were All Asses Because They Fired Me For No Reason At All

Stories About All The Women I Slept With

I believe that it's time to protect the art of memoir so it maintains its proper place in the Temple of the Arts.

May I have had enough of the Gift to help make it so.

Plus, I have another, secret agenda.

Dearest Anna, the oldest, the youngest:

You close doors now. You speak in whispers on the phone and when on the phone and when I approach you put the phone closer to your head and your voice turns even quieter.

You enjoy your privacy. You need it. Out of the bedroom that you and Katya share, you have carved out for yourself a quiet corner, a den, a cubby-hole, a refuge.

You read big books and you don't hear or see what goes on around you.

In short, you are working hard at becoming a teenager.

You have always been you, I am sure. You were you when you came to us, and I am convinced you were you for the four years you spent in Peterburg.

But the you is now deciding what kind of face or faces it will show the world. These years, these attempts – they are so tenuous.

I see you working towards portraying a tom-boy.

I am happy. I think this is a good choice, and it will work for you. What a compelling combination: A tomboy with an extremely sensitive, inward sense of self.

I know that some fathers say that their daughters will 'always be daddy's little girl.' Not I. You have always been you, and as you grow and blossom, you come into yourself more fully.

Dearest Katya, Katya, Katya:

You have had challenges in school. You love math, but it doesn't love you.

You are so proud of what you have learned. Last night you made up for yourself a math book. You decorated the cover carefully, with different-colored markers. You used tape and a piece of construction paper to make a pocket for your special math pencil. You did you math for an hour last evening – we worked on it together.

Even while driving you kids to school this morning, you worked in your math book. You were 'making stairs' by adding or multiplying numbers until their columns increased. I was so proud of you, your devotion, your persistence, your pride. And the Russians had claimed you were learning-disabled!

Today one of your school's learning specialists called and told me you were far behind in math.

Damn.

She wanted to give you a comprehensive math test and then to work individually with you, hoping that you might work yourself up to grade.

Damn! I would shield you from any hurt or pain.

I pray that this kind woman will figure out a way to turn the test-taking into a positive experience – "Katya, you have made so much progress, we want to measure it!" And then to say, "Katya, you have such a gift for math, I want to give you some extra challenges."

Oh, how I hope it turns out that way.

Damn! I would shield you from any hurt or pain.

Dearest Anna:

In March of 2009, you and your Brother and Sister were staying with me – it was my turn on the 'custody merry-go-round.' This was during a medical transition for me. Having retired and having eaten up my "COBRA" benefits, it was time to find my own health care. I ended up with the Veterans of America Hospital and Clinic.

It was the greatest of moves; care is excellent, and cheap, but the doctors there had different ideas about what drugs I should take.

In the first week of April, xxxx, then a new drug for me, apparently started to work against the xxxx that I had been taking, such that I woke up feeling like a real person and I felt like a real person all that day, and I went to bed feeling like a real person too.

For me, it was heaven. Gone were the aches and pains and bone-tiring fatigue that had been nipping at my heels for years. Gone were all the flu-like symptoms that for two years had been making me a bad father, a bad spouse, and a bad librarian. Gone too were druggy hazes that sometimes replaced the vague aches and pains.

This was too good to be true.

Yes, it was too good to be true.

Friday I felt tired, and I 'asked your permission' to go to bed early while you watched a 'Scooby-Doo' movie – I didn't feel well. I figured it might be the start of a cold that was making its way around your school and had hit you three, seriatim. Saturday afternoon, I fell a few times and paid no mind to it. An old clumsy man – someone to laugh at. Then I fell a couple more times, and I became a little concerned. I asked you and your Brother and Sister to play outside, which you did, while inside, I started vomiting. My head spun. I started seeing things.

Then you, Katya, the quiet one, announced that you wanted a toy because you had come up short on our past few trips to toy stores and used clothing shops and garage sales. You, Katya, the middle child, sometimes get overlooked. I figured we could go to Target, a little over a mile west of where our trailer stood. But we discovered that the McKnight Road entry ramps had lines of orange cones that blocked passage. The road was closed and so we needed to find that 'alternate' route.

We found it, but that Target store was closed, it being already about nine-fifteen on a Saturday evening. Maybe the Target near Maplewood Center would still be open, I thought – it stood in an area that was much more developed than that first Target that looked out at a shuttered modern-style brick church, warehouses, and the unreachable arc of Highway 36.

Just one exit down, to the west. White Bear Avenue. Turn right, and soon we would be at Target, I figured.

But what had happened? I must have missed the turn. It wasn't this far to the second Target, was it? I turned around to get back to our initial route and re-trace it. But I couldn't find my initial route, or any route. It was as if someone was playing a joke on me and kept changing the street names.

My heart beat hard and the back of my shirt stuck to the seat and my hands started shaking. I kept them on the steering wheel so that you kids wouldn't notice. I drove on, getting more and more confused. And for some reason, I saw no stores, no gas stations, no houses with lights on. It was as if I was wearing blinders.

I was, in medical parlance for us geriatrics, suffering an episode of 'spatial disorientation.' In newspapers you can read about old people intending to drive a block to the drug store for a newspaper and somehow ending up in North Dakota.

But this particular geriatric person had two terrified kids in the back seat and you, Anna, in the front seat of our little Honda Civic. You all wanted a toy. You wanted a store with bright lights and aisles and shopping carts, including special kids' sit-down types that always got stuck between aisles or smashed into piles of merchandise with crashes you could hear all over the store. Or, if there was no Target open, you wanted to be home, in our trailer.

I was terrified.

I drove on. And on. I traced and retraced. Now, there were no lights to guide me. Where in hell were we? I continued to pretend a casual lack of concern, but inside, I was horrified. I didn't know any of these streets. I didn't see any freeway or highway lights or overpasses or underpasses, just signposts giving off names that might just as well been written in Chinese or Urdu. Giant piles of gravel or sand sprang up ahead of us, forcing me to make more turns to wherever it was we were going.

I saw that we were in some kind of industrial park, then we were in an area of modest homes and no street lighting or illuminated street address signs that would at least tell me whether I was going north or west or whatever.

One hour of this. The sweat glued me to the car seat. Silence.

Soon you, Anna, sitting in the front seat, looked straight ahead and said in a low voice, "We are lost, aren't we." It was not a question, and there was a finality to it that demanded no answer.

"I just need to get to the next big street," I said. "And then we turn left and everything will be fine. We'll hit the toy stores tomorrow."

But now you were not looking at the road or at the objects that our headlights momentarily illuminated. You were looking at me. "You are sick, right, Papa?"

I nodded. Crazed as I was, determined as I was, I felt tears and they blurred my vision at a time that it needed all the help it could get.

Then, Anna, you incredible nine-year-old girl, took charge. You calmed your Brothers and Sister. You gave me explicit instructions, and you made damn sure I followed them.

I was seeing that strong, take-charge Anna who, in another country and in another time, when you, not even four years old, had cared for her younger Brother and Sister, before neighbors called authorities and social workers came and took you three to the orphanage.

"There's the stadium, by the high school!" you called out. But it wasn't a stadium; it was some kind of lumberyard.

We drove on. By this time, I was totally disoriented and had decided to approach the first person I saw and ask for street grids, for intersections and important roads. But there was no one to ask. And it was that kind of upper blue-worker class neighborhood where husbands and fathers keep rifles close to their doors, just in case some hobo like me comes at night, ringing their doorbells.

"Look!" you called out suddenly, and you turned my attention to the left. Yes. That was something! It was a freeway! I knew enough about this northeast section of Saint Paul. I knew the location and direction of highways and freeways, at least.

But I had slid deeper into my internal panic, deeper into the pool of another world's water.

So you, dear Anna, took complete charge. I became your puppet.

"No, I said turn right!" you shouted. And so I would go up to the next exit and then re-enter the freeway, travelling now in the opposite direction.

Yes, it was a miracle that we weren't hurt. Even I, deep in my drugged state, could realize the miracle that was taking place.

Luckily, no matter how disoriented I became, I remembered rules of the road and I followed them. I drove slowly, making sure I obeyed all traffic laws. I didn't want to crash and hurt your kids. I didn't want to be stopped by police, who would surely take you children away from me.

But then we couldn't get back on to the damned freeway. Where were all the exits and entrances? We passed a green directional sign and I turned and read it. "We are driving alongside 694!" I announced. "But I can't see an entrance ramp yet. Oh, wait! There it is!"

"Oh, Papa!" you exclaimed so proudly.

But our adventure did not end there. The entrance ramp was closed – under construction. But we had to get onto that or some other freeway – I knew them, and I knew where they came from and where they headed. Finally we managed. This was the northeast quadrant's intersection of Freeway I-694 and I-35, the crazed and crooked junction that splinters two interstate freeways, spitting one out towards the North and the other one to the East. The junction, like usual, was being re-aligned, and there were orange cones all over the place, like a field of orange dandelions. Everything was chopped up, but then the overhead sign told me that we were headed in the wrong direction and that in an hour or so we would be in Anoka, birthplace of Garrison Keillor and the town that David Letterman said sounded like the name of a brand of toothpaste, and about fifty miles from where we needed to be. So I looked to see where we could turn around, where we could get off the freeway easily and then just as easily get back on, but going now in the opposite direction.

"I'm scared," said Katya quietly, from the back seat.

"Me too," announced Alex. "I want to help, Papa."

"You can," I told the six year-old boy. "You too, Katya. You are big kids. You can read to me the signs that you see." Through the rearview mirror, I could see you, Katya, curled up in your seat, wedged to the door, crying.

Having a limited vocabulary, Alex spelled out most of the signs. "White Bear," "Century" – Papa what does 'b-o-u-l-e-v-a-r-d' mean?" Now we were headed in the right direction. The closer we got, however, the more I seemed to be losing my way.

You, Anna, snapped at me, enough to keep me alert, and you spit out directions. "Right Lane!" Then, "Slow down!" Then, "Here!" sung out in a commanding voice.

Yup. We had taken the Century Avenue exit from I-694, but how could we get from there to our trailer, our home? This was a complicated chunk of urban terrain, with roads winding around ponds, swamps, and lakes.

"Left!" you commanded, and soon we all cheered as we spotted the giant illuminated orange sign that said, "Mills Fleet Farm," the big store just over the hill from our trailer park. It was like the beam from a lighthouse during a terrible storm at sea.

But I somehow managed to circle the store and end up in a parking lot in front of a movie theater. Anna, you got us back on the correct road and soon we were on Hadley Avenue again. "Slower!" you commanded. "Even slower than that!"

I had lost it.

"Slower!" you commanded, and you grabbed at the wheel.

Then, all of a sudden I remembered – things were coming into some kind of focus finally. If we turned right, we'd be on the northern roadway that follows Highway 36. I recognized the terrain now. We drove slowly, around the curve where the road narrows, then down the hill to the stop sign, approaching the tiny billboard that said "29 Pines Mobile Home Manor," and we made a cautious right turn.

We drove about five miles an hour. Three short blocks later, you, Anna, told me to make a left turn and in a few seconds, we reached the last trailer in the row. We were home, under the street light, our street light.

Home. Home. Home. I'd never tire of saying that beautiful word. Home. You, Anna, hopped out and opened the garage door, your arms spread as you faced us in the car -- You, like the rescuing angel that you are, now illuminated by that Honda's holy headlights. I drove into the garage, hitting the gas each time we approached the high ridges in the sidewalk or stubby driveway. That was a challenge, even in daylight, even when I was not crazed. I had to step on the gas hard and then hit the brake quickly, as soon as the Honda's front tires made it over that particular hump. If I did it wrong, we would end up stuck sideways on the street, or I'd crash into the front of our garage.

The Civic leaped off the street and into the garage okay, but I broke the outside driver's mirror as it smashed against the garage wall.

Blam! We were in. Luck was finally with us on that awful night. I turned off the engine, and all four of us got out of the car and cried and hugged one-another before we unlocked the trailer and turned on the lights.

Home.

So we stood there, in the middle of a cool April night, an old man with three young children, a man charged to protect you children, a man who had promised a Russian judge and the world that he would care for you three and raise you -- I had failed you miserably.

Home.

We all kept hugging one-another and we were too tired to go to bed. Each shared his or her tale. Alex said that just at the moment we were turning around on I-694, he had seen a speeding black car from the other side slide off the pavement and land deep in a ditch that separated the freeway's two directions. Yes, I now recalled seeing that too.

"See, Papa!" Alex, always the optimist, said. "That could have been our car sliding off the highway, but you took good care of us!"

Alex, I love you. I love your optimism, your care for people and things. "It's not your fault, Papa. You didn't know the medicines would make you sick."

"It's not the doctor's fault," you said then. "He didn't know that taking these two medicines together would make a person sick."

"It's not the fault of the people who make the pills. They didn't know two of them would make a person sick."

I love each of you. How and why had I put you in the face of such danger?

I spent that Sunday and the Monday next going through, seriatim, all the side effects that are listed in four-point fonts on drug packages. The two drugs that had made me feel like a person for a while – they had joined forces and ganged up on me. Vomiting. Dizziness. Disorientation. Fatigue. Loss of appetite. Inability to urinate. I got them all, and when I was done with them, the hallucinations and disorientation stopped, but only after getting lost again with you kids the next night, this time on the way to Veterans Hospital and we were low on gas and far from home and I had forgotten my wallet and didn't know yet how to use the damned, complicated GPS machine whose voice told me to download some damned software or something.

At a closed gas station, all of them being closed and only the pumps were open, but only for credit cards, but mine were at home. A kind man gave us five dollars, and he would not give us his name. I hope he reads this. I hope he knows how much he helped us, how grateful we are.

Two days later, the doctor at the Veterans' Center said this was a new, unreported adverse drug reaction – he didn't know which drug or two drugs caused it, but he suspected xxxx, which I had been taking for a while, and xxxx, the new drug.

Since then, technology has come to my rescue. I bought a GPS system. I push one button, and a calm and reassuring voice tells me the best way to get home, when to make a turn, how many feet it is until I make that turn....

Since those awful days, usually on freeways, you kids, Alex especially, ask me if I know where we are. I am happy that you ask me, happier that I can tell you.

"I know where we are, I know where we're going, and I know how to get there."

I wish our lives were like that.

Dearest Children:

Thinking about the drug reactions I just described and talking about other drugs I take, you might think to yourselves, when you are a bit older, "Hey, wait a minute! Those are drugs for depression."

Yes, they are indeed drugs for depression.

I think I was born depressed and I discovered much later that I had cried continuously for my first month or so on earth. It turned out that I was not getting the nutrition I needed from my Mother's milk. She stopped nursing me and, following Doctor Spock's advice, as did every other mother in those post-war years, she started feeding me a store-bought formula. I cried a lot less. In later years, my younger Brothers and Sisters were all bottle-fed.

Amateur psychologists who know me draw all kinds of conclusions about that weak milk.

I hate even the sound of the word 'depression.' I've read too many articles about the deaths of artists or writers or musicians or poets, the big 'D' word appearing far too often.

I'd get depressed ever time I accomplished something. That doesn't seem right, does it? But there was always a big let-down, after finishing my PhD thesis, for example, or graduating from a program or passing the Texas Bar and the Minnesota Bar, or getting a law degree or a library science degree.

I got depressed too when bad things happened, and once the overwhelming numbness dissipated – the drowning death of my Brother when he was eighteen, break-ups of a multitude of romantic affairs gone sour, through college and after.

But, I really didn't know the meaning of the word 'depression' until I moved out from you three children. Now I know the breadth as well as the depths of the 'Big D' – they beyond my mind's capacity to comprehend. If something bad should happen to one of you children, I sometimes fear that I wouldn't be able to hold myself together, but I know I would, just for the two remaining children

Oh, Kids: Here's even more of that medical stuff, to show you what led up to those crazy night rides you experienced.

I have not had good luck when it comes to doctors figuring out what is wrong with me. It took a heck of a long time and many doctors to decide I needed emergency heart surgery in 1993. It took them a long time as well, to find in 2004 why I was so run-down.

I went to a lung doctor in Saint Paul. "Must be your lungs" he said. But the tests came back, and the problem was not with my lungs, he reported. That doctor sent me to another doctor who suspected allergies and referred me to an allergist. The allergist ordered me angrily out of his offices when it turned out I didn't have any regular allergies, any exercise-induced asthma, or any asthma at all. He sent me to yet another doctor closer to home, but he could find nothing wrong. I got more and more tired and lost more and more weight as they shuttled me from doctor to doctor.

After two years or so of this, I took myself back to Hennepin County Medical Center, the place where they had found my heart blockages a decade before, and had fixed them. I was happy to find out that the clinic would take me, even though I had moved to a different state. A doctor of internal medicine, not a pulmonary specialist, took one glance at my chest X-Ray, one of the most rudimentary of diagnostic instruments. "You have problems with your pleura," he said. "I'd say major problems."

"Pleura?" I asked.

"Yes," said the Doctor. "Think of your lungs as two balloons that are present inside two bigger balloons. Your lungs are fine, particularly when noting your decades of cigarette and pipe smoking. But there's something not right with your pleura." He pasted the X-rays onto the illuminated screen. "See all those specks? Those are asbestos tailings. They have worked their way from your mouth and nose and then through your lungs and out into the pleura. This process takes decades, and it leaves your pleura scarred -- stiff and immobile. They won't let you get the air you need."

This was not good news at all, but at least I could sue someone and get rich, like other people whose stories appeared in the paper. I thought of all the big companies who had asbestos claims against them. But neither the doctors, nor I, could think of a potential defendant – the 'villain' who had exposed me to asbestos. I wondered if maybe it was the Navy. A request for health records indicated that mine had been 'lost in a fire.' Anyway, it couldn't have happened in the Navy. "You didn't stay in one place long enough to get that amount of asbestos," said the doctor. "This process took decades."

For some reason unknown, the pleura started acting up in 2005. I lost my appetite suddenly, and I lost forty-seven pounds in short order. I lost my energy too.

The doctor was not sure that I didn't have mesothioloma, asbestos-related cancer. "We've done some tests, including a PET Scan, the best way to determine if the spots are malignant," said the doctor. But he wasn't at all comforted by the results. "There are a few cells, a few areas where I am not sure about cancer."

"So?" I asked, dreading the answer.

"We need to go in and do a full biopsy of your pleura. It will hurt afterwards, and you'll be in the hospital for about ten days."

They put me in a room that was empty. Then, one evening later, they brought in a room-mate – a black man with cocaine problems and other issues, including the lack of ability to NOT talk. "What you doing to me here? No, poking now, you hear? You pokes me in the side and then the front and when you're all done with that, you poke me in the butt. Man, what is with you people here? Poke, poke, poke – That's all you know. For Christ's ever-loving sake, get me out of this poke poke place! Get that needle away from me and go poke yourself!"

"How many times you been poked?" he asked me.

"Too many times, friend," I answered. "Too many times."

My cells were not cancerous, they discovered. The operation had hurt more than I thought it would, but I was home and back to work in ten days.

They are watching those spots, to see if they develop into cancer. "They may," say some doctors. "They will," say other doctors. Each day for me is a gift.

The lung doctor asked about my 'activity level.' Luckily, I had already received my degree in library science (you remember me leaving for classes in the evening or for marathon all-day classes on the weekends). But the doctor said that wasn't enough. "You need to retire. Driving twenty-seven miles to work and then working for nine hours and then driving home – it is too much."

So I retired 'for health reasons,' as they say. I had to leave the profession of law librarianship, which I liked and in which I had even made a small name for myself, after having spent most of my life trying to figure out what to do with myself as far as making money and careers went, and I was making enough money almost to support us.

I became depressed.

Other events piled on top of me. Between about 2005 and 2008, my Mother died of a stroke, and two Brother died, one of a heart attack, the other from pancreatic cancer.

Me? I was losing my energy, my weight, my breath. I was unable to talk for fifty minutes without losing my voice, even when I stuffed my mouth with sugar-free cough drops; that meant I couldn't teach anymore. And I couldn't use the stairway in the library – it was enough of a workout just to walk to the elevator. I couldn't be a law librarian anymore.

Those pills I mentioned earlier are mostly the anti-depressants that the doctor tried in order to arrive at the exact mixture that would give me as normal a life as possible. The acute reaction was just one of those things. None of the medical literature mentioned any problems with patients taking those two medications.

The doctor gave me other medications. I didn't even want to be happy; that was asking for too much. Just feeling normal – that was all I wanted.

Dear Young Adults:

Depression. No fun, huh? But there is some interesting news and some hope for improvement. The doctor at the VA seems most competent, better than most doctors whom I've seen.

He says that I am probably a manic-depressive. In a way, this could be good news. Knowing more about the disease, they can better treat it.

What's the difference between being depressed and being manic-depressive? A manic depressive person has highs and lows, both extreme. They don't necessarily have to follow a 50/50 schedule. Some people can be high most of the time, while others can be low much of the time (that's me).

Looking back at my life, I can see some potential high's. These are periods when I've been totally absorbed by something, don't want to do anything else, can't focus on much of anything else, and don't want to eat and I sleep poorly. Studying for bar exams, being involved in fiery and short-lived love relationship, teaching some classes, writing long works (including this manuscript) – these all give me highs. Most of early 1970, when I was in Russia, it was a high.

"High" in these instances is not at all like being drunk or taking drugs. It's quite the opposite. My senses seem sharper as I totally get wrapped up into something.

The process of adopting you three young adults was definitely a long-lasting high for me. One of the reasons I lost so much weight is that I had no appetite. I was too 'wired,' especially in Russia but also at home.

Lately, I have my highs when you three are around. I have my lowest lows on the day after you go back to your Mother's house. Then I slip into a regular low, until you return.

Dear Alex, Anna, and Katya:

I had figured out a way to get around the limited hours that the divorce decree allowed me to see the three of you.

I began to do volunteer work at your grade school. I started out in the library, where they were happy to have me because I have a recent masters degree in Library Science.

It worked out great. How clever I was! I got to see you nearly everyday. Maybe it was just passing in the hallways or meeting over lunch, but by 'grafting myself' to your school lives, I got to see you everyday and was able to converse with your teachers, watch how you inter-acted with others, and pay attention to how you were doing.

I worked in the library for a little over a year. I processed new books, helped with re-numbering books in the collection, shelving books, and checking them in and checking them out.

After a few months, it seemed as if everyone in the school knew me. I began to tutor students having reading challenges, and I helped the teachers assemble their classroom work and I helped decorate the halls sometimes.

Wow. I was able to do what most parents wish they could do but few manage. I was able to penetrate the psychological wall around your school lives.

This is how it usually goes between many parents and their children: "What did you do in school today?

Answer: "Recess."

But luckily for me, I was in there, in the middle of the fray. You kids and I had plenty of things to talk about.

Then something happened. I was given fewer and fewer challenging tasks. One job for more than a couple of months involved cutting paper – Someone had donated a couple boxes of note pads to the school, but the top of each page had a rendering that sort of resembled the ceiling of the Sistine Chapel. There was Moses, in a flowing robe, and, holy sh*t: There was also a woman with two boobs hanging out.

Those were the parts of the sheets of the paper that I cut out for hours on end.

A few people, staff mostly, and not students or faculty, seemed to have changed their relationship with me. They were now distant and quite formal. The principal would stop me each day, and sometimes twice, just to ensure that I was alright, that I didn't need anything, that I was being 'accommodated.' She'd stare deep into my eyes.

The word 'accommodated' struck me. Every administrator hears that word in the context of employment law or education law. In other words, the principal was afraid I might do something for which I could later sue them, or I might hurt myself or others.

Yes, this was the time that I had to change doctors because of losing my job and its insurance, and I had turned to the Veterans Administration. For me, the care was almost free and it was great, but the changes in medications sometimes caused problems, as you well know.

I mentioned to a few people that weekend from hell with you kids. I should have kept my damned mouth shut. Worse, I had to leave work early a couple of times because I was throwing up.

Poet Robert Burns already said it. "O wad some Pow'r the giftie gie us/To see ourselves as others see us." I wonder what else I did that made people nervous or suspicious. Did I perhaps stagger, or say the wrong things to the wrong people? I will give them the benefit of the doubt.

I went to the principal, rather than waiting for her to come to me. I quit. Abruptly. I merely said that I used to enjoy volunteering at the school, but not anymore.

My career as a grade school voluntary assistant librarian was over, but luckily, our connection with the school continues. I regret that those damned privacy issues prevent me from naming that wondrous place. The teachers and staff have created miracles for you. Regular classroom teachers, speech therapists, learning specialists, school district professionals – the list goes on. Bless them all.

Parents of students are invited to come to the school and have lunch with their children. I take advantage of that on Mondays – fifteen minutes with Alex, then fifteen minutes with Katya and Anna. Thus, I am able to work it out so that I see you every other day.

Dear Alex:

Last Wednesday I said I wasn't feeling well and I was going to take a brief nap on the lower bunk in the girls' room. You said that you too were tired, so you crawled into the narrow bed with me. Then you remembered your large, stuffed Scooby-Do and Teddy, your big stuffed bear. "They will be lonely without me," you said.

So you went and got them and put them to bed with me. Then you thought about Astronaut Man and your horse. They came to bed with us too. And what about Viking Man and Iron Man? Surely they'd be lonely.

"I am ready to sleep," you said finally, but first you had to make sure we were safe. So you went and got your pirate's sword. Then your regular sword. Then your army rifle. Then two other rifles. Then your police uniform and your Batman uniform and your firemen's hammer and a badge.

By then, it was time to get up.

Dearest Darling Katya:

Your smile animates your whole face, and then that face can transform itself back to pure sadness or indifference, and you do it so quickly. Your frowns and your brave moments and times of exasperation and your sadness – you show them all, without reserve. I like taking you to Como Amusement Park, just to see the incredible smile that spreads across your face as you spin around on a ride, or race downhill on a roller-coaster.

Plus, you have another face. It is the very essence of a state called 'suffering.'

I recall the day, just weeks ago, when Anna accidentally shut my truck door on your fingers. I witnessed the surreal appearance of your suffering – the essence of it.

Your face was pale and contorted – utter anguish, but, Katya, you were lucky – no dismemberment, no cuts, no signs of damage whatsoever. I was at the rear of the truck and didn't see the accident. I looked at your hand and decided you needed some ointment; that is, you needed some ministrations, and the application of ointment, while doing nothing to the wound, would make you feel better.

And then you really started sobbing all over again and you said, "Papa, can I sleep next to you tonight?"

What a sentence for a divorced Father to hear. I wanted to hold you and hug you and not have to leave that evening but stay with you there, just in case you might awaken with a nightmare. And what about Alex and Anna? What kind of Father was I, that I had abandoned you kids, except for the few piddly visitation times during the week?

I have a little more empathy now for divorced parents who kidnap their own kids.

Dear Katya:

I recall another Katya scenario in your repertoire. The first time I saw it was when you were about five years old and Anna was seven. You had apparently fallen off your bike down the road, and there was a small bit of blood running down your knee to your heel.

There you were, with a look defining absolute pain and helplessness. You kept your balance with your right hand on the fence, while your older Sister helped you along, urging you onward. You limped as if each step brought unendurable pain. Anna walked alongside you, patiently and concerned, like a good nurse.

What a scene. No camera could do it justice – your pained expression as you limped, Anna's ministrations along the way.

I think this serves as an emblem reflecting the relationship of you two. Katya needs Anna. Anna takes care of Katya. It was all in your faces, lovely and beautiful faces that they are. Russian faces. I hope I am around long enough to see how that relationship between you two girls evolves, and how your faces will change, and how you will remain 'being there' for one-another.

Dear Katya Katya Katya:

We speak of children as if they were bread loaves – how well will they rise? I wonder how you will turn out.

Did you know that to call you 'darling' or 'dear' in Russian, it could be 'Milaya Katya.' I like the sound of it. "My dear Katya" would be 'moya milaya Katya.' I like the sound of that too.

You have come so far. Your Russian citizenship papers show a tiny photo of a girl about three years old. The photo looked quite different from the way you look in photos now, but there was no denying it – These were pictures of Katya. Your medical papers listed you as a deaf-mute, but one day you apparently decided to talk and to hear, just as you apparently decided to pee all over the doctor holding you up to have a good look at you, the final days in Moscow.

In life, you will do what you want to do, and few things will be able to stop you. I need to give you wide latitude. I am not trying to force you to take music lessons or to take up a sport, for instance, like your Brother and Sister. You prefer to be alone or with your play animals or your real animals, or to read. Okay.

Just yesterday, you and I were kicking a soccer ball around the sidelines while Anna was involved in a real soccer game on the field. Even from a distance, I could tell that Anna was not happy with the state of things. Whenever she plays with her team, she's wrapped up in the heat of the moment on the field, in a game that requires total attention, and yet she always knows when I pick up my book or when I start conversing with someone else. It hurts her. She is the oldest sibling and often doesn't get her due. Sometimes she demands total attention, but this is an unfortunate demand when you are the oldest of three children.

I recall visiting you three kids in the orphanage. Any time I started up a conversation with any of the other Russian kids, Anna jumped between us and commanded the kid, in Russian, to 'get the heck out of there.' I think she had experienced too much sadness already in her young life. She didn't want to be abandoned, even for a minute.

Anyway, the soccer game was going on during a beautiful Minnesota June evening, before the blistering late-summer heat makes its way from Texas to Minnesota. Katya, you and I were playing off to the side. We weren't such a good match. I'm afraid that my having only half my lung power, plus having a fused lower back – this gave you advantages.

I got short of breath and so we quit playing. "I don't want to play any sport," you said. It was not defiant, and I don't believe you were looking for an argument. "I hate sports," you continued.

"Me too, dear," I answered. "I was always the last person anyone picked to be on their team."

You laughed. "Oh, I know what that is like!"

"My Father was a semi-pro baseball player," I said. "And he wanted me, his first son, to follow in his footsteps. I hated baseball and I hated all sports. I hated the school gym teacher because he hated me and he liked calling attention to my ineptitude in whatever sport they were playing at that moment."

"Were you sick or something, Papa? Is that why he didn't like you?"

"No, not sick. But he, like many others, called me 'Four Eyes,' because of my glasses. Not so many grade-schoolers in those days wore glasses, and mine were thick, like the bottom of pickle jars. I have since had Lasik surgery, which allowed me to toss the thick glasses and to see things clearly from a distance. But I can't see a thing up close, no matter how hard I try, so I wear glasses all the time; the upper part is nearly blank plastic, the lower part magnifies.

Why do I hide behind a pair of glasses? I hate putting on and taking off reading glasses, for instance, just to look at the face on my watch, or to look closely at your face or at the numerous wounds you must show me daily."

When I got my first pair of glasses, in first grade, they were still called 'spectacles.' The word make me think of Benjamin. I wonder if he had to hold on to his spectacles as he flew his kite.

You laughed, Katya, when you heard me say how much I disliked sports, especially those on TV where the fans scream and the announcers shout all he time. My embarrassment at revealing these things was worth it because you flashed your enduring smile. "Did you ever do <u>any</u> sports, Papa?" you asked.

"No. When I was about forty, I tried golf because it is relaxing, according to my Brother Tim, rest his soul. For me, it was a waste of time. You don't burn off calories or help out your heart by zipping around in golf carts and yelling at caddies or screaming at foursomes ahead of you. Tim worked hard to teach me this 'relaxing' game. On one of the holes at Como Park, his tee shot flew into a sand trap, down a steep hill. I stayed up on the fairway. Soon, I heard a couple of nasty words coming from the other side of the hill, and then a golf club, not a golf ball, shot up into the air. Then another club – I think it was his 'nine iron.' Then another club and finally, an empty golf bag.

So much for this 'relaxing' sport."

"But what about baseball?" you asked. "Your Father really wanted you to play?"

"He made me stand for hours, throwing the ball up against the wall of our building in the Projects and then catching it. 'Keep doing it until you can catch ten balls in a row," he commanded. "Then come and tell me."

"Well?"

"I never got beyond four. I was hopeless, and my eyes were bad with astigmatism so I had a hard time judging distances, especially off to the side. This didn't make for good catching or batting. Things got better for me when my oldest then-living Brother, Frank, showed interest in baseball. He could catch and pitch and hit and run. I wasn't jealous of him at all. I was glad he came along so I could get away from the darned sport."

"I am so glad I have a Papa who doesn't do sports," you said. "So many kids are really serious about it, and their parents too. Look at that Father with the red face over there, screaming at the boy in the yellow and black shirt."

"Katya, I promise that you won't have to do any sport that you don't want to. You will have to figure out a way to keep your heart and your whole body in shape some other way, though."

"Like swimming?"

"Well, maybe, but I found it too lonely and you had to take too many showers."

You laughed your cute laugh. "What about running?"

"I ruined one knee and two ankles by running. Of course, running shoes back then in the seventies weren't as good as they are today. My exercise now is walking. I take long walks and I think up things to write about while walking. But what are you going to during your summers if you don't do sports?"

"A computer class. Then an art class that might be okay. And then reading and then reading some more."

"That sounds like a perfect summer," I said.

You had indeed come a long way. You were speaking clearly, understandably, and without stammering or stuttering. I think you stammered the most when you didn't want to say something, or when you were nervous or felt pressured.

I could tell that Anna was irritated as you and I talked. "We better go watch the game or we both will be in trouble," I said.

"I love you, Papa," you said as we raced towards the spectator section. You made it first, of course.

We were now about twenty feet apart. I turned and I sensed what was coming next – it had become our ritual, one that had begun in the school hallways on custody days, when I came to pick you up. You sprinted towards me, and at the very last minute you leaped up into my arms and I held you on high like a baby. You kissed me. I kissed you, and then I let you down. You are getting bigger, and my back is not improving. Your leaps are becoming more painful for me, but in no way do I intend to give them up.

"I want to read and read and read, all summer. Can I sometimes read out loud to you?" you asked.

"Absolutely! I couldn't think of a better summer, and I'd like one like that too."

We were now sitting on a lawn chair, you on my lap. Out on the field, Anna's performance took a sharp turn for the better. Her coach remarked on it. "Hey, Gramps, stay close to the sideline! It brings out the best in her!"

Gramps. How many times had people made that assumption? And why not? I didn't get angry, just a little bored at correcting people.

My dear Katya, keeper of small animals and the maker of miniature skis and swimming pools and cardboard houses for all, you have a strong character. You probably didn't talk for your first three or four years because you didn't feel like it. Your choice of clothing does not always generate approval by others. "To hell with it!" you probably say to yourself. You like those red striped pants and those orange socks with blue stripes and that tie-died T-shirt and your purple sweater, and the colors are all stunning. Who cares about wearing polka-dots and stripes and multi-colored pieces at the same time? You wear it all with great pride that to some might seem defiance.

You have two close friends at school, and you seem well-liked by all, including your teachers. Mrs. Richards, your second-grade teacher, had to split up you and your two best friends because you weren't paying enough attention in class. There were just too many important things to discuss. You had come far, being at one time a hesitant and mute little girl.

I described already the way you make your bed and ride your bike or scooter, and steer other peoples' boats. I love that fiery, happy look on your face.

But, best of all, I liked what I saw this past weekend, when we went to Como Park and spent too much money on rides. I saw you on the roller-coaster, alone in the last car. Later, I saw you sitting alone in a ride consisting of swinging chairs that twirled in a circle faster and faster and faster and higher and higher. What joy I saw! Your sparkling eyes, that incredibly large smile of yours under that incredibly large forehead of yours -- There is something about rapid movement that brings joy to you. Sometimes on rides, you smile extra-hard and wave at me.

The doctors say I will forget things as I get older, but I swear I will hold on to those images of you always.

Dear Katya:

As a young person, you had a peculiar fascination with animals. You had come to the right house. There were six cats and four dogs, including dear Ruthie, a brown Labrador mutt. One day, years before you came, we were taking Ruthie to an obedience class, which she desperately needed, and we happened to walk by the 'Adopt A Stray Pet' section of the pet store. It was stacked with cages of lonely cats and dogs, waiting for a family. That day we walked out with Pasha, a beautiful shepherd-Husky mix who, it turns out, had horrible misalignment of his hips and that's probably why he had been given over to the animal orphanage. He was fine after surgery and after a couple thousand dollars.

Before their obedience training, in the winter, I took both out on leashes for a walk up and down the alley, as well as for the performance of certain creature 'obligations.' The alley was covered with ice. The two dogs knew not the meaning of the words 'heel!' or 'stop!' I felt as if I was water-skiing.

Now your 'other' house boasts of a third dog, a puppy named Elf, who is part husky and part Akita. I took with me the two old dachshund rescue dogs, and Vivian the cat, who had been with me through two marriages and the death of one spouse. You still have five cats at your other house -- Obie (which got shortened from 'Orange Bastard' because he was so ornery until we moved out of Minneapolis).

Away from South Minneapolis and its tiny lots, and almost out in the country, Obie has room to roam and to lord over other creatures. The folks at the treatment center not far from your Mother's house have 'adopted' him. He goes there frequently and plays cute until they give him a big plate of food. They think he is not fed otherwise.

I don't know how that tubby cat manages to carry off that deception. Then he returns to your Mother's house, strutting down the driveway as the more timid cats look on. Then he begs for food from you kids.

Mrowbie (onomatopoetic) comes next, then Ivan, who had been with me through two marriages and three moves. I had chosen him at the Minneapolis Humane Society the day we handed over our donations and spread the ashes of Kate, my dear late wife.

Sadly, there are pet limits at the trailer park where I moved and so I couldn't bring Ivan with me. It was a hard choice, like the one Solomon suggested.

Ivan was prospering in Wisconsin whereas Vivian merely survived. She didn't like the dogs at all. They knew it, and so they chased her all the time. Soon, she spent most of her time hiding in the cracks of the damp basement that was made from stones scooped out of the glacial ridge a couple of centuries years earlier.

Vivian? She was the one who needed to move.

Me? The divorce settlement gave me the two aged dachshunds (Lulu and Gretel), ladies who had been thrown out, no doubt, from a puppy mill when they had become too old to bear children, and Vivian. Poor Gretel had breast cancer and a few weeks ago the nice vet at the Banfield Pet Center removed two big tumors. The lumps came back.

Gretel took her last breath on the front seat of my car, in my lap, as I was rushing her back to the vet.

We had a funeral for Gretel; each of us said what we liked about her, or we talked about our favorite memories of her. We buried her in your Mother's back yard, where Gretel used to jump and run, pretending she was a big dog with long legs. We buried her on your Mother's property since we don't know how long I will be where I am. Since Gretel's death, Lulu has slowed down. Maybe she wants to follow Gretel.

Katya, you treat these real animals as if they were toys. You hold them, fondle them, drag them around on a leash. I can just see that look of strained patience on Lulu's face whenever you show up. She knows her afternoon of repose has just been canceled.

What about your toy animals? You treat them as if they were real. You place them in strategic places around your Mother's house as well as around my trailer, so that they can see all that's going on. Each inch of territory is covered by someone's steady gaze, the same way that a well-constructed sprinkling system will hit each square foot of a well-tended lawn.

You made water skis for one plastic dog out of popsicle sticks, and a pool made from an empty food container. You dress these creatures, talk to them, argue with them, and sometimes punish them when they misbehave.

Your big pink pony normally sticks its snout up to your bedroom window, looking out over your Mother's front yard, the garage, the gully, and anyone passing on the driveway. Thanks to Alex's medical set, the pets you bring here are all in good health.

Today, some two years later, you asked me for my shovel and you dug two holes in the yard. You took two containers from the kitchen, and you asked me to turn on the outside water spigot. I had turned it back on because it was spring and there was little chance of a deep frost again that year. You filled the containers with water. You put down dollhouse furniture. What were you doing? You turned this part of my yard into a miniature spa and restful resort for your small plastic turtle.

You are always on the look-out for empty boxes and containers. You have an urge to make homes for your dolls and toy animals. A shoe box, for instance, makes an ideal studio apartment, once you cut out a door and a couple of windows. You and I built a wagon for hauling animals, sort of like a miniature circus wagon. We used a furniture-moving platform and an old wooden drawer from a discarded chest. It was clunky, and a real carpenter would wince if he saw it. But it works. I built a crib for your dolls too.

I have two giant storage areas that are attached to each side of my trailer. Both are a mess, containing my stuff, over which was placed my Brother Tom's stuff, after he died, over which was placed some of my Mother's things, after she died. I can't find anything that I need, but I somehow manage to come up with the things you need.

I put in a pet door and built a makeshift ramp so the animals could get outside when they wanted or needed to. Copying me, you built a little house for your stuffed dog on one of my bookshelves, and then you built a small ramp for it, using a board and putting screws into it every few inches, for traction. Now your dog can get down when necessary or when it wants.

All your toys need homes, Katya. You need a home. You need permanence. I hope you can found that after the divorce, knowing that you now have two parents who love you and two houses to visit.

I'm so sorry I let you down.

It is hard to write or think about it, impossible not to remember it. Your face, its look of panic. Your voice. I wish for once that my memory would make an exception and help me forget, rather than see those dark and horrible silhouettes of the recent past.

Dear Alex, Katya, Anna:

For now, you think it's cool that your Papa is sixty-four, but I bet that some day you will be embarrassed. You and I may attend a Father-daughter dance, or perhaps that's an odd rite reserved for Catholic high schools, such as the one I attended. Or you'll go to parties or you'll be on team or in activities where parents are involved, and I will be the only person there who is old enough to be the father of everyone else there.

Your schoolmates already comment on my gray beard and my gray hair and my wrinkles and stiff gait.

I don't care that I am old. It took me a long time to get my life in order. For doing that finally, after so many years, I received three wonderful rewards – Alex, Katya, and Anna.

Dear Katya, Anna, Alex:

You are thrilled and proud that your Papa lives in a narrow, metal house that has wheels, now rusted and without rubber tires, underneath.

You have made many friends here in the trailer park, in the community, only for the 2.5 days or evenings weekly that you are here. Mark lives three trailers up; he has a hip replacement thing that is costing his parents a lot of money. They can't afford to buy a 'real' home, which trailer people call 'stick houses.'

Alex, your closest friend here is perhaps Chad. He is fun to play with even though there is 'something wrong in his head.' The right words don't come out sometimes, or else words come out but they are not understandable. You are patient with him. "He can't help it," you say, just as you say it whenever anyone does something wrong, including your Papa, who does it often.

Someday, you will hear the term 'trailer trash,' and soon thereafter, you might grow to dislike the place where your Father lives. It will be a test of character to see how you react.

Some people think that only 'trash' or bums or alcoholics live in trailer parks, or people who are too lazy to work, or people collecting welfare payments even though they could work, or people too lazy to look for a job or to hold onto one.

Things are not that way. Most of the people living here have a job and often two jobs that don't pay enough, or else there is a medical problem in the family that sucks up the money. Many other people here can't find good, well-paying jobs because their skin is the wrong color or their eyes are funny or they say 'gracias' instead of 'thank you.'

Among the scant pile of alternative living arrangements, buying a mobile home was a logical choice for me. Buying a 'real' house was not possible, Social Security Disability payments notwithstanding, and if I had rented an apartment, I doubt you would have been happy with your visits there. The apartment owners would not allow pets, there would be no place for you to play, no privacy for me, and the building would outlaw any kind of fun.

This trailer is good for me. It offers quiet and solitude, and it has opened my eyes to many groups of people I might otherwise not have met. I see that last advantage applies to you too. When you are not in the trailer, you are in a place that is vanilla, lily-white. Here, you get lots of diversity.

My Mother gave me money, right before she died, so I could buy the trailer. This, she said, was payment for the couple months' work I'd done cleaning up Brother Tom's house and getting it ready for sale. Tommy was gone, unexpectedly, and now his possessions had to go too. My Mother and I gave away stuff, to family, then to friends and neighbors. What was left, we donated. After that, we threw out stuff, and put other stuff into my storage rooms.

We made a big mistake when we donated Tom's items to the xxxx Charity. I recall one day when I was dropping off things at the back entrance to xxxx. Your Mother was always picky when it came to buying things --- Clothes had good labels, for instance.

As I was dropping off the stuff, I noticed that two of the workers were loading a truck with bales of clothes, tied tightly together by wires.

I checked around and found out. The xxxx charity does not sort through things, clean them up, and offer them for sale in their stores. No, they sell clothes, for instance, at a dollar or two for a truckload of baled clothes.

Where do those clothes end up? In stores that look like charities but are not. Store signs such as xxxxx and xxxx are not non-profit stores. They buy things from charities for a song, and then they sort through the stuff and put out on their shelves items that surely find a buyer.

The only 'charity' part of the deal is the small stack of nickels and pennies they use to buy the things from the charity stores. Then they sell the things, and many people think they are buying from a charity. Not so. Xxxxx and xxxx are for-profit companies which no doubts pay their managers a high wage and pay their workers, (many of whom might live in run-down trailer park communities) a few bucks an hour.

But I digress. Back to the community.

This 1977 Marshfield Trailer gives me the shag carpeting, green tiles in the hallways, kitchen and bathroom, swag laps, and dark wood paneling, bought in 4 x 8 sheets, from places such as Mills Fleet Farm, just over the hill.

My trailer is a step back into the 1970's, a time in my life when things were good for me. A 2001 décor wouldn't be so hot for me, except for the presence of three young adults. With them, I can endure much.

I rent the spot for $424 a month, and so far, in nearly two years, I have had only one major expenditure; the thirty-two-year old Maytag Clothes Washer retied and gave up its ghost. It had served well during its long life.

I was sorry to see it go; I couldn't find a replacement in the correct color – 'Harvest Gold' had gone out of fashion about thirty years ago.

The furnace and water heater and roof all are in good shape, and the trailer came with a new water softener which, someday, I may figure out how to operate. I worry about the chipped harvest gold electric stove and the old harvest gold clothes dryer, but so far, they have behaved well.

So, in the final analysis, I live in a trailer community that has seen days, much finer than those today. My trailer is falling apart – the combination of age and xxxx fake wood, and ice and water are taking their toll.

I sit in that crumbling trailer, my body giving out on me. Vivian, my cat, is fourteen years old and falling apart. Lulu, my dachshund, is remarkably old. I don't know exactly how old because we adopted he from a rescue operation,, but she had a white snout when we adopted her in 2002. She had 21 teeth pulled, and she takes just about as many pills as I.

Viv and Lulu and I look at one-another and wonder who will be the next one.

Oh. Every time that you see an 'xxxx' or an 'xxxxx – That means there is a company or article involved, and it for they are protected by copyright. I don't name names. I don't like people yelling at me or sending warnings via U.S. mail, return receipt requested. I also don't like anyone, especially wealthy companies with battalions of lawyers, yelling at me.

Living in a trailer park has opened vistas for me. The parks don't leave room for B.S. "You are what you are, and you ain't what you ain't," in the words of Ann Landers via John Prine. You are stuck living in a trailer park community, just like everyone else here, so there is no room, literally and figuratively, for pretense.

But do you know what? It's almost like a family here; yes, a family with its share of dysfunction, but no more than other families (except for my family of origin, perhaps). One time my carbon dioxide monitor went off. It was a horrible noise, and all three of you kids plugged your ears as I led you out of the trailer and a block away.

Nothing was wrong, it turned out; I guess the alarm just needed a new battery and wanted to make sure I knew about it. Well, within just a minute or two, and during normal work hours, mind you, at least twenty-five people rushed towards my trailer. One guy was late because his wheelchair got stuck in the mud. Another guy had a spiffy carbon monoxide tester. He lugged it over, and he found no traces of the gas.

Very many families here have an expensive medical problem (witness Mark and Chad), so there is no money left over for a 'real' house or apartment. Are you listening, Barak Obama and senators and representatives and governors?

Many people learn to love the trailer life and would not exchange it for a 'real' house. You meet a great variety of people, whereas your other house is in an exurban, vanilla area. Here we meet all kinds of people; we get along with all of them, I think, except for the lousy mechanic who took my Civic, collected my money, and didn't fix it.

I don't have a retirement fund or insurance proceeds. The remaining small chunks of it went to Russia, and it was money extremely well-spent. Or the money went into improving a house which I no longer occupy, or the house before that, in South Minneapolis, which neither your Mother or I now occupy.

Imagine, your Mother was about twenty-five years old when she bought a house. That is really something special; most people that age have problems paying rent for studio apartments.

I will be in the trailer for a while, and not minding it much at all.

When you are not around, I am alone. Completely alone. I prefer that, most of the time, for the times that you aren't with me.

Dear Anna, Katya, and Alex:

Today, Saturday, we celebrated Fathers' Day, because you will be in another house on Sunday.

Memory. Somebody told me about her, or else I had read somewhere about her – A young girl who loved her Father and lost him when she was young. Sometimes, strong feelings and memories about her Father unexpectedly and suddenly appeared. It was as if she was four years old again and her Father was with her. Why?

She found the answer herself, without help from anyone. Her Father used Old Spice Aftershave Lotion, and whenever her Father hugged her or held her, she smelled his aftershave. Now, when she was around other men who wore Old Spice, the aroma was strong enough to pull her back to her earliest years, to the Father whom she loved and lost.

What is it about memory?

Last Wednesday, it was my custody day and we had to stop by your Mother's house that used to be our house, to drop off Alex's baseball gear and to pick up a few things for Anna. The house and yard were empty. I didn't go into the house, although I could have, I suppose, under the pretext of watching out for you children.

I chose to stay outside, in the yard.

I took a long look around, from the driveway where I had parked. Going further would have made me feel like a trespasser on someone else's property. I looked around, at as much as I could see from the driveway.

It had been about two years since I had been in that yard or on those grounds. The old two-story house sits on three-and-a-half acres. I looked at the half acre or so that lies between the house and the road and the neighbors' driveway. (They have an easement that allows them to use a common driveway running past your house to their house, down the hill from your Mother's house, closer to the river.)

A steep hill divides the lower portion of the property from the high ground around the house and the road. A grassy meadow lies at the other end of the property near the river, I knew, even though I couldn't see it. Why is the ground so level there? It used to be a power company access road that ran along a lake, but the lake disappeared when the State took out the dam downriver, creating a state park, and letting the falls gush forth in their full fury, and the power company no longer needed a road that led to a swamp downriver from your Mother's property.

I recalled that because of various sales of property over the century, the lot on which I stood, your Mother's lot now, was even more oddly shaped. When your Mother and I were buying the house, the land surveyor had a heck of a time figuring the boundaries – there were metal stakes and buried lead pipe in irregular lines all over the place, like a tangle of cables and cords that you might find behind a computer. Big chunks of that land, which used to look like a hand, are now someone else's property. So, it's sort of like the way a person eats around the outside of an apple or chews on a cob of corn.

I was standing up at the road, the highest part of the yard, not far from the house. About one-hundred feet of property runs along that road. The whole yard was overgrown and a big mess when we moved in. Buckthorn, a crazily invasive bush, had taken over in many places and, as had a strange kind of Bavarian Bamboo guaranteed to choke whatever you planted. Not to mention a multitude of fat vines that wrapped themselves around trees, sucking the life out of them.

Memory. I had dug up that hundred feet that running alongside the road. I had planted a row of lilies along half the road -- Lilies were free. They grew wild in the gully that lay on the opposite side of the driveway. I dug into these piles of free lilies, with the capable help of you three young adults, and we hauled them by wheelbarrow and planted them along the road. It looked pitiful, a disaster. They were just little pale weeds, flopping on the ground, looking like they never would survive, never become erect again.

When your Mother and I had moved in, seven years earlier, a bunch of hydrangea plants hugged the north side of the house. I took little clippings from them. I planted about a fifty-foot row of those small clippings up by the road, behind the lilies. They looked more pathetic than the lilies, and there was a very good chance that winter temperatures and snow plows and road salt would do them in.

Well, they survived beautifully. On this visit, the hydrangeas were about four feet tall and filled with beautiful white blossoms. I had also taken about forty feet of driveway leading towards the river, between the house in question and the neighbors' house, and I had planted a stubby row of hydrangea cuttings on both sides of the drive – pathetic little sticks that they were. The neighbors must have been embarrassed coming down that drive, when scraggly cuttings lined their passage, as if they were signs of mortality, like the skull that monks used to keep on their tables. But no longer were these rows of hydrangea pathetic. The sticks have grown into gigantic hydrangea bushes, heavy with flowers, bushes that have to be cut back so they don't cover the driveway.

Memory. I was looking at all this. Much of it was my handiwork (often with the help of you three young adults), and I was feeling nothing. Yes, I had precise memories of what I had done, but there were no feelings attached to those memories. This was the opposite of the woman who loved Old Spice Aftershave but didn't remember why, until she probed.

Shouldn't I have been angry or at least sad that I lost all this? Shouldn't I have wept even?

The work that I described is just a start. I busted up two concrete foundations behind the house and down by the lilac bushes, with a sledge hammer, while wearing a post-surgery back brace. This had been just a few weeks or months after my second lower back surgery, and I fear that the sledge-hammering was not part of the surgeon's suggestions for recuperating, and that it may have helped lead me towards a third surgery.

The gulley behind the garage had been a dump for years. Old tires and layers of rotting carpet and old cabinets littered the area. I cleared it out. You helped. We met big families of very unhappy wasps who considered the rotting carpets their private domain.

As I now looked over the pretty gully, I was not angry then, and I have absolutely no anger as I write this. You remember how that gully used to look, right? I yanked out buckthorn and bamboo and I chopped down scruffy trees.

I can write more. When your Mother and I moved into that place, barely affording the mortgage, we couldn't see half of the property from the house because a wedge of dying trees and buckthorn bushes and killer vines wrapped around trees and dead trees -- they formed a dense triangle that cut off the view of the meadow. I learned how to use a chain saw, more or less, and I cleared it all out.

I remember going to the doctor for some unimportant reason at the time, and he led me into another room. Soon, an administrator entered, all the while looking at the floor, as if her job was not administrating or nursing, but inspecting the clinic's linoleum.

"I am required to ask you this," she said. Her cheeks were red and the pen in her hands shook. She coughed a dry cough and then she opened her mouth, as if to speak, and she spoke, "Are you being abused?"

I knew not what she was talking about, until I looked at my arms and saw that I was covered with scratches, cuts, and bruises, as was my back. "Oh!" I said. "No! That's from clearing buckthorn, and worse, from digging up a stubborn juniper bush whose root ball was the size of a Buick."

You can pull up a young buckthorn plant with hardly any effort at all. But wait a few years, and when the plant is fully grown, it takes a lot of work to dig it up. In that way, buckthorn is like some people.

I recall all this about the house and the yard and the nervous hospital administrator and the buckthorn and its scars and scratches on my body. I feel nothing. Perhaps I am one of those despicable males accused of being 'separated from their feelings.' But I seem to have had feelings otherwise.

And a final note, kids, because you were participants. The acre up between the house and the road? It now looks like a park. Many rock-lined paths meander around tamaracks and maples and hosta and various other expensive plants that I neither bought nor knew the name of, some of which came from your Grandmother's yard.

Hah! Those rock-lined paths. I bet there are five hundred stones lining those paths. You three young adults and I dragged most of them up from the hill that's way down towards the river, where the glacier had so graciously left them for us, eons ago. Your Mother helped sometimes but often she was busy with some other kind of landscaping necessity.

When you and I ran out of stones that lay on the surface, we learned how to tap the ground with hammers and shovels, and sense the edges of underground ridges just waiting to crumble. Alex, you became an expert at finding those ledges. We pounded at them with hammers and dug up pieces of rock with shovels and crowbars.

What a job we did. Sometimes it took almost a half hour to get one big rock uphill, through an area thick with trees and vegetation, and around a rotting fertilizer wagon that had stood there so long that trees had grown right through it. Somehow, we four managed to get those rocks up the steep hill, across the property, past the house, and up to the new paths. In the process, we broke a heavy-duty garden wagon and an extra-heavy-duty metal wagon, and we did violence on a new wheelbarrow that soon looked like it had been run over by a tractor. Not to mention chipped shovels and bent crow-bars. I rewarded your work by giving you rides in the wheelbarrow downhill, as we went back in the summer heat to our cache of rocks.

I remember all that, and still more – the giant scraggly bushes, on the dark side of the garage, that needed to be dug up and tugged at and axed out of the ground – it took a whole morning and afternoon, squeezed between my work at the College and the courses I was taking at another college.

When you three came to live with us, you were happy to help me trim tall tamaracks while high on a ladder during which, I confess, my knees shook. But a father's knees should never shake in front of his children. I chopped off dead branches which you caught and dragged into the gully where later, we would chip them into small pieces so that they would become food for the trees and bushes and flowers, including the bunches of lilies that wouldn't bloom because they received too little sunlight. We spent hours on those aged trees, no doubt planted over a hundred years ago, when the village was born.

What is it about tamarack trees that, as they grow, the new branches block the older, lower branches from the sun, and the lower branches die?

Is there a lesson for us, hidden deep inside those tree trunks?

But looking over all these things and remembering how we shaped them and nurtured them, I had no feelings, no aftershave memories. It is all dead within me.

But that's a trifle. How about you three children? I bet that if we went back to Peterburg, you would look at the orphanage and at the people who took such good care of you for two-three years, and you would remember nothing, would make no connections.

Maybe you have pounded down the Russian parts of you, making room for the three Americans who stand in their stead.

And, for you, no doubt, your early years are filled with too much pain to remember, and so the little file clerks that work in the rooms and file cabinets of our hearts tuck away the memories in places we can't reach? I could surely see that in your circumstances with Russia, but not necessarily in mine. Divorce is such a commonplace thing these days.

Memory.

I hope that these few pages of discussion that concern your first years in America will help you remember them. Maybe. Maybe not. I don't know. Perhaps that is why I am not known as a memoirist and don't want to be called one now. This book is about you, not me or anyone else.

Maybe, like in movies and books, you three will experience one 'Old Spice' moment, and then all of your memories will come back.

Will you break down and cry when your memories of Russia come back, or will you laugh, or simply reminisce?

I don't know.

Dear Anna:

I am so proud of you. You came to America knowing no English and you started kindergarten eight weeks later. You adapted fast, and well.

You are all-American now, through and through. You did a thorough job on yourself, in record time.

You play soccer. You said last year that you enjoyed it, but it almost looked to me that you really weren't getting involved in the game, and you seemed to make a point of staying far away from the ball. When the ball was near you, it sometimes seemed that you were being overly polite, stepping out of the way so your opponent could kick.

This year's soccer started out the same way, but then one evening you kicked the ball hard, nearly from the center of the field, and you made a goal. Everyone cheered. Your eyes lit up; you became so animated it seemed as if you'd changed physically. From then on, teammates have not hesitated to include you in their most complex maneuvers, and opponents learn quickly to avoid you. Anna Jack is known to 'kick butt' out there on the field.

You are proud to tell me that you are a tom-boy, and you are; yet are a charming young woman who appreciates feminine things.

This year, you started to study violin. I am proud, and happy. The violin is my favorite instrument. Did I ever have lessons? No. "We don't have space or money for any damned pianos or horns or whatever it is you want," my Mother said. "There's already enough god-damned noise in this apartment," my Father added.

In high school, I joined the school military marching band (there was no other choice) just so that I could learn to play an instrument. The only open spots were in the clarinet section. I looked forward to learning to play it, even though I have ever been fond of the clarinet, presuming that I could then transfer some of that knowledge over to another instrument, a violin maybe.

What happened? The crabby band leader handed me a clarinet and a music book and he told me where to buy reeds. "Come back when you know how to play the clarinet," he said. That marked the beginning as well as the end of my musical training. I went through a couple packs of expensive (for me, at least) reeds, and all I could do on the clarinet was screech. I brought the clarinet back to the music room at school. Today, when I hear a clarinet solo during a symphony, I remember those music 'lessons.'

How's that for an 'Old Spice' memory?

I am happy for you, Anna, and, I confess, a bit envious. Yes, your parents are divorced, but I believe that all three of you young adults are being brought up well. You have two good houses that want you and that are good for you. I wasn't so lucky when I was your age. Time will tell how well you have been brought up. Is the old axiom true? Is it better to live with divorced parents living in different places than it is to live with parents who live in the same house but ought to have divorced? You are from the former category; I am from the latter. I think that the former is better, but you might tell me otherwise.

Please do to the violin playing what you did to that soccer ball: Kick butt. I hope that soon you will hit a note or play a few bars on the violin that will animate you just as that long goal in soccer animated you. May it compel you to practice harder and play better.

You have big, beautiful eyes. The first time I saw them was on the video tape we received before we went to Russia. There you were, the last kid on the video, of course, because you were the oldest --- being the oldest has its disadvantages, no? You sat with your elbow on the breakfast table, your arm pointing upward. You were slowly, rhythmically tapping on the edge of your toast, remember? You were glaring at the camera man; it must have made him nervous.

I have rarely seen such expressive eyes. You have lovely blond hair, and I think you will be tall. I suspect you will, at any age, leave behind a wake of once-hopeful males as you choose the one who's right for you, just as I chose three young adults who were right for me.

Except that they forgot their Russian.

Dearest Katya:

You are a loner, and probably always will be. But this is not out of shyness. You speak your mind. You wear what you want to wear, rules of fashion be damned! I wish I had photographs of some of the, um, 'interesting' wardrobe ensembles you have come up with.

I love you for it. Your independence, your ability to find happiness all by yourself, deep in your self, is such a big and strong-running part of you, I doubt that it will ever disappear.

You can read later about my childhood days and high school days and you will see that I too was a loner, but mine was more out of shyness or fear, I think, whereas yours came simply from desire.

I rebelled, and somewhere in the process I became cynical or bitter or vengeful – all of them being petty emotions. You, on the other hand, are a loner simply because you want to be a loner.

How lucky you are. I predict an unusual but fulfilling life for you. I know I am not wrong.

My Dear Friend and Partner, Alex:

You are a young man of great determination. All it takes for you is to see someone do something once, and you then will know how to do it, no matter how complex. After that, you will want to do the thing all by yourself – no help from anybody please, including me.

You put me to shame many times, but I love it and am proud of you. One time, I was having trouble closing the trunk on Blackie. (All our vehicles have names. Blackie is the 1997 Honda Civic. Ruby I was a Ford minivan. Ruby II is a 2000 Dodge Dakota four-door pickup with a tough magnum V-8 engine that both you and I love, except when at the gas pump, which is too often. Whitey is a Ford conversion van that gave us plenty of room and that offered us nice things such as inside running lights and curtains on the windows. Two men came in a Ford Focus, and one of them drove off with Whitey, to take it back to their bank, probably.

But back to Blackie, the Honda Civic. The trunk wouldn't close, so I went to the back of the car and I started fiddling with it. You saw me, apparently. You looked over the situation, and you took action. You opened the driver's door and yanked out the thick rubber floor mat that jammed the trunk-opening lever on the floor.

How did you know that? I might have figured it out after an hour or so, but you went directly to the cause of the problem.

And another time I had spent hours looking for my big new rechargeable red flashlight. You came over to the trailer on your usual Wednesday. I swear I had not used that flashlight when you were here the prior weekend. But, when I mentioned that I couldn't find it, you walked directly to it, digging it out from a mass of rubble in one of my lower kitchen cabinets where, because of my back, I rarely venture.

How did you know that?

A few years ago, it was difficult for me to watch such a determined young man held back by speech problems. Like your two Sisters, you received special help with language at school and during the summer. Happily, all three of you have emerged successfully. We are all very grateful for the help of these trained professionals who worked with you three during school and over the summer. Their results have been miraculous – only a person with extraordinary powers and sensibilities could produce such results in such a short time.

All three of you carry a faint Russian accent – just enough of one. It's not the guttural English of some Russians who overcompensate on their r's and th's. That is the accent that comedians make fun of. You are much better off.

In kindergarten, Alex, you were having great difficulty with the 's' sound. The language tutor was teaching you to think of an initial 's' in a word as a 'separate word.' Thus, you would utter the 's' sound, pause for a millisecond, and then finish off the word, such as in 's/nake, and then, miraculously 'snake,' with no pause, no two words.'

Sometimes this didn't work. I recall one time when you and I were driving in Ruby I. We were talking about traffic laws, and you wanted to utter the word 'stop,' but you got hung up on that initial 's.' I swear that at the times when you got hung up on an initial 's,' you would 'hiss' for an extremely long time.

Ssssssssssssssssssss. Through the rear view mirror I could see the sadness in your face. Embarrassment. Shame. You were stuck.

Ssssssssssssssssssssssss.

It was difficult for me to sit behind the steering wheel and do nothing, as the speech therapists instructed. I wanted to slam on the brakes, turn around and grab you, and tell you not to worry about it -- You'd have the damned 's' sound down by college, so forget about it!

Sssssssssssssssssssssssssssssss.

Torture. For you. For me.

Ssssssssssssssssssssssssssssssss.

I so wanted to finish the word for you, but the teachers had commanded us to give you and your Sisters all the time you needed to complete your challenging sounds and words. I swear this particular 's' went on for several excruciating minutes.

Sssssssssssssssssssssssssssss.

I feared looking into the rear-view mirror again, and seeing once more a face filled with sadness and failure, a person stuck and unable to do anything about it. It was like standing on shore and watching a person drown. They told me to do nothing, but to wait and to hide my feelings.

Sssssssssssssssssssssssssssss.

Hell. Suspended. Interminable.

Sssssssssssssssssssssssssssss.

Then it was quiet, completely quiet. I turned around, dreading what I might see.

You grabbed the arms of your booster chair, and then you looked straight at me. "Darn, Papa!" you said. "I just cannot say the word 'stop'!"

We looked at one-another and both of us laughed, your laughter being the result of complex thinking. You knew that by not concentrating or fearing the letter 's,' you could utter it with no problem. But when you 'tried,' your trying made it difficult.

What a guy, Alex. I have so enjoyed our times watching men chop down tall, aged tamaracks across the road from where we lived together, or build a bank near the hospital or tear down buildings or drive trains or work with high wires from a cherry-picker. (We both realize, of course, that women do all this as well, but we also realize that it seems that more men than women do these kinds of jobs.)

You know, being such an aged Father certainly has its limitations, but it has some great advantages too. Because I am retired, I can devote a lot of time to you and your Sisters; my schedule is flexible. I can be there when you want me, and during other times, when you're not around, I take care of other things that need attention (ripping up moldy carpets, repairing a water-stained ceiling, etc.). Not too many Fathers have such flexibility. Had I not retired, I would have continued leaving as you got up in the morning and returning at your bedtime. We would not have become so close. It is difficult to distinguish sometimes between choices freely made and that which is preordained.

I am a lucky. You have had a lot of projects. You built a toll booth after we had driven to Texas. You've constructed numerous forts and houses with the scrap lumber and myriad other things that are stuffed into our two giant sheds. You built a store, and made your money bills from newspaper. You opened up a doctor's office and treated all the stuffed animals in the trailer, emptying out my supply of bandages and medical tape on more than one occasion.

I have no idea what you will become in terms of a profession. You are adept at so many things and interested in so many things. I must hang around to find out.

Your Sisters? I ask. They do not answer.

Dear Ann, Katya, and Alex:

Have I remembered enough things for you? Will you remember them and tell your own children, years from now?

Those children of yours may ask about your Father, their Grandfather. He was the man who brought you to this country. You may wonder about me, long after I am gone.

Read on, please. I well tell you, among other things, how I was drawn to you.

Dear Young Adults:

I hope that your interest in your past will grow. I hope that somehow that interest will inspire you to study Russia – its language, literature, poetry, music, and culture in general. I have been obsessed with those things for over fifty years, and there isn't a drop of Russian blood in me. You three, you three Russians, must get at least equally obsessed. As Russians, you must. As children of Sankt Peterburg, it is your solemn duty.

After all, I am just a middle-European hodge-podge of nationalities, but you are Russians, through and through. Better yet, you come from Peterburg, the city that has been so crucial in all the areas I mentioned above. Learn all of this. Pass it on to your children.

Will I include too many details in telling you my story, or too few? Well, that depends on how well I can write it. A one-page legal document can seem at times to be longer than <u>War and Peace</u> – it takes more effort to get through a turgid legal document than it does to read a compelling story of any length.

Remember the scene in the movie "Amadeus," where Mozart plays for Emperor Joseph II who, it is reported, dozed off during the performance? After the concert, Mozart was brought to the Emperor, expecting the praise he normally received. But the Emperor did not blanket Mister Mozart with praise. Mozart was aghast. This is what the Emperor said:

> My dear young man, don't take it too hard. Your work is ingenious. It's quality work. And there are simply too many notes, that's all. Just cut a few and it will be perfect.

Mozart is truly shocked. Cut out part of his great work? Remove a few critical 'bricks' from his intricate structure?

Mozart's response was about as sarcastic as it could be, given the times. "Which few did you have in mind, Majesty?"

It's not hard to imagine Mozart steaming under his collar while biting his tongue.

Which notes? Indeed!

Well, my childhood was bizarre, to say the least, as was my adult life. Becoming a father at age fifty-nine doesn't happen very often. I am two years younger than your maternal Grandfather.

Who exactly is your Father? Let's go back to the beginning of the beginning.

My own Grandfather, like many of my relatives, died of brandy, beer, and cigarettes. He hated the old folks home where he was sent towards the end of his life because no one wanted to live around him. Even in this old folks' home, they gave him a private room because no one wanted to be around him, even the comatose patients, I guess. His last words were, "Get me out of this damned place." Evidently someone heard. He died soon thereafter.

Oddly, my own Father seems to have carried on that tradition of hating old folks' homes. Twenty-nine years of emphysema had wrecked his body, and he had reached a state of physical deterioration that even my Mother, the eternal care-giver, could no longer face. We put him in a nursing home. It looked like a nice enough place to me. "I'd rather die than live in this dump!" he said. He died that night; he hadn't been there a week.

Emil Jack, my Grandfather's father and my Great Grandfather, was born in Germany, sailed on the S.S. Cimbria, and became an American citizen in 1897. He was a Mississippi riverboat man who fell and broke his neck while descending a long stairway that led down to the river. The newspaper reported that the railing gave way to his weight.

I don't know how much he weighed then, or what he looked like. I don't know why he came to America, how he became a riverboat man. I didn't ask my Grandfather. Maybe I was too wrapped up in my own life then to inquire about my ancestors. What a loss. Neither Grandfather nor Great Grandfather had written a book about their lives. I know so little.

Emil had been returning to his sons in Lilydale, the shanty town across the Mississippi River from Saint Paul that has since been done in, thanks to the 1965 spring floods and to the complicity of the city.

I have a copy of the 1917 newspaper article about Riverboat man Emil Jack and his 'untimely' death. The great era of the Mississippi riverboats had passed, the article noted, when the railroads came in, years before Emil died.

His rowboat was waiting for him, ready to take him, not across the River Styx, but across the Mississippi to his Lilydale shack.

He must have been a strong man, at seventy-five years of age, to row across the Mississippi while the river's current worked to push his boat down to New Orleans. His line to Lilydale was straight – he had made no allowances for the river's currents, the same currents that, downriver, claimed my Brother, Jimmy, in 1965.

How odd that Emil was heading towards his rowboat that rocked alongside a shaky dock at the edge of the very river that had sustained him for most of his life, that then abandoned him, leaving him like so much junk on the shore.

My Father's Mother, Anna, died when my Father was in the sixth grade. He and my Grandfather lived in vacant buildings on the West Side. My Father lived in Saint Joseph's Orphanage for several years, just around the block from where I went to high school decades later. He never told us about the orphanage, but my Brother, Michael, the official family historian, found out.

During one family argument (which of the hundreds was it? I don't recall) I was listening to them argue from behind a closed door. My Mother yelled something about my Father being married earlier, and that his Son was asking for money. I never found out more. No one wrote a book, like your Father is doing for you kids.

My Father brewed beer in our basement, until one batch blew up, all over the laundry my Mother had hung. I recall picking up the bottle caps that had flown all over the place. That was the end of his homemade brew hobby.

Dearest Alex, Anna, and Katya:

Finding out about your Father's kin – does that lead you to understand your Father more? I don't know, but I write with the assumption that it does.

On my Mother's side, things were not much better than on my Father's side. My Mother came from Moravian kin, who had farmed in Glencoe, not far from New Prague. Her Grandmother, Christine, must have been no taller than four foot-seven. How overpowered she looks in the sepia photos that show her, almost cinemagraphically, shrinking, while beside her stands an imposing man with a giant moustache, a wide hat, and a great belly that he seems to take pride in, cupping his hands tenderly around its lower edges, as if it was a baby or a pet.

Josie, my Mother's Mother, she of the evil eye, was born in Foley, Minnesota, where she met Paul Ford, he of a normal-sized belly that needed no support from his hands. He had lost his job in a lumber camp, according to family legend, legends often hard up for happy stories, but failing once again.

Grandfather Paul was 'Pennsylvania Dutch,' which not at all meant that he was Dutch. What, you Russian-rooted kids might ask? The people in Pennsylvania apparently didn't want to say 'Deutsch,' the German word for 'German,' and so they called them 'Dutch.'

Short Josie and the non-Dutch Paul Ford moved to a shack in Waite Park, a suburb of Saint Cloud, Minnesota, at the edge of what one might consider the Lake Wobegon area – Garrison Keillor had studied at Saint John's University, not far from Saint Cloud.

But this edge of the prairie was not so mellow and nice. My Mother lived with her parents and with two brothers and five sisters in a shack meant for four.

Work was nearly impossible to find during the Depression, of course. My Mother was born in 1921, and so she and the Depression grew up together. She and her sisters worked at the hospital and they brought home the patients' leftovers. There were many colds and other illnesses of contagion in the Ford residence.

I was afraid of my Grandfather, Paul, and we had to live with him and Short Josie of the Evil Eye in South Minneapolis for a while before I started kindergarten and after my Father's accident.

Grandfather Paul hated kids. In fact, he hated the whole world, ever since he had been a bootlegger in the 1930's, and had gotten into a fight with one of his customers. Grandfather Paul, the mean one, punched the non-paying customer in the face. The man had rotting teeth, and Grandfather got a bad case of gangrene.

Going to a doctor was out of the question, given the expense of it all, even while his kids worked at the local hospital in Waite Park, cutting down on food expenses. The hospital, I bet, refused to grant discounts to parents of employees or to treat people who couldn't afford to pay for the care. The amputation of his arm ultimately was free, thanks to Anker Hospital in Saint Paul, the hospital that cared for indigents, of which there were many in those days. Well, perhaps they didn't actually <u>care</u> for the indigent patients, but they did treat them, and, a person might ask, how well did they <u>treat</u> them?

After Grandpa's operation and until the end of his life, he staggered around, perpetually off kilter because of his missing limb, and no doubt also because of the vast quantities of liquor that he manufactured and then drank. He screamed and mumbled in his stupors. I never heard his real voice.

I still always leave the toilet seat down, nearly sixty years later, after Grandfather Paul, the mean one, beat me with a razor strap for leaving it up one morning. He had sat down without looking and in the process dropped his self-rolled Bull Durham cigarette into the toilet bowl. He was shaking his whole body then, or what remained of it, as if ready to punch me with his fist that was no longer there.

When my Mother really, really got earnest in her fights with my Father, she'd say, "You son of a bitching bastard!" (There was never a real lot of syntax in my Mother's swearing; it was just an attempt to string together as many bad words as possible.) "You're just like Paul!" she'd say. "Christ, I'm going to call you 'Paul!'"

I brought this up at a family reunion, long after Paul was gone and long after Grandmother Josie, she of the evil eye, was gone too. I didn't fear her so much because she came to take care of us whenever my Mother was in the hospital having a baby, which was often. As long as she could watch her television programs, she was fine, although she didn't cook very well -- everything tasted the same. Most of the time she just sat in the easy chair, covered with doilies on the back and on the arms. She glared at us without blinking. That's why I started calling her 'the Grandmother of the Evil Eye.' She disliked my Father so much that he got the evil eye whenever the two were in the same room, even if just for a few minutes.

This Grandmother, who never swore during her life despite numberless reasons to swear, many of which revolved around Paul, suffered a stroke, many years after Paul, the armless one, had died. The stroke left her in a hospital room where she spent hour after hour cursing a blue streak, such that the nurse-nuns asked to be transferred to a different floor and the non-nun nurses had to bear the brunt of her filthy language as she let out decades of anger and resentment against Paul, who was too dead by then to hear them. Her cussing was something akin to the noise her pressure-cooker made on the stove – you always had to be careful so the pot didn't explode.

So at this particular Ford family reunion, dozens of years later, at the Cottage of Ill Repute (I will explain soon), I brought up the subject of Paul for one reason or another. Perhaps we were tallying alcoholics, to see whether the Jack family or the Ford family had more.

"Paul, a drinker?" One of my aunts pounded the arm of her folding chair such that it nearly folded and toppled her, but certainly taking away some of the serious effect of her words as she wobbled on the flimsy planks that served as a cottage porch floor. "Paul? Paul drinking? Where ever did you get that idea, Billy? Paul was a saint! A saint, I tell you!" said this Aunt, whom I will call 'Youngest Child.'

Memory. What an unreliable historian.

The 'Cottage of Ill Repute?' Okay. After Grandfather Paul died, Grandma Josie spent twenty-five years of her life living with child Number One, whose husband had done quite well with his job in the main post office. He drove new cars and smoked long cigars. The Widow Josie became their maid, baby-sitter, dish-washer, etc. But when Josie got old and took sick for housework, she moved in with her youngest daughter, a woman who had fallen on hard times, losing a husband and a daughter to suicide and a son in a fire, undoubtedly related to his alcoholic intake, and all of that within a few years' time. Still, youngest Child took care of Josie as she became more and more feeble, unable to do even basic things, like getting out of bed or placing tabs on a bingo card.

When Grandmother Josie finished up with all her swearing and died in the nursing home, Oldest Child took all of Grandmother's few belongings (bingo winnings mostly), saying that she had cared for 'Ma' for so many years and was entitled to whatever pittance there was.

But Grandma Josie, she of the Evil Eye, had not been a burden to Oldest Child, ever, but rather a blessing. It was Youngest Child who had taken care of a now-feeble Grandma who didn't help anymore but instead needed help.

Cosmic justice sometimes makes brief appearances. Oldest Child sold all of Grandma's possessions, and with the proceeds she bought herself a pontoon boat for their summer cabin on a small, round lake near Annandale, whose residents came up with the novel 'Round Lake' as fitting for their lake.

Enter Cosmic Justice. The pontoon boat proved to be Oldest Child's undoing when she went out fishing one morning, prepared to enjoy the spaciousness of the pontoon and the comfort of its lawn chairs. How much different was it from their rickety old wooden boat with its hard benches. That morning, she had forgotten her minnow bucket and so she headed back to shore. There, she found Husband in bed with Neighbor Lady. The shrieks of Oldest Child no doubt terrified everyone around the round lake called, poetically, 'Round Lake,' including Husband and Neighbor Lady.

So both sides of my parents' families had, um, interesting histories. I am lucky to remember these things, because everyone else seems to have forgotten. They practice the art of 'Let bygones be bygones' so much that many of their unpleasant memories have disappeared.

Dear Katya, Anna, and Alex:

Lilydale. Mention Lilydale today in the Twin Cities, and people will think of a pricey neighborhood, of condos mostly, gripping the bluffs over the Mississippi and offering views of both the Minneapolis skyline, bigger but further away, and the Saint Paul skyline, closer but smaller.

But I knew a different Lilydale. It was not on the bluffs but down near the river, at river level, in fact, and it was one of the most surreal locations in which I have dwelled. My Great Grandfather and my Grandfather came from there.

You can go there today but you will hardly see anything. The town is gone, except for the one-room school house which they have been promising for decades to make the centerpiece of a new state park, but is now falling apart under its own weight. Decades later, there is no state park, just a levee overrun by weeds and buckthorn. But if you get out of your car and look closely and push through thick shards of weeds, you might see the remnants of a road or part of the foundation of a house.

Behind that one-room school house lived my Dad's Uncle Carl and his wife, Alma (I think), and his child, Young Carl. The Senior Carl farmed to the west of his house, and he also served as Justice of the Peace. He often went up to Highway Thirteen, on the bluffs that were then bereft of condos, that didn't become popular until decades later, and he stopped people who were speeding. He invariably led them down the scary, twisting, unlit, and poorly-paved road that led to Lilydale from the west end, and there he collected the speeding fine. For a fee, he showed the speeding drivers how to get back up on the highway. Most of them seemed more than happy to pay for the guidance from this pit of horrors and bad dreams, back up to the highway.

There were two ways out of Lilydale, then, each offering its own perils – the corkscrew steep road lacking pavement, guardrails, or lighting on the west end, and the flat road to the east, offering its own perils. Funny, people talked about roads that led 'out of' Lilydale, but they hardly talked about roads that led 'to' Lilydale.

Carl's house was the 'mansion' of the town because it had a basement. To the east of Carl lived his brother Frank. This brother never liked throwing anything away, so he kept things in his yard – old sofas, old refrigerators, old stoves, and old cars. Besides, Lilydale was a dumping ground for the big city people anyway. Frank farmed a little, corn and tomatoes mostly, drank a lot, and raised rabbits.

My Mother hated Lilydale, perhaps partly because she knew that every time her Husband went down there, particularly with his Father, both would come up the hill stone drunk. To prevent this from happening (although it never helped), she often sent a kid or two along, thereby reminding the men of their obligations up the hill. I was often the kid.

It didn't work.

My Mother often received phone calls from Carl's house. I think that was the only phone in Lilydale. The caller was Carl's wife, whose name I don't recall but it might have been Emma or Alma. She spoke in a thick German accent that years in Lilydale had not softened. She screamed into the phone. "Yours, that dirty bastard, he went and got another case and then mine, the dirty bastard, drank half of it and fell down, and then yours…"

I wish I could write her words phonetically. 'Yours' was pronounced with a hissing 's' at the end (Alex would be proud). 'Bastard' was pronounced something like 'Bayes-terd.' Emma or Alma, or whatever her name was, made it a point to emphasize all of her 't's,' such that she often spat when saying (or shouting) 'baye-sterd.'

The 'yoursssss' invariably referred not to my Father, but to my Grandfather. My Mother's voice got louder each time she repeated the same phrase: "'Yours' you say? He's not mine!" But my Mother was married to my Grandfather's son, who was my Father, and so Emma could scream 'Yoursss!' as she gave an account of the weekends down at the river.

My Grandfather's real name was 'William,' the same as mine. But he was always called 'Mozh.' I asked everyone, including my Grandfather himself, where the word 'Mozh' came from. No one knew. My best guess is that it was somehow connected to 'morsch,' a Slavic word for 'walrus.' Pronounced fast enough, especially when shouting when half-drunk, 'morsch' could sound a lot like 'Mozh.'

Now in Russia and some other Slavic countries, people who carve a hole in winter ice and dive in while wearing only a summer swim suit – they are called 'walruses.' There are still walruses in Russia; In December, they cut their holes into the Neva River near the walls of the Peter and Paul Fortress.

My Grandfather boasted that he dug holes in the ice of the Mississippi almost every year when he was young, and had dived into the frigid water. Walrus? Could be. Not much is certain about Lilydale. Sic transit, etc., etc.

Most city people then did not know that Lilydale existed. Those who knew called it a 'shanty town.' This was an accurate description, except for Carl's house with the basement. Frank's house was pretty much a shack. All his inside walls had horizontal mud lines of various hues and thicknesses. They started at the floor and went almost to the ceiling. These were the marks left by various floods. Frank had penciled in, next to the particular mud line, which year that line was formed. Actually, I don't think Frank could read or write and so it was probably his daughter Esther, she of the jutting front teeth and the swinging purse, who wrote the dates on the walls.

There were several streets that ran north-south, and a few that ran east-west.

No matter which field it came from, my Mother hated Lilydale produce. She threw out the fresh corn or the canned tomatoes or whatever it was that her husband, that dirty, dirty bayestard, had brought back with him up the hill. "How in hell you made it up that god-damned son-of-a-bitching road, I'll never know!" my Mother usually said.

She was speaking of the southern route to Lilydale that started out at the foot of the Wabasha Street Bridge. The road started out in the industrial section of Saint Paul's lower bank, passed the York Brewery halfway up the hill, and then ran straight west for a while as it passed under the High Bridge that stood on high between the bluffs. Soon, and without any warning, the road took a ninety-degree angle to the right and then immediately another ninety degree turn to the left, just as you were righting the car from its swerve to the right. A blackened wooden single-track rail road bridge ran low over the road, exactly at those turns.

If you missed either of the turns, you could end up flattened against a railroad bridge timber support pole, probably bringing half of the bridge with you, or you could slide down a few feet into the Mississippi. In the winter, ice on the road encouraged the latter.

After the bridge, the pavement gave way to dirt and dust that blew into Grandpa's Model A Ford, even on the rare occasions when its windows were closed. For a long while, you had to drive a few feet back from the river, along the river, and just a few feet up from the river. The road had big holes and it had crumbled in places. After the road crossed Pickerel Lake, you were in Lilydale. A white wooden sign announced the town at its southern border, but the sign was old, faded, dirty, and unpainted. You could only see the 'L' and the 'I,'' and that only after stopping the car and squinting. The name, then, was 'LI,' and that's sometimes what I called it, being a code Mother didn't know.

For fishing, you had your choice of the river's main channel or backwater you just passed, known as 'Pickerel Lake.' Mozh preferred Pickerel Lake. It was more peaceful there than in the river, and there were fewer dead fish, their arching faded-white bellies rising high in triumph or defeat, and dead turtles, upside-down on the banks, and pools reflecting in murky tones the colors of the rainbow, and with dead, black ducks within the rainbow circles, and it was easier to anchor your boat and open up your case of York's beer and maybe even throw a line or two into the water, in Pickerel Lake.

No fancy rods and reels for Mozh. He preferred extra-long and extra-bent bamboo cane poles. It was said that one time, Mozh had drunk too much beer (this part of the story is easy to accept as truth) and that he was using a live frog as bait. The heart of the story is that Mozh had fallen asleep (or had passed out, depending on your point of view – my mother would have said "stone-assed drunk"), and the frog was sitting on top of Mozh's giant cork bobber, taking in the sun.

Mozh told us that one time he was throwing out his line and he caught a bird that was so big that it pulled Mozh and his line and his pole and his beer cooler and anchor clear across the lake.

I don't know if any of this really happened.

He had a glass eye that didn't move, one thumb that went sideways at the last joint, which made him an expert at rolling Bull Durham cigarettes. A rooster pecked his thumb (his 'tumb,' as he called it), he claimed. He lost his eye in a fight at a lumber camp, he claimed.

There was another story about how Mozh was up on the hills, driving a buggy from one tall river bank to the other, via the High Bridge. I don't think this story is true.

The bridge. If you were from Saint Paul, you called it the 'HIGH Bridge' with accent on the first syllable. Foreigners, they called it the 'high BRIDGE.' And no matter where the speaker put the accent, almost every kid in Saint Paul was familiar with this bridge because there wasn't one mother in the whole city who at one time or another, while talking to her children, hadn't uttered once or twice even, "If everybody was jumping off the High Bridge, would you?"

This remark came after a kid asked for something, claiming that all the other kids already had it. Example: "Mom, can I have a new bike? Everyone else has one."

"If everyone else wanted to jump off the HIGH Bridge, would you want to too?"

Anyway, according to Mozh, and not at all depending on how the person accented the bridge, Mozh happened to find himself in the black buggy on the middle of that bridge, between tall bluffs, during the great storm of 1907. The wind channeled and gained strength as it blew through the path lined by the bluffs on each side. The only thing that saved him, he claimed, is that he used the buggy umbrella as a parachute.

If this really happened, then Mozh could have used his nose as sort of an impromptu rudder. His nose was huge, as were its pores. It looked like an elongated rutabaga. His ears stood out from under his fedora hat. Funny, but old photos of him show an extremely handsome man. I suppose that, as he got older, what happens to many people who are aging happened to him. In other words, his ears and his nose grew, while other parts of his body shrank.

My Mother's contempt for the place was partly because that's where my Father got drunk, because that's what showed his extremely humble beginnings, and, because, anyway, the stuff from Lilydale stank awfully bad. I must admit that fresh corn and even canned goods (in jars, actually, not cans) smelled of Lilydale. So did I and my brothers and sisters – there were three of us then, and I am the only one remaining, which permits me to make up all the Lilydale stories that I want.

In particular, Lilydale's sweet and pungent smells coalesced, and settled in Uncle Frank's house. I don't know where that odor came from. I know they had an outhouse and used bedpans for urine. Perhaps they forgot to empty the pans for a week or two. Combine that with the smell of clothes hardly ever washed (and when they were, it was in river water), and the smell of people who didn't have bathtubs or showers. It was also a mix of river smells that included oil and other chemicals, dead fish (You know you're in bad water when even the carp don't survive), rotting birds of various denominations, and turtles (dead ones have a quite unusual odor and you can always tell them from dead fish).

The biggest fights between my parents came on days that my Father drove back up the hill shit-faced drunk, as they used to say, and how had he ever made his way back on that road, and what would happen to the entire family if he drowned in the river, and, once having made it home, my mother would hide her relief and complain about the odors. Having them in the kitchen for just a few minutes was enough to stink up the whole apartment, for weeks at a time, and the odor never left our various cars and probably did not increase their resale value or please the people who were repossessing them. The fish were most often big and oily carp, which no one ate anyway even though they heard stories of how popular and expensive carp was in France and other fancy countries. One of my Father's grand plans included transporting Mississippi River carp to Paris.

My mother should have known what she was getting into when she married my Father, and perhaps she did know. Maybe she, like so many of us, like me, needed to re-play her childhood drama that included a drunk and angry Father, bad enough to merit continuous wringing of hands. My Mother had moved to the city and was staying with her older Sister, the one with the Pontoon boat and the Cabin of Ill Repute years later. My Mother got a clerical job at the State of Minnesota Unemployment Office on Tenth Street, right next to the Schubert Theater that is now known as the F. Scott Fitzgerald Theater, named for Saint Paul's most famous writer, and the place where Garrison Keillor performs his "Prairie Home Companion."

In those days, my Father had been unemployed for so long that he helped form a semi-pro baseball team whose members were all unemployed. They played people who had jobs and whose employers contributed money and equipment to their baseball teams. Oddly, my

Father's unemployed team often won. Maybe they had more time to practice, or at least time to rest up and swallow a few bottles of Grain Belt beer before the games.

My Father started asking my Mother to the games, and then he asked her to ride with him in his Father's Model-A Ford. On most days, when he didn't have his Father's car, he walked my Mother home, up on the West Side bluffs. To get up to the top of the West Side part of Saint Paul, you used an extremely rickety set of wooden stairs, with platforms changing directions every fifteen feet or so. I am sorry to report that the City ripped down those stairs, and that they closed the giant cave at the stairway's base which served as a bar for those about to make the climb, and which was supposed to be the country's largest underground, or, more accurately, in-ground speakeasy during all the days of Prohibition, when literally all the gangsters hung out in Saint Paul until somebody bribed the Saint Paul Police, or 'turned down the heat' in other ways, or fashioned a fire so bright that the gangster cave was no longer on any policeman's clipboard.

My Mother and Father got married in 1941. The war in Saint Paul had commenced.

Dear Children:

The River and the City. Some attentive readers, and other readers as well, may already be confused. Why is the West Side where it is?

This needs some explaining. Everyone knows that the Mississippi flows north, from Minnesota and south to New Orleans, so if you are looking north, the east bank is on your right and the left bank is on your left. But as the river flows through Minneapolis over Saint Anthony Falls and through the locks and then past the Ford Bridge and its dam, it makes several sharp turns so that the river flows past downtown Saint Paul, while flowing running east-west.

The riverboat captains, who may have included my Great Grandfather Emil until he fell down the stairs, if you believe "The Saint Paul Dispatch" – those riverboat captains going down-river still called the bank on their right the 'west bank,' even though it was really the 'south' bank. They chose to ignore maps and the compass.

Who knew more about the damned river than the river boat captains, right? Especially if they weren't as drunk as my great-grandfather, Emil, no doubt was on the day he tumbled down the river bank stairs that were located in the west part of Saint Paul that is called the 'north side' of the city. Perhaps Emil was sober and he just got confused and disoriented, trying to make sense of all these things, as he walked down that stairway.

It is confusing, to be sure. In Saint Paul, the West Side, as well as the suburb, West Saint Paul, are located south of downtown Saint Paul. The suburb of South Saint Paul is located next to West Saint Paul, and the East Side of Saint Paul is actually a bit north. Enough already. The natives just take this all in and tend to treat foreigners (e.g., people from Minneapolis) as if they are the ones who are disoriented.

It has been said that all this nomenclature was kept over the years, even when people knew better, because it was one more way of keeping strangers out of the city. Minnesota's strange governor, ex-professional wrestler Jesse Ventura, proclaimed that drunken Irishmen had laid out the roads in Saint Paul. He didn't say anything about Irish women.

Dear Anna, Katya, and Alex:

I was the second oldest of ten children. Our family gatherings get smaller every year. Many of the others, around my age, have died, and the cause of death was often alcohol-related.

My Brother, Jim, drowned in the Mississippi when he was eighteen. Alcohol played no part. He had enlisted in the Marines, but he needed a hernia operation first. Being the competitive type, he didn't follow the doctor's orders to 'take it easy' for a couple of weeks. His friends went swimming. He joined them.

I hardly remember his funeral or the days afterwards. I think it was painful and so I blocked it out of my mind, a process that I think you three also have used and that I have used at other times as well. Our memories sometimes block out things to protect us. At times, I wish it did that more often.

Most of my family is gone. Many of my family memories concern people and places who are gone. That, I think, is why many old people choose to dwell within the often-muted, softened shadows of their memories rather than face the glaring lights of their today's, the exposure of so many decays, the fright for what the future brings.

My Father is dead. My Mother. My Sister, Patty. My brothers, Jim, Frank, Tim, and Tom.

I used to collect the 'holy cards' that the morticians hand out or leave on podiums, next to the white sign-in books. These cards sport a picture of Jesus or Mary or Lazarus or Moses on one side, and on the other side they give the bare essentials of the life of the <u>dead one</u> – oh, I mean, the <u>deceased</u> one – we must be euphemistic and circumspect in funeral homes, and our voices must not rise above a whisper, as people hug or hold hands with the 'bereaved's' family members or shake hands or place hands on shoulders – all of this done as people speak in lowered tones showing the appropriate depth of their regret. At the bottom of this card's second side, there is always the name, address, and 24-hour phone number for the funeral home.

Kids, I don't want a funeral.

I repeat.

Kids, I don't want a funeral.

Dearest Kids:

In 1943, my father was driving a city Water Department truck down the kinky road known as Snelling Avenue. It stopped at West Seventh Street, a main artery from downtown Saint Paul to Fort Snelling and the airport. My Father wasn't serving in the Army or Navy because he had rheumatic fever when he was young. Perhaps sleeping in vacant buildings had indirectly saved his life.

According to him, the truck stalled just as it was passing over the streetcar tracks. This long stretch of West Seventh was the place where streetcar drivers made up for lost time and kept to their schedules, nailed to their walls. This stretch of West Seventh Street was near the river bank where Emil, my Great-Grandfather, had died.

I think streetcar 'brakes' in my Father's day consisted of the driver yanking on a lever that sent the wheels spinning backwards.

A speeding streetcar struck my Father's truck, which started on fire. I know this is true because there is a newspaper article, with photos, about the accident, and I still have a copy of that article, which they called, "Death Takes A Holiday." No one had been killed, not even my Father, although he was not yet my Father since I hadn't been born or even conceived.

According to my Father, the only way he got out of the burning truck was to kick at the passenger window until it broke, and then crawl through it. The door handles and the window handles had melted, he said, and the burns and cuts all over his body had not necessarily come from the crash but from crawling out of the pile of scrap metal that a few moments earlier had been a truck that said 'Saint Paul Water Department' on both sides.

One time my Father took me to the junk yard where the carcass of this city Water Department truck stood, weeds crowded through all the holes and cracks. Hardly anything remained on the left side of the front part of the truck It was hard to imagine that at one time, years earlier, an engine had stood there. All that remained was metal, bent and twisted and colored a deep and ashy black, weighing down hundreds of weeds that worked to extricate themselves from this once-burning truck, not unlike the way my Father had extricated himself.

I remember my Father's face as he pointed out for me the truck's melted handles and its tangled bumpers that looked like giant pretzels. There was pride in his face, I think. A pride that perhaps was connected with the fact that he had escaped against powerful odds, that he had calculated in one unbelievably short moment, the way to escape.

I saw, or think I saw, relief on his face too.

And then there was something else – so deeply personal that you could never talk about it. He put his hand on my shoulder. I remember only about two other times that he touched me, not counting the punishment with 'the belt.' It never was called 'his belt,' but 'the belt.' It felt so strange to be touched by him.

Call it what you will, but, except for those beatings, there was no real physical contact between him or me, and, come to think of it, between him and any of my nine brothers and sisters, and with my Mother as well.

But his hand was on my shoulder there at the junk yard. I didn't dare to look at his face and I believe he felt the same way about my face. We just stood there, looking at 'his' truck, and his hand remained on my shoulder a long time. The weeds were tall and filled with grasshoppers. We stood there while grasshoppers landed on us and then, recognizing in no time at all that this was not a good place for a visit or a meal, they jumped away, something like the way my father twisted himself out of that burning truck.

And then, as if trying to negate or minimize his hand having settled on my shoulder for a minute or so, or perhaps longer, as we walked out of the junk yard, he said, "Be careful when you drive."

Dear Children:

These are the memories that helped shape your father, for better, for worse.

It was said that my Father spent a long time in the hospital. He claimed that they had to give him many pain pills because of the burns on his body, and this is why, later, he drank too much, and in his final days, managed to double up on his pain pills by going to two pharmacies.

According to my Father (and my Mother never disagreed with him on this point and probably only on this point), he had a good workers compensation case that would help the family through the roughest parts during the times that he was out of work. A good claim, to be sure. After all, he had been driving a <u>city</u> truck when the accident happened.

No doubt the streetcar company had a good lawyer or more likely, a crowd of lawyers. I worked in a law firm, years later, that represented and protected companies and other entities. I remember that when I was in about sixth grade, something happened to me on a bus. I don't recall once, and can't even think of what I might come up with. Maybe I tripped. Maybe the driver stopped too quickly and I fell. Maybe the bus started to move while I was still exiting – I don't know.

But I do recall almost all the events that transpired thereafter. Three men in dark blue suits talked to my Mother and then talked to me. I don't recall what I said, but it seemed to please them. One of the men gave papers for my Mother and Father to sign. Then the man, wearing a white shirt with starch that kept him from bending much, opened his wallet and gave me a five-dollar bill.

I didn't and don't recall the reason for the visit of these three wise men. Decades later, I asked my Mother and she had forgotten it too. Strange that all this would concern the same transit company that formerly owned the streetcars.

Lawyers. Who ever thought I'd become one?

According to my Father, his lawyer got drunk the night before the workers compensation hearing, and my Father got nothing.

I know for sure that we got nothing because that's the time we began moving around from place to place, and one time my Father's

1947 blue Plymouth was repossessed. This was the time my parents filed bankruptcy, an act that took away much of my Father's pride, or what was left of it after his inability to provide for his family.

One of my earliest memories concerned a year or so after the accident. My Mother was driving somebody else's gray 1949 Buick with a sloping rear end. This car may have been the car of my uncle, the one who was married to the Pontoon Boat lady.

My Mother was fearful of driving, I recall, especially driving down-town, what with all the other cars and the streetcars and pedestrians – men in fedoras, women in small fur hats. We crossed the Wabasha Street bridge leading to downtown, and to the hospital. Crossing that bridge may have been proof that Mother had borrowed the car of my Father's Sister, who lived on the West Side even though her area was south of downtown. But why downtown? I don't remember. Chances are my Father was at the County Hospital, called 'Anker Hospital,' and a person could get there easily without going through downtown. Or maybe the city put him up in one of the hospitals downtown or near it, such as Miller Hospital, where I was born.

I am sad that I don't remember seeing my Father then. I probably had to wait in the car or in the hospital waiting room, or in a room for kids. My first memories of him are after he got out of the hospital and had already started drinking.

He was out of work for a couple years. We lived in a smelly old downtown hotel for a week or so. We lived in various houses up from the levee, near the green houses of the Holm and Olsen Nursery.

My Father and Mother and Patty, my older Sister, and Jimmy, my younger Brother, moved into a basement apartment on Kent and Holly, a plain apartment building plumped down in the middle of a rather ritzy part of town. My Mother and Father were caretakers. I recall staring up at the giant iron heat pipes that hung (well, I hope) on the ceiling over my bed..

The building had a small grocery store in the other corner, at the front of the building, of the basement. Many apartments had small stores in the days before supermarkets or refrigerators that common people could afford. The clusters of two-story commercial buildings that you now see around town? They were food stores, butchers' shops, and dairy stores, located at streetcar stops so people could buy ingredients for supper on the way home. (This, kids, is how it was in Russia too.)

I also remember my Father leaping through one of our apartment's windows, to drive away a burglar. But who would be dumb enough to break into a basement apartment in a neighborhood populated by giant single-family houses?

Another early memory was being shushed and sent to a bedroom when a police car and a hearse pulled up to the side of the building. There was a tiny apartment in the back of the building, and its tenant, an unmarried man, had hung himself.

How does a person remember things from early childhood that happened or else could have happened? A piece there, a fragment here. Memory is an unreliable historian.

Dear Kids,

If you have read this straight through until now, you will note that when I was born, my parents were poor and then they went bankrupt.

I worked hard for a different kind of life – happier, no feuds, no fighting. Love of literature and languages. I went to school. Then more school. Then more school. Five college degrees. I worked as a professor, as a lawyer, and a law librarian and instructor of online legal research.

There's that line about falling apples and apple trees. There's a Shelley poem called 'Ozymandias.' Read it, please. The reference is to something far, far greater than I, way beyond my lowly, one-person, one ordinary person, but there is something to be said for the similarity between my life and the situation described in the poem.

Full circle. I am bankrupt. I am poor. I live in a trailer.

The park manager calls this place of trailers, in various degrees of deterioration, a 'community,' and she uses the word a lot, in her speech, in her printed bulletins, as if she is trying to win us over to her version of the place. Example: "Our community would look much more appealing if we all got together and removed from our grounds (not 'yards,' mind you, but 'grounds,' – no mention of the tiny spaces between trailers) broken washing machine parts on the lawns, and cars without tires in the parking spaces."

There are a lot of stories in this community.

Mine is happier than most.

Dear Alex, Katya, and Anna:

So where or when did Russia first come into my life?

When I was in the first grade at Saint Stanislaus School, we began each day with Holy Mass. Every morning, at the end of that Mass, we prayed to the Virgin Mary herself, going right to the top, begging her to convert Communist Russia to Roman Catholicism.

How odd that a Church that warned us all about the wiles of women revered one woman so highly. Whichever archbishop or cardinal wrote those prayers for Russia's conversion -- They wanted kids' mouths to stumble over every line, forcing them to dwell on their meanings perhaps. They were a mouth full, especially for us first-graders:

Hail, Holy Queen, Mother of Mercy, our life, our sweetness, and our hope. To thee do we cry, poor banished children of Eve. To thee do we send up our sighs, mourning and weeping in this vale of tears. Turn then, most gracious Advocate, Thine eyes of mercy towards us. And after this, our exile, show unto us the blessed Fruit of thy womb, Jesus. O clement, O loving, O sweet Virgin Mary.

Pray for us, O holy Mother of God.

That we may be made worthy of the promises of Christ.

Let us pray: O God, our refuge and our strength, look down with favor upon Thy people who cry to Thee; and by the intercession of the glorious and Immaculate Virgin Mary, Mother of God, of Saint Joseph Her Spouse, of Thy blessed Apostles Peter and Paul, and of all the Saints, mercifully and graciously hear the prayers which we pour forth for the conversion of sinners, and for the liberty and exaltation of our holy Mother the Church. Through the same Christ our Lord.

Amen.

Maybe the Cardinal or Archbishop figured that this major battle required a male or two on their side also, so we prayed to the mightiest of the angels right after we prayed to the Virgin Mary:

Saint Michael, the Archangel, defend us in battle; be our protection against the wickedness and snares of the devil. May God rebuke him, we humbly pray: and do thou, O Prince of the heavenly host, by the power of God, thrust down to hell Satan and all the evil spirits who roam through the world seeking the ruin of souls. Amen.

It is odd that in that muddle of words that tripped over our tongues, 'Russia' and 'Communism' and "'Soviet Union' were never mentioned. Maybe these were prayers left over from an earlier era, with a fight against some other monster, and the bishops hauled these prayers out from the attic. As if Russia would ever go Roman Catholic. The thing about religious people is that they seem to hold the greatest animosities towards those with whom they are closest. A Russian in Leningrad once told me that Russian Orthodox Church members see little difference between Western Protestants and Western Roman Catholics – they are all simply Western Christians, their differences hardly worthy of mention.

The word 'Jesuit' is still a profanity in Russia.

In third grade at Saint Patrick's Grade School, Father O'Malley was an old grouch known to leap out of his confessional box and grab a young masturbator or girl-kisser by the throat, screaming out the sin he had just heard, momentarily forgetting about the sacred 'seal of confession' that was supposed to keep priests even from acting as witnesses against murderers.

This priest came into our classes every six weeks to hand out report cards and to make sure all the children were working up to capacity so as to bring honor to the parish. Once he made me stand in front of the class and demonstrate the proper way to make the Sign of the Cross. He whacked other kids with his cane when they didn't put their left hand at their waist, or when they didn't make distinct points on their foreheads, chests, and shoulders.

He groaned as he braced his hands on the desk edge and sat down in the sister's chair.

There was a danger of sitting in the first row, but that's where I had to sit because I had bad eyes and I wore thick glasses. "You, boy, with your glasses, what evil befell us through the disobedience of our first parents?" he asked.

I swallowed hard. "Through the disobedience of our first parents we all inherit their sin and punishment, as we should have shared in their happiness if they had remained faithful."

I had learned my <u>Baltimore Catechism</u> from cover-to-cover. I knew I was correct, but no praise came from this ornery old coot. "What is your name, boy? Come up here!"

My hands shook as I left the security of my desk, a wood and iron apparatus on rails, along with three or four other desks, each with an ink hole at the corner.

My throat tightened. I was afraid of speaking or of doing anything in front of people, or even in front of one person. I stood up, holding onto the corner of my desk, for support. "My name is William Jack."

"First name first!" he snapped.

"William," I said.

"Hmph! Let's have a look at your report card." He licked his stubby finger and began leafing through the stack. "Ah, yes. William. Come up here and recite the Baltimore Catechism!"

"The whole thing? I asked.

"Just get yourself up here!"

I walked up to the front of the class and stood in front of Sister Saint Joseph's desk, while she stood in the back of the classroom, no doubt crossing her fingers, hoping that her student with his thick spectacles would perform well for the Priest. I was nervous around this particular priest. Who wasn't? Even the nuns seemed to quake.

From where I was standing, I smelled rotting teeth. I started breathing through my mouth which for some reason made me more nervous. I noted thick smudges on his rimless glasses. I wondered how the old coot could see.

"Make me the sign of the cross!" he commanded.

I put my left hand in the proper place, but then I choked, and, flustered, and angry at myself for being flustered, I put my fingers on my right shoulder before I touched my left shoulder.

The old priest leapt out of his chair with the speed you would not expect from such an old and ill person who was weighted down by the third message from Our Lady of Fatima, the message still not released.

He slapped me hard across the face. I nearly fell over, but I grabbed the edge of Sister Saint Joseph's desk.

"That's the pagan Orthodox way!" My face stung. Tears welled up in me, but I refused to cry. Instead, I stood, head lowered as the old priest rambled on, the smell of his bad teeth permeating the room. "You will not amount to much if you cannot fulfill even the most rudimentary requirements of your faith! How can you expect to go to a Catholic high school or, heavens, a Catholic college, if you go around making the Sign of the Cross like that? For shame, child! For shame!"

I saw Sister Saint Joseph. I loved her, just like I loved all my nuns, except for Sister Ann Patricia. Moving from Saint Patrick's school to Saint Luke's school, I was relieved that I wouldn't see Sister Ann Patricia again.

That year, the bishop transferred her to Saint Luke's.

But Sister Saint Joseph I loved. She lowered her head but before that, I spotted her red cheeks and her red forehead.

I had let her down.

Russia. There were 'Red Rosaries for Russia.' In fifth grade, we students made the rosaries out of store string and cheap plastic beads. We made a loop at the end of a long piece of straight string, and we knotted, then added a bead, and then knotted again, until we had ten beads touching one-another and then it was time for the 'Glory Be' and recitation of one of the mysteries, be they joyful or sorrowful or what. When we had finished tying all the beads, we attached the string to a crummy red plastic cross that looked like something you'd be disappointed in if you found it in your box of Cracker Jacks. The cross, you see, marked the beginning as well as the end of the rosary.

We had races to see who could finish first. We sold the rosaries, with all our crooked little knots between beads, the knots being as imperfect as our ability to recite the prayers for the conversion of Russia. The money we collected in our grubby mittens somehow passed through the right hands until it went to work at converting Russia.

These rosaries were like the Jesus or Mary statues that glowed in the dark for a couple of minutes after you turned out the lights. We sold those door-to-door too. This was our way of helping Jesus, of helping his Church convert Russia, along with selling Christmas cards and popcorn balls that we sold to baptize pagan babies. And we held newspaper drives. It was the least we could do, we, the Catholic youth wearing our cardboard and string scapulars that itched and separated us from the unholy, unblessed public school kids who went to school down the street with, horrors, Black kids and Jews.

Jews and Blacks must have been truly evil, because more of Saint Patrick's and Saint Luke's school and School hatred was directed at them than was directed at unholy Russia.

Dear Katya, Anna, and Alex:

I was eight years old, and I remember the newspapers and newscasters and newsreels telling us that Stalin had died. I didn't know who Stalin was, but I was surprised that anybody's death would produce so much rejoicing, and so much dread too. What would come next, people asked? Would the next ruler be kinder than Stalin or worse than Stalin? Would he have the same kind of mustache?

In the newspapers we saw grainy pictures of old and serious men standing on top of a stone platform that had spikes sticking out of it, like a castle tower, or like the grimy exteriors of the tile "White Castle" hamburger chain buildings. Below the tower, missiles on wheels passed, looking like giant bugs whose wings had been pulled out by some sadistic kid. Soldiers marched behind the missiles, in almost a goose-step. Those of us born right after the end of the war but before the 'Baby Boom,' still knew what a goose-step was.

We had air raid drills, not knowing what was to come next. Terrible horns blew inside Saint Luke's School, while sirens outside shrieked. We all did as we were commanded – this was no time for frolic or silliness, girls and boys. This was a matter of life and death, and of survival of our Holy Mother the Church and our beloved Pope Pius the Twelfth, who is ill and who has been carrying around that awful burden of the big, heavy secret from Fatima for years.

There was little to worry about, though. We were ready for whatever the Reds dished out. With Civil Defense shelters and home backyard bomb shelters, for the rich, at least, we could survive a missile attack or a hydrogen bomb. If the bomb fell when we were at home, no problem: We'd spend a little time in the local Civil Defense shelter or, if we were rich, in our own bomb shelters. Maybe the bomb would fall while we were all at school. No problem. We'd sit in the Civil Defense shelter until the nuns gave us the "All clear.' Soon afterwards, all of us kids could return to our school desks, dust them off a bit perhaps, and resume dipping our pens into our built-in ink-wells, practicing the Palmer Method of handwriting. When fountain pens came out, I preferred Esterbrooks.

Or maybe God or Mary or Michael the Archangel would finally hear all our after-Mass prayers, and Russia would become Roman Catholic. Then we'd switch our prayers over to the salvation of pagan babies, I supposed.

But it was better to be prepared for the enemy's bombs or the enemy's missiles, just in case God didn't hear the prayers we uttered daily, after Holy Mass. Or what if we got a new enemy, and God was on their side too?

But for the Soviet Union, we had practice drills, along with the usual fire drills. For the bomb drills, we learned how to duck under our desks, crouch, and put our hands over our heads. We Catholics would survive whatever the Communists hurled our way. Our desks were set on long wooden runners, about four to each runner. One time during a practice raid, I knocked the desks too hard as I scrambled to get under them; ink splashed over everyone's school work in the aisle.

I stood in the corner while Poor Sister Mary Edward and the janitor wiped up the mess. Her face, framed by the starched white coif and wimple, was red. She was pissed. "Be more careful next time, William," she said.

"Wow! She didn't even hit him!" said someone.

"He's a suck-ass and a brown-nose!" someone whispered, just loudly enough for me to hear.

It was true, I guess. It wasn't so much that I worked to please the nuns. It was more that they and I shared common interests.

I was what the nuns called 'a good boy.' If there had been grade school awards for 'Biggest Suck-up' or 'Super Wimp,' I would have won.

I had decided by third grade that I would be an intellectual. I was too lousy at sports anyway. In baseball, I was bad at hitting, throwing, catching, and running – that's all. I was always the last kid picked to be on any team.

But I survived, marking my time in the shambles of my world, which the Communists apparently wanted none-the-less. I would leave home as early as I could, and I would spend all my time reading books, because at home, things were not so peaceful. We had our own Cold War there, but that was much preferable to the too-frequent Hot Wars that flared up every time my Father came home with half a paycheck or no paycheck at all. I knew that once I became an adult, I could move away. I dreamt about that day, as well as about the day I could buy myself a car.

I had an older Sister and four younger siblings then, and more on the way in subsequent years, eventually reaching God's quota of three girls and six boys and me. God's quota? For Catholics, it was a mortal sin to use any kind of contraceptive. I recall seeing condoms behind the pharmacist's counter, craftily stuck in a dark corner. One fellow student somehow got a box of those things and he passed them out. It was years before I'd know what they were for, and then many more years before I needed to use one.

God's quota? God or the Pope (it made no difference) not only forbade Catholics from using birth control, but there was an obligation to, um, do the nasty at least once a month, on a day that was, um, one of the better days for doing the nasty.

When other Catholics assured my Father that God would provide for all ten Jack kids, my Father answered, "I'll believe that when I see God's name on my paycheck."

During Sunday mass, no matter the weather, my Father sat outside in his car. In winter, he crouched low in the driver's seat, his overcoat up to his ears, his mittens hitting one another, while his breath formed designs on the windshield. He refused to go into a building that housed so many damned hypocrites, as he said – all those pious Catholic families that had one or two children.

My Father tended bar in the evenings and on weekends, as a second job. It was beneficial in three ways: It got my Father out of the house (which made my Mother happy), it brought in extra money for bills, and it provided free beer to my Father. He seemed to imbibe at least as much as he dispensed. It was an honor to be brought into a bar with him on Saturdays, and set on a tall bar stool. "This is my oldest son," my Father would declare proudly.

Later, the orange ring around my mouth from the three or four bottles of orange pop that I drank – that was 'Exhibit A' in the ongoing trial conducted by my Mother against Father. Later, my Father ordered me to drink Seven-Up, which I still don't like much.

My poor, overworked Mother wailed loudly and often. "Be quiet, damn it!" she'd yell at my Father. "Do you want the whole god-damned neighborhood to know you're a drunken bastard?"

They knew. My Mother's "Be quiet, you drunken bastard!"

was much louder than any noise he ever made.

On weekends, he was not allowed out of the house alone because forcing him to take along two or three kids lessened the chances that he'd stop off at a bar, or at least would lessen the duration of his visits, she figured.

She was wrong. His favorite bar was near the railroad crossing at Seventh Street, not too far from where my Great Grandfather fell to his death. My Father told us to sit in the car and 'watch the trains – he'd be back in a minute.'

The trains came by about once every half-hour. We'd see about six trains, and then Father would come out, his eyes glowing, and his legs looking as if they wanted to fold. He was so happy to see us that he usually wasn't angry about how we had fiddled with each knob and every control on the dashboard of his green 1950 Mercury, screwing up almost everything about the car. On the way home, he told us about the important people he had met. Why, he was going to partner up with one of them and buy a big house on Summit Avenue. The owners lived in France or something, and would be happy to get rid of this headache, a house that they never visited.

Our apartments were ones of disorder. No, not physical disorder. Nine of us could fit into a two bedroom apartment with a small pantry off the kitchen and the dining room serving as an extra bedroom. Toys were always put away, as were clothes. The rule was: If you leave something out, that means you don't want it anymore. That rule meant that if I got up from doing my homework at the kitchen table to go to the bathroom, when I returned, my books and workbooks and pencils would be in the garbage.

The shambles and disorder came from raw feelings, unmet needs, insecurity, fears, unpaid revenge – whatever. The hatred and contempt between Mother and Father bled down into the children. I hated Patty, the one Sister older than I. I hated Jimmy, the Brother directly below me in the birth line. Eventually, the whole family was divided up into teams – those who favored my Mother and those who favored my Father. I was on my Father's side, which made me the automatic enemy of my Mother, as well as all the kids on my Mother's side.

It was hard to read a complex novel such as <u>War and Peace</u>, at home, although the title would have been appropriate, without the 'peace' part, and not to hear all that was going on in the apartment. Neighbors in the halls would look the other way when I passed. The apartments stood around three-sided courtyards, such that the acoustics no doubt rivaled those of the Hollywood Bowl.

I wanted out. I became a scholar. I always had a shoulder bag or cheap briefcase containing 'my papers,' whatever they might be (maybe the Latin text of the Mass, which I was memorizing, or newspaper articles, or catalog pictures of clothes I wished I had so I could look like all the others in school, or poems).

I switched schools often, my parents barely staying ahead of the eviction notices, so it was hard to make friends. Or was it that I was about as good at making friends as I was at playing baseball? There was Jefferson Public School for kindergarten, then Saint Stanislaus for first grade, still down on the lower West Side but higher than the Italian levee that flooded nearly every spring. Then we moved into public housing for my grades two through five, and we were bussed to Saint Patrick's school. This lower-middle-class parish was stretching its budget and increasing its contempt for the poor by taking in us public housing brats.

We were a separate breed. We had our own winter sliding hills off the back end of the playground. We stuck together. It was as if we had 'Projects' written on our school uniforms. We were not like the others. Our clothes had holes in them and buttons missing, and our shirts had been washed too many times and were nearly transparent. Not to mention our shoes, that sometimes had soles flapping. In that respect, I was pretty lucky. Being the first boy of the family, I got the clothes that relatives and neighbors gave to us, and then they were handed down through the long chain of Jack boys, until the items were of no value at all.

Dearest Alex, Katya, and Anna:

I wish I could convey to you the fear and loathing that characterized America's attitude towards the Soviet Union during the high points of the 'Cold War' between the two countries.

I was barely twelve years old in 1957, when the Russians shot a metal ball into space that went spinning around the globe and even dared to spin across the United States. We watched it one night from a hill near the Cathedral of Saint Paul, on Summit Avenue. It was a faint light, hardly scary, although people were staring at it wide-eyed and speaking in hushed tones. The end was near. If they can put a satellite into space......

The trembling nuns commanded us to study extra-hard – the world was in for a hard time of it. Surely that third secret of Our Lady of Fatima, which the Vatican never revealed, concerned this red menace, the nuns reminded us. No wonder Pope Pius XII always looked so sad. We boys and girls had to pray for him daily.

After Sputnik, and after the next Russian satellite, which was occupied by Laika, a dog who was allowed to starve to death in outer space, the newspapers filled up with stories about why Johnny couldn't read and why Ivan was good at math.

The free world would get little help from me on that score. I was lousy at math and science, and I hated it all.

Federal money sprouted freely from many fountains. Russian departments were formed, and Russian émigrés living in America, no matter their trade or craft, were dragged off the streets to become college professors and department chairs.

There were scholarships too. Thank you, Soviet Union. Because of you, I had a nearly free ride through graduate school. As long as I continued to study Slavic Languages and Literatures, I received enough money to pay tuition, buy books, and help with living expenses. I hope my study of Old Church Slavonic, a Bulgarian dialect of the 800s, helped our fight in the Cold War. Same goes for my delving into the possibilities offered by a Structuralist approach to Russian Expressionist poetry that hardly anybody read. I'm sure it made a difference for us all. Thank you, Federal Government.

Dear Children:

I was in love with every nun I ever had -- Not just 'loving,' mind you, but 'in love.'

In seventh grade, Sister Lucille taught us to love and fear literature. She made us memorize poems, most of which I can still recite today. How odd that fifteen or so years later, poet Joseph Brodsky would too command that we memorize poems. This was the way to reach the heart of the poet.

In eighth grade, Sister Raphael taught us to love the predictability and flexibility of language, and marvel at how these two apparently opposing forces coexist. She threw away the math books and the science books and the history books and for most of the day we diagrammed sentences on the blackboard, reciting as we wrote....."'New' is an adjective modifying the noun 'year,' which is the subject of the sentence, and ...."

From her, I learned to love and respect language.

Sister Lucille in seventh grade. Sister Raphael in eighth grade. They cleared the way for literature and linguistics. I wonder where I would have ended up or how I would have ended up, without those two good nuns and the ones who came before.

My Dear Children (Lord, I sound like a priest when I utter than phrase. I think I will change it.)

Dearest children:

Read on, about Russia.

I don't remember if it really happened – that's the problem in recalling things from childhood, for anyone, but particularly for a person who suffers from an overactive imagination or who reads too much (real events can get mixed with sections of stories). Some things that never happened appear vivid, while other things that happened are submerged so deep in memory that you don't remember them.

But Khrushchev did visit Minnesota in 1959 – I know that. And he did ride in a convoy of limousines that snaked down Summit Avenue, Saint Paul's elegant street that was a little bit down on its luck in the 1950's. Old, crumbling mansions lined the street, as did towering elms whose arching branches met over the middle of the avenue, forming a darkened canopy. In a few decades, the elms would be chopped down because of Dutch Elm Disease. Naturally, the paint that was used to mark the afflicted trees was red.

My grade school then was Saint Luke's, a nondescript, tan 1950's two-story brick building located on the same block as the gray Romanesque monstrosity known as Saint Luke's Church. It stood, like a bulldog, guarding the corner of Summit and Lexington Avenues. No Communists passed there, at least as far as anyone knows.

Except for the Soviet Premier.

"This is Nikita Khrushchev himself!" Sister Saint Peter had said as we walked down the stairwell single-file. "Remember the terrible things he has done to the poor Catholic boys and girls in Poland and Hungary. Imagine being taken away from your parents and put into a state school, in rooms with no windows! We Catholics must stand on the curb as the Khrushchev convoy passes, yes, but we will turn our backs, in protest, as his limousine passes."

If all that did happen, I am sure I turned and sneaked a peak at the Premier, but I honestly don't recall. That was almost my one and only face-to-face encounter with a Soviet leader. But I must mention Gorbachev, who drove down the same street in 1990, as the Soviet Union was crumbling and East Europe was flexing its muscles the way

Popeye did in the cartoons. Gorbachev had flown over in a Soviet Tupulov plane that seemed nearly unable to remain aloft.

When I discovered what was inside that plane, I understood why it was not very air-worthy. Gorbachov was on board with his team and with a brace of secret service agents. In addition, the plane carried about six Soviet limousines. Nothing is heavier than a Soviet limousine; well, perhaps an aircraft carrier is. These limos looked like Lincoln Continentals on steroids.

Soviet cars, it was said, started out as imitations of foreign cars during the lend-lease programs earlier in the century. Many other Soviet commodities started out that way as well. There was a story that an early version of the Moskvich sedan had an engine copied from that of a Chevrolet sedan given to the USSR during the lend-lease program. The original engine block, the story goes, had a crack running across it, and all Soviet iterations of engines carried the same crack. Maybe so, maybe not. The answer may still lie in somebody's memory, but not mine. I looked at one Soviet engine once, in 1970, but I saw no crack line.

We sign-holders got a wave as we held high a long peace and friendship poster that was painted on the back of a twenty-foot roll of wallpaper. We stood across the street from Saint Luke's Church. The sign was written in Cyrillic, which became a matter of great concern to the Police. "What did it really, really say?" they wanted to know.

Dear Anna:

I heard you mention the word 'heaven' today. It surprised me because I thought it was agreed that no religion would be forced upon you. The other day you wanted to say grace before dinner. This makes me nervous but, on the other hand, so much of the Western cultural heritage is tied in with the Catholic Church in particular, and with Christianity in general. So I am ambivalent about you saying grace.

I stopped going to Church when I was a sophomore in high school. I'd usually leave home in time for the latest Sunday Mass, to deceive my parents, but I'd spend the hour or so looking at dirty magazines in a shady drug store on Selby Avenue, in the direction opposite the church. By the way, what was nasty then is now so commonplace that it isn't even considered mildly nasty.

Why didn't I go to Church anymore? Well, if you went to Church, you had to file up the center aisle and go to communion or else everyone in the Church would know you had committed at least one mortal sin and were damned to the fires of hell. But, if you went to communion, you had to go to confession too. And, maybe you did things in your teenage years that you wanted no one, not even a priest, to hear about.

The priests usually sat in tiny, windowless boxes about the size of a phone booth, along the side walls of the Church. On each side of those booths stood tiny enclosures, about the size of an out-house, for you to kneel and, when your time was up, enumerate all your sins since your last confession. The priest went from side to side, using a series of small doors that raised when it was your turn and lowered when you were released to perform your penance. It was dead-silent in there, although once in a while I could catch the muttering of the priest, and sometimes even the cries of the penitent on the other side of the window, but I couldn't make out the words.

The clicking of the tiny door on the other side meant that it was just about my turn. Then the slit would open on my side. The priest would listen to my sins, then give a bit of advice, and penance (usually saying a rosary or two at the communion rail). Swearing got you a couple of rosaries. Masturbation? Well, one time I saw Father O'Malley, of Saint Patrick's Parish, leap out of his phone booth, grab his teenage male penitent by the ears, and escort him from the outhouse to the doors of the church.

For our reading sessions during our high school 'religious retreats,' I used the cover of Thomas Kempis' Imitation of Christ to conceal what I really was reading. When I learned all possible vocabulary words for the female body from Henry Miller's Tropic of Cancer and Tropic of Capricorn and from Lady Chatterly's Lover when it was finally allowed to be published in the United States, I turned for some reason to the Russians.

I don't know why. For one thing, the books were dead serious. You didn't read them casually while watching network programs on your Motorola or Muntz TV with an oval screen and a giant dial you turned to select one of the three stations. Books pulled you into a different world, away from continual family fights, and you remained suspended there until the author let you go. I was very much into escape during those years – there was a lot of screaming at home. All that paled, however, when compared to the travails of the Russian characters.

I read Dostoevsky (Crime and Punishment, The Brothers Karamazov) and Tolstoy (Anna Karenina, War And Peace, Childhood, Boyhood, And Youth) and Gogol and Chekhov and Turgenev and others, in junior and senior years. I wrote poetry during trigonometry and calculus class.

I studied Latin for four years, loving it, although my junior-year teacher knew no Latin. He was a bookkeeping student yanked out of the Brothers' preparatory school because baby boom enrollments in Catholic high schools were swelling, and there weren't enough Christian Brothers to go around. Maybe they were too busy making wine in California or punching kids in Chicago. He didn't know syllabic verse from syllabo-tonic verse, and he beat out the rhythm of "The Aeneid" for us once, banging a desk with a long window pole, thereby ruining Virgil for me forever. "Ar-MA vir-um-QUE can-O. Tro-JAE qui PRI-mus a-BOR-is." Those words still reverberate in me sometimes.

My sophomore Latin teacher was Professor Brown, a seminary drop-out who was terrified of hormone-riddled sophomore males and of life in general. He was a pencil-thin man who frequently adjusted his glasses by using his middle finger, resembling the one-finger salute. We made fun of him horribly.

We all had cribs (cheat sheets) that we used for translation, because without them, we were lost and would never finish the first thing on the class syllabus. Moses Hadas (whom we called "Moses Hot Ass") was our favorite translator because he remained closest to the Latin syntax and word order. When we translated on our own, we came up with horribly garbled messes – "Catullus, having been married to the previously dead former ex-wife...."

After a while, our Latin Professor began using Moses Hot Ass too.

In my junior year of high school, I started spending many evenings at the home of Kathy Strehlow, the girlfriend of one of my friends. She and her parents had the time and inclination to discuss politics, religion, and life, with several confused high school boys. When I was there, which was often, I felt as if I was putting one foot on solid ground while the other foot remained mired in quicksand. This was a normal family. They had lived in the same house for years. They had the same phone number for decades. Imagine.

Dear Kids:

Let's go back a little so we can clarify some things. A big change waited for me in the middle of fifth grade. My Father's regular salary and his bartending salary meant that we were making too much money to remain in the projects. We were <u>real</u> people now, almost, because we moved to an apartment building in Saint Paul's affluent and sometimes smug neighborhood. I started going to Saint Luke's School for grades five through eight.

Saint Luke's parish encompassed Summit Avenue and the parallel fancy streets – Portland, Holly, Laurel, Lincoln, Goodrich, Fairmont, all with gigantic four-square houses filled mostly by big Catholic families. Our family of ten was not unusual; others had eleven or sometimes sixteen children. Why so many? I already talked about condoms and the obligation to, um, do the big nasty at least once a month.

There was a clear hierarchy in school and in the parish and neighborhood. At the top were the superbly privileged kids who lived in the mansions along Summit and Portland and Lincoln Avenues. Many of those kids went to private schools and wore the best clothes, with labels showing. Next came the simply privileged kids who lived in more regular houses or on the edges of the parish, where, to the north, the blacks were getting closer and closer, and to the east, where the Jews were moving out.

Then came the kids who lived in nice apartments, then those who lived in less-nice apartments on the fringes of the parish. At the very bottom of the list came the un-privileged children of caretakers. We lived in basement apartments, trading rent or portions of rent for services. We were something like urban sharecroppers.

I emptied garbage cans, painted porch railings, vacuumed halls, and filled the coal stoker on cold winter mornings. I had to use a shovel that was bigger than I, step deep into the coal room, fill up the shovel, struggle with it over to the conveyer belt that fed the furnace stoker, and toss in whatever coal I hadn't managed to spill, picking up all I had dropped along the way (probably a good half of what I had when I started). I loved the smell of coal; good thing, that. My clothes and my skin smelled of it.

True, at Saint Luke's we all wore uniforms that should have made us all look alike and should have blurred the hierarchic distinctions. Still, those distinctions were as clear as if we wore numbers or letters.

Why? How? I don't know and I still wonder about it. Maybe it was the confident grins that came from girls who had gotten lots of dental work (this was in the days before fluoride was added to the city water supply – some protested that it was a communist plot.). A watch that a boy might wear, a necklace that a girl might wear, and new shoes – those things separated the elite from the masses. My clothes were hand-me-downs or give-away's, or they came from shopping at Goodwill or at St. Vincent DePaul's (The Salvation Army was way too expensive). My Mother preferred St. Vincent DePaul's Store because they didn't put prices on anything – they'd look at you and then decide how much something cost. My Mother made sure all of us went with her to the store, and we all wore battered clothes.

Where do you suppose they buy their clothes?

They buy their clothes at the city dump.

The melody was fetching. I heard it enough times. And I wore glasses, ugly ones that came from charities such as the Wilder Foundation. Few kids wore glasses in those years. I think that when I was in first grade at Saint Stanislaus School, I was the only kid in the whole school who wore glasses. The day I got my first pair, I hid under the stairwell until the Czech janitor found me out and brought me to the principal.

And I had chipped my two front teeth, right after they came in. My Sister was chasing me into the bathroom because I hadn't dried the dishes. I slipped and fell against the edge of the tub. My teeth remained chipped for about forty-five years.

To save money, my Father bought rejected wieners from Peters Meat Company. Some of the wieners had giant bends in them, or bulges. There was something horribly sinful about the shapes of some of those contorted wieners. He bought rejected "Seven-Up" candy bars from the Pearson Nut Company out on West Seventh, very near where he had his truck accident. Our "Seven-Up" bars might have had only six pieces, thus being, more accurately, "Six-Up" candy bars, or maybe they had two brazil nuts and no caramel.

I never, ever understood why the students and their parents, no matter where they were in the hierarchy, didn't like Blacks or Jews. Lucky for me, I never learned to hate groups. I somehow escaped that and I don't know why. I have reserved all my hatreds for individuals, not groups, and I feel this is a more effective use of the energy that drives hatred.

Yes, the lovely atmosphere of the Crocus Hill neighborhood that spread from the Cathedral up to Saint Luke's – it was a gentile sort of place; on Sundays people dressed in white and women with gigantic bonnets played croquet in a tiny park at the top of Ramsey Hill. Why? Were they posing for a photograph? Were they pretending they were in a Rockwell painting perhaps, or maybe they were they were celebrating their heritage, or dreaming they were in a movie about the 1880's?

And what a heritage it was. This was the part of the city where upper middle class families fled in droves because the blacks were invading. What caused this invasion? Were the blacks out to capture the neighborhood or rape all the white women? Did they want to play croquet too? No. The kind city fathers had dug a long, wide trench through the Rondo area, literally cutting out the heart of the black neighborhood, so that some day Freeway I-94 could run from downtown Minneapolis to downtown Saint Paul. The blacks needed to find a new neighborhood, and they moved south-west, closer and closer to Saint Luke's parish. All the time I was in grade school or high school, I never saw a student who was black. And they say there was no prejudice in the North then?

And what about those Jews? We in Crocus Hill had been lucky. While the whites played croquet, the Blacks and the Jews tended to stay with their own – the Jews living about a mile away, down around Victoria and Hague. The blacks had lived further north, around Iglehart and Marshall Avenues, before the freeway pushed them out. When I needed to go to the Saint Paul Public Library downtown, I could take a Selby Avenue bus; they ran fairly frequently. But, I was warned, I was liable to run into blacks on that line, Jews too probably, although I had no clear idea of what they looked like. Better to take the Grand Avenue bus, the nuns cautioned. It came less often, but there were only whites on it.

I am sorry to report that my parents shared in these prejudices.

One of my earliest memories is of a shaking old woman pressing her face against the back screen of a second-story apartment behind the building where we lived in the basement as caretakers on Kent and Holly. She wanted to give me a toy and was going to drop it down from the window. I couldn't tell what it was from the distance.

Just then my Father came around the corner and yanked me by the arm. "Don't ever talk to people in that building!" he commanded. "They're Jews!"

"What's a Jew?" I asked.

"They're – they're different from the rest of us. Stay away or they'll rob you blind."

It made no sense that this person anxious to rob me blind was offering me a free toy. I didn't get it. Later, I heard people tell stories about going into apartments of Jews and finding dead animals hanging from the ceiling or Jews swimming in animal blood in their bathtubs.

I had never been around blacks; my Father took great detours to avoid the black areas. When we lived in the McDonough Public Housing Project, there must have been some kind of 'de facto' segregation there, because even in the projects, in this god-forsaken pocket of the poorest residents, all the Blacks lived in one section, on the opposite end.

We were forbidden to use the community house or its playground because Blacks played there, and they even swam there too, Good Lord! Instead, old yellow school busses with torn seats took us to some dismal "Paul Savage Club" for good Catholic boys that was located in a brick warehouse building on the industrial edge of downtown.

It was there that I learned I could not swim. They offered swimming lessons only for those who could swim. That logic never quite made it with me. I also learned that I was lousy with tools, and not good at any sport whatsoever.

I hated those nights spent at Paul Savage. They didn't let you read – it was a place for socializing, they claimed, and people there wanted to talk to me about as much as I wanted to talk to them. I hated the bus rides there and back too – there was punching and spitting in the back seats, particularly at outsiders wearing thick glasses. I guess there were no Blacks or Jews to pick on, so they chose me.

The lovely, placid veneer of Saint Paul that is still celebrated, had, in essence, worn thin in places, if it had ever existed at all. The city had been a major hangout for gangsters in the thirties, and it was said that the city's government was the most corrupt in the nation. Even as a young adult, I wondered what vestiges remained.

Jews were not allowed in Saint Paul's 'Town & Country Club' until late in the 1970's, a decade after I had caddied there. What was the matter? Didn't Jews replace their divots on the golf course fairways? And a Jew or a Black as a member of the Minnesota Club or of the Athletic Club? Forget it. Even white women were denied membership.

That's how life was in the city of Paul – imperfect, but trying. Just like another country that interested me. I tried to follow things going on in Russia. After Stalin, names came, and then went. I would read them in the headlines or hear the newscasters on the radio pronounce them. Khrushchev. Beria, but he died and they yanked his lengthy profile out of the Great Soviet Encyclopedia and replaced it with a long article about the strategic importance of the Bering Straits. Molotov. Was he related to the cocktail? Bulganin. Malenkov. Their names were as harsh and guttural as the appearances in newspaper photos and in newsreels of the men bearing those names. All the newspaper and magazine photos, all the newsreel shots, were dark and grainy – the country must have been that way for real, I decided.

But it was intriguing that from such bleak circumstances, beautiful art and literature emerged. Somehow, that appealed to me greatly. I had the makings of a Russophile.

Dearest Children:

We Catholics were told it was alright, and not a sin, to hate the Soviet Union for what it did in Poland and Hungary in the mid 1950's. We read all about Cardinal Midzenty. We got some Hungarian refugees in the parish when I was in fifth grade. One's name was Karl, and he was my age.

For some reason we hated one-another – I don't remember why. We got in a fist fight on the playground – I don't know over what. Then for some reason, during a stall between punches maybe, I asked him where he was from, and he said Budapest. I asked him whether he was from Buda or from Pest. He was impressed that I knew that Budapest was two cities in one, and he stopped punching me.

I don't know how I knew.

Dear Kids:

I wanted to be a priest as far back as the first grade. The nuns encouraged me. At school, I sat on half my chair, reserving the other half for my personal Guardian Angel, who probably needed a break from all that standing around.

Why didn't your Papa become a priest? I was determined to go to Nazareth Hall Seminary after eighth grade, but Father Sutherland, a kind and erudite priest at Saint Luke's, talked me out of it. He didn't actually forbid me. He simply told me I couldn't go, and he'd make sure no parish priest would write a letter of recommendation for me. He doubted that I had a 'true vocation,' whatever that was. "Go to a Catholic high school for a few years," he advised. "You can always switch over to the seminary later, if you still want to."

I don't recall the reason for his hesitation with me. He knew something I didn't. I decided to go to Cretin High School, run by the Christian Brothers because the only Catholic alternative was Saint Thomas Academy, but it was way more expensive. I feared public high schools. There were girls there. There were tough guys there who would no doubt take turns punching me or stomping on my glasses.

Cretin was eighty-five dollars a year, and they let you work in the library or office for a penny a minute, applied directly to tuition costs. The military uniform wasn't too expensive, if bought used, and you didn't have to buy any other school clothes. The second-hand clothes shops still carried a lot of World War Two and Korean War gear, which suited Cretin just fine.

To pay my tuition, I cut lawns in the summer and shoveled snow in the winter and caddied and did whatever else I could for money. I started 'babysitting' for a woman whose lawn I cut, except that the 'baby' was her senile Father who kept thinking my name was Jake and I was working the coal mines with him in Pennsylvania. "Got up a good load today, Jake, eh? We'll get more tomorrow." Poor guy. He did indeed look like a baby, so pale and too thin to have wrinkles, set immobile in that crib-like bed with railings.

Dearest Ex-Orphan Children:

You have had incredibly different lives so far. No one would argue that.

I wonder, did I ever have a 'normal' life? Does anyone? I turn to high school.

Poetry and censors and Latin Masses and communion hosts and, yes, I confess, things Russian, sort of got pushed aside as I began high school. There was a war going on, inside me. Puberty had come, without an invitation. Hormones raged over the scarred battle scene that was my ever-changing body. I'd wake up some mornings, look at myself, and conclude that I was someone else or I'd wish that I was. My whole face broke out with pimples, as a sign perhaps of the turmoil within. I had to shave at least twice a week. Sometimes I was called 'pizza face.'

My skin was not all that erupted. So did my mind. I rebelled. I can't remember when or why it began. I was second-to-the-top student in my freshman year of high school and had few friends. In sophomore year, I became something of the class clown, composing fake, sarcastic daily bulletins that were prized whenever they escaped confiscation. My grades dropped, but the number of my friends increased greatly. My attendance at church went from bad to 'certain eternal punishment in the fires of hell.'

My Father was outraged when he saw that my grades in Latin in one year had gone from 54 to 95 to 62 and then back up to 97.

One day, I spotted a blue city Water Department truck parked outside. I sank low in my chair. I knew what I was in for. My Father had used his city Water Department badge to get into the school. He had done this before, for me, and for my brothers and sisters. No good ever came from it.

There was a loud bang on the classroom door. Before Brother Martin could open it, my Father came storming in, holding a large monkey wrench. His greasy thumb pounded my report card. "How in hell can a person go from 95 to 62 and then 97 in one subject? Are you crazy or something?"

"We grade on things other than mere knowledge of Latin," the Brother said meekly.

My Father ripped up the report card and threw the pieces on the floor. "You wouldn't make a pimple on a Latin teacher's ass!" he said. My Father had only finished third grade.

This was probably one of the most embarrassing moments of my life, before that as well as after. I have never felt my cheeks burn so hot, except perhaps when I graduated from grade school.

There was a grade school graduation dance party in Ramaley Hall, above the liquor store on Grand Avenue. I was terrified. I didn't know how to dance. In those days, the dance moves were all set in stone – not the free-form stuff that passes as 'dance' today. There was the waltz and the fox-trot and the polka and others, but I could do none of them.

For some reason, I had done my Father wrong early on the day of the party. He came after me, ready to beat me with the belt that all of us kids feared. I ran and locked myself in the bathroom. Somehow and for a reason I do not know or remember, my Mother was on my side that day. She snuck my sports coat, a clean and ironed and starched shirt, my clip-on bow-tie, and creased and cuffed pants into the bathroom. I slid out the window, snuck down the back steps and then walked the six blocks to the dance.

About an hour later, my heart nearly stopped. My Father staggered into the dance floor. I quickly left with him, wanting to minimize as much as possible the number of kids who would see us. We sat in the car on Grand Avenue, and my Father talked about how he had to work hard at two jobs, and he did all of it for his children and he loved all of them and was proud of all of them, especially me.

It was raining, and the car windows steamed over.

Dearest Katya, Anna, Alex:

The real world, the outside world, managed to seep in through the cracks of Cretin, that bastion of American middle-class Catholicism. While I was a junior, a grim and tired-looking President Kennedy appeared on WCCO TV, KSTP TV, and KMSP TV one October night. Satellite photos of Cuba stood behind him, with circles drawn around some white rectangles.

The Christian Brothers had us pray for our own safety, and several students talked about quitting school, driving down to Florida, and figuring out some way to get to Cuba and fight. They were sure there was going to be a war, and so were a lot of other people.

I was skeptical. After all, this was Russia, the home of Pushkin and Chekhov and Gogol – what would they want with guided missiles? First of all, I had just learned that Khrushchev's infamous remark of some years earlier ("We will bury you!") – the remark that had been repeated in the newspapers and on television and from pulpits in America – was taken out of context and was poorly translated. It could have more justifiably read, "We will surpass you," but I'm sure that 'bury' sold more newspapers.

And I had always wondered why that image of Khrushchev pounding his shoe on the lectern at the United Nations had terrified so many people. He looked so inconsequential, so unthreatening, and almost clown-like in his baggy clothes. And anyway, he had given Richard Nixon a hard time during the 'Kitchen Debate' in Moscow, and anybody who gave Richard Nixon a hard time was a friend of mine.

I read up on this Cuban Missile Crisis, hunting out whatever viewpoints I could find in Saint Paul. The best I could do was at the Saint Paul Public Library, where a London newspaper article talked about Soviet missiles now being ninety miles from the United States in Florida, but American missiles being right at several Soviet borders, in Turkey, Germany, and the Aleutian Islands.

And I remembered the whole brouhaha earlier about Francis Gary Powers, the American U-2 pilot/spy who was shot down over Russia. I remember Eisenhower on television vehemently denying that Powers had been spying, and I remember the not-so-vehement admissions that came forth a few days later. I recalled the terror that the name 'Joseph McCarthy' brought to people, and I saw some of his anti-communist harangues on television. In those days, the TV screen was about as big as a dinner plate, but still, McCarthy looked formidable. I disliked that man so intensely that I pretty much stood for whatever it was that he was attacking. It was Communism. "Russia is trying to take over us!" he claimed, waving his now-famous list of Communist spies working undercover in America.

My skeptical view of life at Cretin High School was now extending out to the whole universe. My high school mentality honed in, like an ICBM guided missile, on the fact that Powers' escape kit included condoms. I wondered if he had bought them himself or if the government gave them to him.

They played the scratchy radio loud over the Cretin speakers when Walter Cronkite announced that the Soviet ships had turned back from the American blockade around Cuba.

"I am sure the Pope, our Holy Father, has saved us!" said Brother Martin.

Months later, in the public library, in a London newspaper, I read about the then-secret agreements in which the Americans withdrew some missiles from Turkey and Germany in exchange for Russia taking back its missile sites from Cuba.

Dear Kids:

Do not pay too much attention to my bad grades, please. You three are all doing very well. Don't follow your Father's example.

I barely graduated from Cretin High School. I was too much a smart-ass. I once asked our religion teacher why the Catholic schools in Louisiana were segregated.

"We don't want to create any fusses," the Christian Brother answered.

"Is that how the Church was in Germany during Hitler's time?"

"We will discuss this some other time," he answered. "Right now we are scheduled to start math, and we all know how bad you are at math."

For this and other transgressions, I was demoted to private and my punishment was to spend the last weekend of the school year flanking. That meant that I had to march back and forth in the hallways, while carrying a rifle on my shoulder, for twelve hours straight or I wouldn't graduate.

Because my poetry-writing had caught the attention of my drama teacher, I got a four-year scholarship to Saint Thomas College, a small Catholic liberal arts institution in Saint Paul that has since reinvented itself and become a business and management mega-institution.

I turned it down and decided to go to the University of Minnesota, over in the sinful, protestant city of Minneapolis. Brother Wilfred, a man of about three hundred pounds and the assistant principal at Cretin, told me I was committing a mortal sin by turning down such a blessed opportunity and exposing myself to so much godlessness and temptation. "If a bus hits you or if you fall off a cliff, you will go straight to hell!" he said, resting his hands on his desk as if he was a lawyer concluding his final argument to the jury.

The Brother stared at me, waiting for me to announce that I had changed my mind. After all, hadn't I seen the photos in the paper of those beatniks at the university? Among them was a guitar-playing, harmonica-blowing singer who later changed his name to 'Bob Dylan.' I could lie and say I heard him sing in person, but I didn't. By the time I graduated from high school and was attending the University, he was already in New York.

I did graduate from Cretin High School, but barely. I was a buck private in a military school, an agnostic in a Catholic school. This was not good.

And why such a name for a school as 'Cretin,' a word that is defined as someone with an extremely low intelligence, often the result of too much inter-marriage between relatives? Well, Bishop Cretin, for whom the school was named, was born in the mountainous parts of France. Apparently there was a lot of in-breeding and hence a surplus of village idiots, who were called 'Cretins' or 'Blessed Ones' or 'Holy Innocents.' There is something similar in Russia, although I don't know if intermarriage is a part of it; there's a long tradition of the 'Holy Fool.' You can see a rendition of a Holy Fool if you go to the opera and watch Modest Mussorgsky's "Boris Godunov," which you should do anyway.

Dear Children:

I felt lost and totally inconsequential on the University of Minnesota campus. There were 40,000 students, none of whom knew me or wanted to know me. I was an English major, then a philosophy major, then a history major, and I thought about architecture and medicine until I found out you had to be good at science. I thought about taking Russian literature, but those courses were for juniors and seniors. I wondered how to get out of the basic math and science requirements.

I was too timid to approach any women, in those days called 'girls' or 'co-eds.'

I wanted to contribute poetry to the university's poetry magazine, "The Ivory Tower," but I looked at what they published and I looked at my own verse, and I could see the worlds between them. Anyway, the poetry published was way too profound, and the name of the magazine's editor, Garrison Keillor, was obviously made-up. No one would be born with a first name like 'Garrison.' I think he was two years ahead of me at the University, maybe more.

Dear Kids:

President Kennedy was killed while I was between classes, drinking sodas and shooting pool at Coffman Memorial Union, at one end of the long mall on the university campus.

A friend with a portable radio ran in and told us. We didn't believe him, but then we ran to the radio room with the news. They thought we were fakers, or on drugs. "Please turn on the radio and hear for yourself," I said. They tuned in WCCO, listened for a few moments, and then turned on the loudspeakers throughout the building, broadcasting the news. All the TV sets were on, and it didn't matter which station people were watching, because all the stations were showing the same thing.

Walter Cronkite, the stern grandfather of television newscasters, read from a sheet that someone had just passed to him. His hands were shaking. He took of his glasses and wiped his eyes. You would never expect him to show any emotion, any personal connection with that which he broadcast. But on that dismal November morning, rules were broken all over the place.

On the University mall, students and faculty and workers and whoever's – for the most part they simply stood, seemingly not knowing where to go or why. I sat on the floor of the student union, my knees drawn up to my chest.

No one moved or said a word for a long time. Then there were some sobs. After a while, people left the building silently, slowly, and often alone.

He was the hero for people my age back then – everybody's hero. With him, I believed, died hope in the realm of American politics. Never again would Americans become so attached to their president. His death made me really sad. I resolved to get busy with politics. Something had to be done.

Kids:

I kept my promise to myself, and I got involved in politics in 1964, in my sophomore year. I became Vice President of 'Students For Eugene McCarthy.' He was worlds apart in ideology from Joe McCarthy, and was no relation, although people sometimes confused the two since they lived in adjacent states (Minnesota and Wisconsin). I was campaigning for Eugene McCarthy when he was running for the U.S. Senate. He was just about the first politician to speak out against the war in Viet Nam. I stood with him on the stage at the university, but I couldn't see much because I was wearing a pair of contact lenses – they had just come out. My lenses were about the size and shape of a football. I never got used to them, although I tried many types many times for the next fifteen years. When I managed to overcome the discomfort and wear them, everything blurred and I couldn't see a thing. Thus it was on stage with McCarthy.

I ignored my studies and I got the grades to prove it. I walked in on my astronomy midterm exam, not knowing there was a midterm exam that day, and not having attended classes for a couple of weeks or so. Astronomy was one of the 'soft science' courses that I had taken to get around the university's science requirement.

Do not, please, follow my example when it comes to education.

This was before the days of the military lottery. Things were heating up rapidly in Southeast Asia in 1964 and 1965. All unmarried non-students were liable to be drafted.

Kids:

The campaigning and the working nights at The Lexington Restaurant and the occasional studying wore me out after a few months. I didn't finish Fall quarter. I didn't register for Spring quarter, and about one week after registration closed, I received word of my impending draft in March of 1965. What to do? I was opposed to the war in Vietnam.

I checked into becoming a conscientious objector, but there was some queer logic which said that, in order to qualify, you had to be opposed to all wars, not just the stupid ones that we shouldn't have been in. This seemed back-ass-wards to me.

I thought of sneaking up to Canada, but I lacked the guts and, yes, the commitment. Yet, if I did nothing, I'd end up in the infantry, probably in Viet Nam.

I took the coward's way out. I enlisted. I decided on the Air Force, but it was a cold and windy winter day in Minneapolis, and the Navy recruiter was closer.

Dear Alex:

Yes, Alex, you are proud when you tell others that your Papa became a 'soldier,' in a manner of speaking. I was a sailor, to be more precise. United States Navy. I went to basic training in 1965 in Great Lakes, Illinois. For our 'service week,' most of my compatriots had to get up at four in the morning to work in the galley, preparing the over-cooked eggs and the watery oatmeal that they served at breakfast. Me? I was chaplain's assistant. I was his altar boy, and the most challenging part of the day for me was to go to the galley late each morning and get doughnuts for him. Being a chaplain's assistant, I didn't have to walk in formation or, if walking alone, run. All the others had to do those things.

I don't remember how I ever passed the swimming test in boot camp, but I must have. Or maybe the Chaplain got me out of it. I couldn't swim until thirty years later, when I admitted it finally and took lessons.

I did very well on the Foreign Language Aptitude Test, called the "FLAT." They had you read a paragraph or two of a fake language and then they'd ask you a couple of questions about it, also written in the fake language. Taking Latin probably helped me. They offered me language school, and this being the Navy, you could request what you wanted and they would try hard to give it to you, except that, in this case, your second language choice had to be Vietnamese and your third choice had to be Chinese.

I figured I'd better make a good first choice, one they might likely need, not French or German or Spanish. Russian. I was drawn to it. There was no need even to think about it. Yet, I remembered Tolstoy and Dostoevsky and reading about how great Pushkin was in the original and how lousy he in translation, so I picked Russian. So Russia was once again part of my life.

And, it changed my life, and it led me to you.

Dearest children:

I had gone to Boot Camp via train. This was during the great spring floods of 1965, and the train was diverted to Canada. I arrived at the Great Lakes Naval Station two days AWOL. This was not an auspicious beginning.

How odd, that my first trip away from home coincided with the demise of Lilydale. The shanty town so familiar with floods succumbed to the hundred-year flood of 1965. How high was the water from that flood? We didn't know. Uncle Frank didn't write the year of this flood on his wall. He didn't have a wall anymore.

During earlier floods, Uncle Carl put his rabbit cages high into the trees. Then the uncles loaded up their junk trucks and drove up the hill, on the bluffs until the waters receded. They had stocked their vehicles with enough beer to wait out the river's wage. After the waters receded, they'd squabble about, for instance, the fact that Uncle Carl's garage ended up on Uncle Frank's property, and that too much of Uncle Frank's junk had ended up in Aunt Elizabeth's yard.

But there was nothing to fight about in 1965. Why? Yes, it was what they call 'a hundred year flood,' meaning that a flood with as much ferocity would hit only once every hundred years, but there was more to the demise of 'Lower' Lilydale.

Over the years, the city of Saint Paul had been putting up dikes along the river, to protect the city and its property and its inhabitants on the north side of the river. I recall the 1950's when hundreds of barrels bobbed in the flood waters after Kaplan Brothers' scrap metal yard, across the river from Lilydale and downstream a bit, had flooded. I recall in 1950, in Kindergarten, when policemen in hushed voices ushered out Italian kids because their levee town was flooding. The rest of us looked on. The teachers told us to pay attention to class and to get back down to work. Still, we kids had to wonder what was going on. What would send a dozen or so policemen to our school? Who were they going to arrest? Why were they taking away so many kids?

The city was evacuating the Italians who had created their neighborhood on the flats on the north side of the river. The City built up the flood wall so that the Italian community would be spared from the next one-hundred year flood or even from the next one-thousand year flood. Downriver, The City built tall dikes on both sides. On the north side, the dikes protected Sheppard Road and the businesses along the bluffs, such as Booth Cold Storage, which took advantage of the caves in the bluffs. Across the river, they put in dikes to protect Saint Paul's airport and the little town nearby that had risen to house the workers at the packing plants in South Saint Paul.

But Lilydale was not a part of Saint Paul, or a part of anything. It had no spokesperson, no lobbyist, no power. What this meant is that when the crazed Mississippi tumbled over Saint Anthony Falls and then stumbled over the Ford Dam, all its anger swirling around the wide curve where the Minnesota River joins forces with the Mississippi. Kept away from other parts of the city, the river now was free to plunder and destroy its last adversary, Lilydale. It stood like a single soldier in a battle that would never be won.

No flags were lowered when it died.

Uncle Frank did not write the year of that flood on his wall.

He didn't have a wall anymore.

This happened while I was leaving home for the first time, sitting in a Milwaukee Road train that was diverted, because of the floods, all the way to Canada.

I was joining the Navy, protector of waters.

Dear Kids –

You will learn, I think, that grief follows happiness, and happiness follows grief.

On the Milwaukee Road train to boot camp, next to me sat another recruit. "I can do a perfect Jerry Lewis imitation," he said. He couldn't, by any means. He didn't even come close. "I'm not going to boot camp," he explained. "I'm joining the USO, to entertain you military guys."

'My, what the Navy recruiters were doing these days to fill their quotas,' I thought to myself. This unfortunate kid got off the train the same time as I did. He explained his situation to the MP sailors present, and they quickly whisked him away.

I saw him, in civilian clothes two days later, as I was standing in line to get my first Navy uniform. His head was hanging low and his hands were behind his back, like 'Dead man walking,' a prisoner being led to his execution. They were leading him to the train station.

My trip back home on leave, then, was my first time in an airplane.

I got on that plane, one with propellers, and an hour or so later, the plane skimmed over the Mississippi, approaching Wold-Chamberlain Field. I started to choke, and I grabbed at my neck. I figured it was just part of flying.

The plane landed. My parents picked me up and we drove home, ate, and then I went to see some high school friends to show off my Navy whites.

The phone rang. I knew right away it was for me. I don't know how I knew, but I knew. I picked it up and my Mother said, "Jimmy's dead."

My Brother had drowned in the Mississippi at about the time my plane was coming in for a landing, over the Mississippi. He had been the athletic one, while I was the intellectual. He was trying to swim across the Mississippi even though he had just had a hernia operation so he could join the Marine Corps, and the doctors had warned him to take it easy for a few weeks.

The mighty Mississippi's current of legend and song got him. He fought off the two friends who were trying to rescue him.

I was numb for a long time. I don't recall the funeral or the weeks after.

Dear Kids:

In July of 1965, still numb from the death of my Brother, I reported for duty at the Naval Postgraduate School in Monterey, California. It was quite a change from boot camp and its succession of barracks that we moved to week after week (Camp Porter, Camp Dewey, Camp Moffett). This Monterey Postgraduate School was the former Del Monte Hotel, and the steaks they served enlisted men covered the entire plate. They even asked how you wanted your steak done and what kind of vegetable you wanted to go with it.

That luxury was short-lived.

A week later, I reported for duty at the Defense Language Institute at the Presidio of Monterey, up on the hill, above the wharf. The school was run by the army, and looked it. Rows of wooden two-story barracks stood across a field from rows of grim wooden one-story rambling buildings that served as our classrooms. A cold, clammy breeze blew in from Fisherman's Wharf and Cannery Row, which then was still a smelly string of decaying fish industry buildings, since having become a 'tourist destination' like too many places in the world. The barking and complaining of the sea lions kept me awake at night until I got used to them.

The language students came from all branches of the military, although most of them were Army. My Master at Arms, the demagogue of the barracks, was an Army sergeant, studying Vietnamese. He talked to himself in Vietnamese a lot, exaggerating the sing-song of the language. He was failing his classes, and he took his anger out on us sailors.

Giving us new students the royal tour, he threw three blankets at me. "Okay, swabbie," he said. "Now I know you sailors call the floor a deck and the walls bulkheads, but here we have floors and walls, see? Now show me how to make up your bunk. I know you swabbies call it a rack."

I looked at the three blankets in my hand. "I don't know how, Sergeant. In the Navy, we had one blanket."

"You mean those cheap sons of bitches only gave you one blanket?" he bellowed, as if to an audience.

"We only needed one blanket," I said. "They heat our barracks."

I was put on report and ended up peeling a roomful of potatoes in the back of the mess hall (appropriately named) until my hands were numb, raw, and bleeding. To the credit of the Master at Arms, we became friends later. I wished him well as he left the barracks; there were tears in his eyes although he held his head on high. He was headed for the Infantry and Viet Nam.

One evening I walked down to Monterey Bay and put my hand in the water. It was the first time I touched salt water.

Dear Katya, Alex, and Anna:

Your language (Russian) did not come easily to me. It took a lot of work and a lot of memorization. At language school, we reported for classes in the low, rambling buildings, and we were marked as 'newbies' by our red books – everyone else's books were gray.

Andrei Govorov, an ancient refugee from the Russian Revolution some fifty years earlier, was our instructor – he taught all the new people, one week, for each new class. He had delirium tremens, and we called him 'Shaky Jake.' Who wouldn't have a drinking problem, being doomed to teach first-week Russian to class after class, year after year? Later I met his wife and spent evenings at their home, where he repeated how he had studied piano at the Conservatory under Rachmaninov. To prove it, he played Rachmaninov, but all he proved is that he had a bad case of the shakes and couldn't hit the right keys.

His wife had been married four times, had lived in Egypt, and loved to shriek at her current husband for his drinking, which only drove him to drink more. Shaky Jake couldn't help repeating over and over, compulsively, all the mistakes that his first-week students made. It was driving him crazy, or at least to the bottle.

I did well in first-week Russian, so well, in fact, that they decided I had been placed too low. I was moved up to the advanced class.

I fell in love with my grammar teacher. Her name was a mouthful – Olga Vladimirovna Chebyshowa. She was a stubby old maid, about sixty years old and about four feet, seven inches high – thicker than tall. She had a deep voice and laughed like a man. She liked me when she found out I was interested in Russian literature.

She began to invite me to her house, where I talked with Nina, Olga's aged, thin Mother, who told me about life in old Russia, before the revolution. She didn't speak a word of English, and tears welled in her eyes when she spoke of her youth in Russia. Each story began, "Kogda ya byla molodoy…." ("When I was young….").

I visited them two or three times a week, and I did odd jobs for them around their tiny cottage in Pacific Grove. "You have such an ear for the language, such a sense of the literature!" Nina said often. "You must become a writer!" I think she filled me with her stories so I would write about Russia.

Two decades later, she and her daughter would change my life in an unusual way. Read on.

We moved on from the red book to the gray books – a new one every week. Each day, we were given a long dialogue, stuffed with military terms in Russian, to memorize for the next day. These things were single-spaced and on a legal-size paper, and they got longer and longer as classes progressed. They contained odd dialogues:

Good morning, Petyor Pavlovich.

And a good day to you, Maxim Ivanovich! Long time, no see. Tell me, is that a duck there in the sky?

No, that is not a duck. That is a Class 72 Soviet self-directed, auto-firing guided missile with retrofitted Tupulov engines.

The brain is like any muscle, I learned. The more it is used, the more it can do. Soon, after much stumbling and sputtering like an engine that wouldn't turn over, I became able to memorize those long dialogues in the morning, while getting ready for reveille's revelry.

Reveille blew at six in the morning. It wasn't a real bugle, but a recording of a bugle that blared out on all the giant loudspeakers placed on poles around the school. It was an old record. The scratches woke me up before the recorded bugle blared. Thirty seconds later, the Master at Arms grabbed his night stick and whirled it around the insides of a galvanized garbage can, just to make sure that no one slept past revelry.

At the last of the scratches and the bugle and the garbage can rumbling, we dived into our clothes and rushed outside to the field, where we fell into formation in the damp fog. When dismissed, we ran back into the barracks, undressed, shat, showered, and shaved, and then headed for breakfast. The food was so awful that we welcomed the days they served C-Rations that were close to being destroyed because they had exceeded their expiration dates. We learned to hide bread and peanut butter in the barracks so we wouldn't have to waste time standing in line to eat food that we didn't want.

Andrei Govorov and his wife plied me with Russian food and made me promise to study Russian language and literature when I got out of the Navy. Nina and Olga ensured that I would. I had found something that interested me without end. Russia.

The more I knew, the more I wanted to know. I had become insatiable. I was a full-fledged Russophile.

I joined the Russian choir, led by Nick Volkov, who knew not how to direct a choir, but had us sing Russian folk songs well anyway.

Russia. Why did it feel so right for me? Why did I know I belonged to it?

I finished language school at the top of my class, but I couldn't get a Top Secret Clearance because of my leftist leanings, my friends, and my activities, and because I wouldn't tattle on military classmates, this, before the days of 'Don't ask; don't tell.'

Instead, the Navy sent me to a clerical school in San Diego. I didn't complain. Most of my fellow Russian students ended up in isolated Adak, Alaska, wearing headphones and staring out windows to see miles of unbroken snow. I fared much better. Read on.

Dear Children:

After two months in San Diego, my orders arrived in a brown manila envelope that my Chief Petty Officer slapped down on my desk.

Staff Headquarters, Fourteenth Naval District, Pearl Harbor, Hawaii.

This was an odd place for a Russian specialist, no?

I didn't do much for the Navy in Pearl Harbor; the country barely profited from the months they had trained me. I lived in a barracks not far from the tall water tower painted with Hawaiian design. I worked in a personnel office, and I ordered books from the mainland. I read Tolstoy and Pushkin and Dostoevsky and Gogol and Turgenev and Chekhov, in Russian. I read on the Navy's time, and I went to night classes at the University of Hawaii, on the Navy's dime.

The more Russian I read, the more I wanted to read. Others in the building and in the barracks thought I was a language specialist, coding and de-coding secret documents that, they could see, were written in a stubby code.

The 'Vityaz,' a Soviet geodesic survey ship, had run low on supplies, and was allowed to pull into Honolulu Harbor in 1966 or 1967. I put on my civilian clothes and went aboard during the open house that they held in exchange for being allowed to dock there. It was the first time I had encountered Soviet Russians. I had sometimes feared that the Russia I loved was a thing of history – that I would hate the Soviet Union.

But I marveled at these Soviet Russians. I felt a strange kinship with them, and even with all the signs and ship's instruments written in Cyrillic. It didn't feel like pride at knowing their language – I don't know what it was, but it was comfortable. I was happy I could understand their language and they could understand me. It was indeed like a secret code, and I had the key. But the connection seemed more than that. I don't know why.

I was surprised to learn that these 'Vityaz' scientists and ordinary sailors were extremely well-read, not only in Russian literature but in English and American literature too. There was some kind of magical rapport there. I knew I was not one of them, and they surely knew I was not one of them, but they were drawn to me, it seemed, as I was to them.

In 1968, Soviet troops marched into Prague. The Prague Spring was over. "How can you study that awful fucking language?" a student at the University of Hawaii asked me.

I remembered the words of my émigré teachers in Monterey – "The Soviet Union is not Russia." Still, I was drawn as much to the Soviet Union as I was to Russia. I knew of the horrible Stalinist terror of the 1930's, and I knew about Nazi atrocities in the 1940's. Your city, children, then called Leningrad, was surrounded by the Nazis for over nine hundred days. They used suburban palaces and churches as stables. I bet that the Nazi line extended beyond where you three kids were born.

Still, I was drawn to that country, but warily and with my eyes open. It was in no way a 'workers paradise.' Few actually believed that, though many were compelled to act as if they believed.

Dear Young Adults Hiding inside Kids' Bodies:

After I got out of the Navy, I continued studying at the University of Hawaii. I think I was only one of about three upper-class Russian majors, so I got lots of personal attention. Professor Dubrovsky, I think, liked my strong interest in Russian literature. He spent a lot of time with me, explaining little nuances in the materials I was reading, things I would have otherwise skipped over.

I worked as a school bus driver, and as a 'latchkey' guardian of kids at a small private school. Before jumping onto the school bus and loading it up with kids, I played with them for an hour or two, after school hours and until their parents came by to pick them up, or until it was time for me to hop on the bus with those who remained. The kids had unusual names like Clinton Watanabe and Lionel Wong. I think this reflected the diversity of peoples on Oahu Island. My challenges included maneuvering around winding mountain and hillside and valley roads, and also reading the street signs, all of which seemed to have started with the letter 'K.'

Evenings, I worked in a clinic. My job was to sit at a reception desk and contact doctors when a patient called in with something that couldn't wait until morning. The doctors wore state-of-the-art (then) little black boxes on their belts, and I worked at a machine with many levers. Touch one of those levers, and a loud buzz would go out from that particular doctor's belt. I wonder how many concert or theater performances I ruined with my lever-pulling.

Doctor Eastman was head of the clinic, and he told me about a small cottage for which he needed a tenant. I volunteered immediately (Waikiki was a place for partying into the night, not a place for studying).

So I rented the doctor's tiny former garage/cottage on Manoa Road, in the shadow of Mount Tantalus and not far from the university.

One day I was driving home from school, going up and down Manoa Road's many dips and tips. I was still a mile or so from home, and between me and home were about five dips and tips.

Suddenly I got a vision for the briefest of durations. I saw the tiny cottage, and I saw big gray snakes lying over the roof, from the ground on one side of the building to the ground on the other side.

Well, what of it?

As I got closer to home, I saw thick but slender curls of black smoke up ahead. Arriving home, I saw that the doctor's house had burnt down. Half a black shell, the bottom of a black boat – that was all that remained where their fine house had stood. The firefighters had run several gray fire hoses running across my cottage, that stood between the fire and the hydrant. They looked like snakes.

I don't consider myself a person of extraordinary power or perception.

Dearest Children

Writing these letters and 'whiting-out' the sections about your adoptive Mother and her family – it's like trying to compose an exceptional piano concerto for someone with only one hand.

Impossible?

Maurice Ravel composed his famous "Concerto in D for piano left hand," for his pianist friend, Paul Wittgenstein.

The pianist had lost his right arm during the First World War. Sadly, it was a Russian who wounded and captured him.

I will do the best I can for you, my children, given the limitations I have.

I wish I could write about your Mother and her family. I wish they could have added their letters to this as well.

But I can't do that. I repeat. I don't like people yelling at me or suing me.

The First Amendment lets me write my memoir. In deference to your Mother and her objections, I have tried to balance my right to write with her displeasure at my writing it.

Besides, everyone has a story. They want to be the main story. No one enjoys being a secondary character, I believe. I know I would not enjoy someone writing their memoir and discussing me. I would demand to see the manuscript and to be kept apprised of any changes.

Dear Anna, Katya, and Alex:

While studying in Honolulu (well, while drinking mai-ties with little umbrellas stuck into the glass). I chased after women on Waikiki beach. Then I heard about a new undergraduate student exchange program with the Soviet Union. The University of Minnesota was one of the signatories, so I rushed back to Minnesota, where I was still considered a resident because I had been in the service. This exchange was not the first Russian language program for foreigners in the Soviet Union, but it was the first that put the American students in with their Soviet counterparts and that offered those Americans courses in the regular university curriculum.

Back in Minnesota now, I walked into the Russian Department office, which was housed in an army barracks called 'Temporary South Of Falwell,' – temporary even though the wooden building had stood there for twenty-five years, since World War Two. A thin woman was sitting in an old chair, her feet up on the desk. A cigarette seemed permanently attached to the center of her lower lip. "I'd like to talk to a Russian teacher," I said. "I want to major in Russian."

"My name is Helene Borisova," she said. "I'm head of the department." It turned out that she was an American who had married a Russian man she had met while working in a displaced persons' camp in Germany.

I took the required undergraduate classes, and I took every Russian class I could. I majored in Russian language and literature, and I minored in history. I loved my teachers. Helene was down-to-earth, all business but extraordinarily funny. Natalya Popovicha was a woman who treated Russian literature with the reverence it deserved, describing the life of writers in hushed, reverent tones, as if their relatives were sitting in an adjoining room. Catherine Kuzmina, a fast-talking, passionate woman, steered me into serious literary criticism, slapping my proverbial laziness or stubbornness or unwillingness to work at capacity.

Vasily Andreev, a kindly old man with fine, Slavic features, taught me old Russian literature, philosophy, and advanced language. He laughed to himself, often for reasons we students never discerned, and he had a hard time criticizing students, no matter how awfully they mangled the language – "It is good. Good try! Not correct. Not entirely correct, but is good try!" Then he'd laugh again. "Is not correct, but very good try." Then his gaze would shift over to the windows, where you could see the Mississippi River, and his eyes glazed over and he turned sad. Perhaps the river reminded him of a Russian river, maybe the Volga.

I applied for the exchange program at Leningrad State University, and I was one of three University of Minnesota students chosen. The problem was, I didn't have the money to go ($2,700), but the university wanted me to go. I was called into somebody's office and told that I <u>had</u> to go – it was an honor for me and for the university. "But I don't have the money," I said, and it was true. I was not stone-walling for a free handout. At the time, I was working as a waiter at Vescio's Pizza in Dinky Town, next to the campus, and barely surviving.

The university came through with an anonymous grant. Thank you, oh anonymous grantor. I know not who you are, but I wrote you a long letter after I returned from the Soviet Union. Again, forty years later, I thank you again. I wonder who you are or were, and what were your motivations. Thank you.

Dear Anna, Katya, and Alex:

1970. I bet your grandparents were born about that time. Maybe I shared the same bus or subway car with your great grandparents, or maybe we bumped into one-another on a crowded sidewalk or brushed up against one-another in a store stuffed with customers.

When you read this, I hope you are willing to read about your Father's early romances. I don't know how I would have reacted if I had learned of any early romances of my father. In that case, I doubt if he had any real *romances*, including my mother. But I had them. If I didn't write about them, I would be leaving out a big hunk of my life.

I was twenty-five years old when I went to Leningrad. It was a good age, I think. I was old enough to believe I was wise, and young enough to be easily fooled. My long trip there started with a flight from Minneapolis to Amsterdam, then on to Finland, and from there, a short flight to Leningrad, made much longer, I discovered later, only so foreigners wouldn't be flying over Soviet military sites.

Few Westerners made journeys to the Soviet Union in those days, particularly in the dead of winter. As the Finn Air flight landed at Pulkovo Airport, I peered out the tiny round window.

Here I was. A 'Hero' Soviet city, as the banner spanning the terminal announced. The airport exterior was adorned with giant red slogans. Here I was, among people who had suffered so much for decades, if not for centuries, and who, in their own right, were capable of unbelievable cruelty. Here was the USSR, our enemy.

But here I was too, at the home of writers and poets whom I had read since I was a child.

Which 'theme' was going to win out?

The terminal was barely visible from the edge of the tarmac where our plane had pulled up for its stop. The engines shut down with a long whine, and the passengers gathered their belongings and dressed for the inevitable cold outside. It was all like slow motion. I was anxious to get out and see what I had gotten myself into. The minutes passed slowly, too slowly.

A gray bus finally pulled up alongside the plane, then two uniformed guards carrying opened bayonets marched up a ramp to the front door of the plane. They wore baggy, drab-green uniforms with pale red stripes on their shoulder boards. Leather ammunition pouches hung from their left sides. Behind them marched a severe-looking woman in a gray woolen uniform. She wore a man-size black fur cap, and two large leather pouches hung from the thick belt wrapped around her waist.

This clearly was not the Russia of "Swan Lake" or "Eugene Onegin," but the Soviet Union of the propaganda machines of the 1950's. Had all those people, and the nuns, been correct then?

I filed up the aisle with the others. As I approached the exit, I swallowed hard, not knowing why. Maybe because I had been in the United States Navy and they probably knew about it and thought I was a spy like Francis Gary Powers, only without condoms. The matron said only one word to me, "Passport!" She examined my passport and then stared at my Soviet visa, while the guards looked on as if ready to draw their bayonets. She stared at me again, then at the documents, then stared at me again. She grunted, motioning with her head, and I was allowed to get off the plane.

The airport bus took us to the terminal about an hour later, and more armed soldiers led us down a series of corridors into a cavernous, dimly-lit stone hall. A few old men in dark overcoats smoked cigarettes in one corner; a pungent odor filling the air. In the middle of the hall, groups of plump, sturdy women sat on rows of long benches that resembled pews. Most of the women wore gray or black or dark purple cloth overcoats with large scarves, thick knots blossoming out from under their necks, towards their chins. A few children, miniature versions of their parents, sat quietly and erectly, staring blankly but not meekly, forward.

A policeman came up to two young men who were talking in a corner of the hall. The police took them out of the building – to where, I don't know. Just getting them out of the terminal? Bringing them in for interrogation or jail or both? I wondered if I had made a giant mistake by coming. Then two other solders, stuffed inside giant gray coats, motioned for us foreigners to pass into a separate customs area, and they shut the double doors behind us.

The suitcases came gliding in on a jerking conveyer belt that looked like a cheap imitation of its Western counterparts. I stood in a long line, waiting my turn at the metal customs table, which was an elongated shallow trough, like perhaps something you'd find in a morgue. Each bag was opened and each slip of paper and book carefully scrutinized.

Dear children, I promise not to repeat the phrase 'long line' in reference to the Soviet Union. Every line that I saw was long. If there wasn't a line, then there was chaos, such as in an otherwise empty store that might unexpectedly receive a shipment of tiny, half-spoiled tangerines.

But I am jumping ahead of myself.

"Hello, I am Peter, and I am a student from Denmark," said the young man in front of me. "You look nervous," he told me. "But there is no need. I know. I have been here before."

The severe-looking matron at the customs desk examined his passport, as if memorizing the data. Then she opened up his luggage, and carefully laid out its contents on her table. Bright lipstick spread over her lips and onto the skin around her mouth, and large swatches of rouge stood out on her round cheeks. Her hair was wiry and she had a permanent, obviously and ineptly dyed a dark red-orange. Her brown and gray roots were showing. It was time for a tune-up. Large, bold streaks of mascara tried to conceal the fact that she didn't have any eyebrows.

Maybe if I studied her long enough, I figured, I would 'know' her, and she would no longer be a threat to me. Strange thinking, that. She seemed somehow nice enough, despite her 'official' sternness. And what about my Navy service? Was there any possible way she – they – the Soviet establishment – would know I had been in their greatest enemy's Navy?

Her face suddenly turned a dark red as she pulled something out of Peter's bag. "Chto zhe eto takoe?" ("What is this?"), she squealed with disgust as she held out a copy of "Playboy." She grabbed the middle of the magazine, so the fold-out of the nude lady with staples at her waist flopped out in full view. "We do not tolerate such capitalist filth!"

"It is for my personal use only," Peter replied, in apologetic Russian made lighter by a musical Danish accent.

She held the magazine behind her back, as far as her arm could reach. "Boris, come here!" she commanded.

A thin man in a thin leather coat with a cracked leather belt, stepped out of a small room off to the side, and took the magazine dangling from her outstretched hand. He folded it and went back into his room. The matron wiped her hands on her jacket and continued the search.

Thick clouds of cigarette smoke, with that same pungent odor, poured from the small room, and the sounds of muffled guffaws and expletives spread out into the customs area. The matron's face turned red. She caught me staring at her, and she muttered something under her breath. 'Playboy just acquired three new readers,' I thought to myself. But then my attention turned abruptly to the situation at hand. I wondered what she would pick on now that it was my turn. My hands tightened at my side and my throat tightened too. I swallowed, but with difficulty – my throat had gone dry.

"You pack neatly," she woman said as she slid her hand up and down inside my flight bag, not unlike the way a veterinarian checks a cow's uterus.

"I try to be organized," I said.

"Where did you learn to speak Russian?" she asked, squinting into my eyes. "You don't look Russian."

"At the university," I said. This did not seem the place to discuss the Defense Language Institute or the American Navy.

"Why does an American study Russian?" she asked in a tone suggesting the answer might be important.

"I want to be able to read the literature," I said. "And to appreciate it."

Her eyes widened and a smile appeared on a face that probably didn't smile often. "Yes, we have our literature. If you understand it, you will understand us. You have come to the right city."

A rapport was established, I felt. It was a good sign – my first encounter, my first success. She passed over my flight bag without further inspection, but then she came upon a roll of toilet paper at the top of my suitcase. My Father had jokingly given it to me during the last minutes of packing. "I heard they don't have any of this stuff over there," he had said.

"Why did you bring this?" demanded the customs lady, drawing herself up to her full height. "Do you think we don't use toilet paper? Do they tell you capitalists that we are animals?"

I thought fast, hoping the right answer would come to me. "We hear stories like that, but I'm here to see for myself." It was all I could think of to say.

"Keep your eyes open!" she snapped. "Conduct yourself well, and please do not tell lies about us when you go back to America!"

My eyes burnt from fatigue and cigarette smoke. It was about eight in the evening, I figured. With the time changes and the overnight flight, I didn't know if it was Tuesday or Wednesday. The soldiers led us outside to an ugly, bubble-shaped bus with tiny windows and a large, almost illegible sign that said 'Sputnik,' the Soviet travel agency for capitalist students. I remembered the fear and consternation that the word 'Sputnik' had produced back home, barely a decade earlier.

"Welcome to Soviet Union!" a woman called out, in English with a thick accent with which most of us Americans are now familiar. "Please to board the bus!"

Hot air blew from the floor boards of the bus, but thick, opaque patterns of frost sheathed the windows, so there was nothing to be seen. The bus lurched and bounced forward. I scratched at the window with my glove, then with my plastic drivers license. I saw the silhouettes of a few nondescript, tall buildings in the distance. Those buildings, kids, were no doubt similar to the one in which your birth parents or their parents had lived.

I bit my lip, doubling my determination not to form bad impressions so early. Dim, hazy lights outside told me that we had come into the city. I scraped hard at the window. Old ladies, bent over with knee-high straw brooms, swept snow off the sidewalks. Crowds of drab figures walked automaton-like up and down the pavement, lingered at bus stops, or queued up at store fronts. Most people carried little net bags that swung from their arms. Small children – little miniature adults – trailed along after their parents, hanging onto their coat sleeves, trying to keep pace. A few couples pushed sturdy baby buggies with wheels clearly designed for all terrain vehicles.

We crossed over a block-wide bridge, and I noticed a glow of lights ahead. The bus, clutch-in, coasted into a wide turn.

And, then, there it all was! Saint Isaac's Cathedral, and then Decembrist Square, with the Bronze Horseman, Catherine's statue to Peter the Great. It was an amazing sight that leaped out at me from out of the fog. The statue stood on top of a giant sloping stone base, and the horse's forelegs flailed motionlessly at the air. Peter, on top of his steed, pointed westward, his horse's hind legs squashing a long, coiled snake. Floodlights illuminated it all, and glistening, fluffy snow gathered in the folds of his cape and across his outstretched arm. I had never, ever seen anything like it.

Oh, Lordy, kids, the beauty and grandeur of your native city! Had you ever even seen its heart, especially in the deep of winter, stuck as you were miles away from the center? And, Lordy, the beauty and strength of the poetry and novels and short stories and musical pieces and ballet written from and about this sanctified place! I felt like I had seen it all before. Of course, I had, in books and in illustrations and in paintings. But still, I felt even closer to the place than that. Perhaps I had read too many Russian novels and poems and had listened to too much Russian classical music.

The driver turned right, coasting around the front of the statue. On the left stretched a granite embankment and the Neva, a wide river now frozen over – people were filing across it. "That's the university!" someone said. "Right there, across the river!" I spotted a squat green building and a reddish, narrow mass stretching backwards to invisibility.

The bus stopped at the intersection. The palace bridge stretched low across the Neva on the left, and I saw a solitary red spire poking into the low fog. "That's the Fortress of Saints Peter and Paul," someone said. "It's the oldest building in Leningrad." Downriver, an old wooden streetcar plied its way over an arching bridge, setting off sparks while a whole flock of trolleys swirled in turns at the foot of the bridge, some heading up towards the bridge, some racing into the darkness. Through the driver's window, I spotted a long pastel building, also illuminated and lined with white columns. A series of story-high figures graced the building at the top of each column. "The Winter Palace!" I didn't need to be told.

I was so excited. I could imagine our dormitory – a nineteenth-century building probably, maybe with columns, along this embankment, and my room certainly would have a view of some river or canal. The bus drove alongside the palace, and then past it, turned left and then crossed a few bridges. I know now that we were driving down the middle of Vasilievsky Island.

"Wow!" I said to Nick, another exchange student who was sitting in the same row as I. "Our dormitory is probably one of these mansions!"

But the bus lumbered on, away from the lights, away from the river, away from the palaces and mansions. Where were we headed? To another city center perhaps as stunning as the first? No, there was only one city center, and we had for sure seen it.

The bus took us down darkened streets, and it stopped in front of a forlorn-looking, five-story building flanked on both sides by a row of barracks-like two-story, crumbling stucco structures. The ride was an eerie one for me. I shivered, even though it was hot on the bus. Contrary to popular belief in America, Russians seem to hate cold; they keep their apartments and buildings and busses at uncomfortably high temperatures.

The 'aftobus' driver leaned back, yanked on a lever, and the bus doors opened. "You are home!" he said in Russian.

"Please to get off the bus now!" said the matron over a microphone that was so scratchy her English almost sounded good.

It was the ugliest hulk of crumbling bricks that I had ever seen. This was 'University Dormitory Number Five,' or the 'Capitalist Dormitory,' as the university students called it. The building housed foreign exchange students who were not from the 'brotherly socialist countries.' Over the building's entrance, a small oval sign illuminated by a single bare light bulb announced 'Shevchenko Street 25.'

Dear Katya, Anna, Alex:

What a dreary dump that dormitory was. I and three roommates occupied a room that was about ten by ten feet. Our four sagging cots with their thin, hard mattresses, almost touched in the middle. A tiny, cheap-looking round table made it hard to move around the dinky room.

At 6:05 on that Monday morning, the scratchy radio built into the wall blared out a shrieking woman's voice, doing calisthenics. ("Ras Dva Tri! Ras Dva Tri! Ras Dva Tri!") That first morning, my roommate Nick jumped up and headed for the radio. "Christ!" he said. "There's no way to turn this dammed thing off, or down even!" He grabbed his pillow, stuffed it around the speaker, and dived back under his covers.

I lifted myself out of bed, shivered as my feet hit the icy floor, and headed down the hallway for a shave. "Where's the hot water?" I asked when I stuck my hand under the icy tap.

The Danes, who had been there for a couple of months, laughed. "Only on Fridays!" was their answer.

I developed a morning routine. At six-thirty, I peeled my stiff, hand-washed socks and underwear off the heat pipe. At seven, a giant woman banged a bucket on the floor. "Comrades, it is late into the morning!" she shouted. "Productive people are already up and braced for work! And even if you have no productive work, I do! I must clean your filthy rooms!"

Twenty minutes later, we students ran down the five narrow flights of the dormitory and out the door into the bracing cold. A half hour later, we barely squeezed onto the back end of a jammed Municipal Bus Number 47, the one they told us would bring us to the university.

I learned the ropes. The trick was to squeeze on board. We Americans were generally too polite for the shoving that feat required, but the morning cold was a good tutor. Then the real challenge came. "Where should we stand?" I asked that first trip.

"What do you mean?" Nick asked. "We'll stand right here!"

"Look at the crowd jammed into this bus!" I said. "If we stand too far back, we won't make it out in time at our stop. But, if we get too far forward, I bet we'll be pushed off, before our stop!"

"God, I'm suffocating!" said Lucia, another student in our group. "I've never seen so many people in such a small place!"

"Hey!" said Nick. "Someone just gave me some money. Look!" He showed a handful of kopecks.

"It's not for you, stupid!" said Lucia. "They're passing money forward, to the pay box, and then they're passing tickets back. Look!" She was right. Whoever stood next to the ticket machine at the rear of the bus collected the coins, deposited them into a box on wiggling legs, and passed up fragile paper tickets with the appropriate change. We passed our money and got our tickets just when it was time to push our way off. The bus dumped us across from a giant building that said 'Library of the Academy of Sciences.'

We were late. We rushed from the bus stop down a narrow path alongside an incredibly long, red building. The wind blew from the Neva ahead, channeling between the buildings. Lucia made me and Nick walk first, as wind-breaks. A right turn at the embankment brought us into full view of the Neva, and across the river I could see the Bronze Horseman.

We pushed through – or were pushed along with – the crowd of students filing through the building's only open door. For heat control, or for crowd control perhaps – or just to confound people even more than the Soviet morning had already confounded them – only one of the six or seven doors was open. On the other side of those doors, the crush of students led to the left, into a cloakroom. We headed up the stairs. "Nyet, Nyet!" said a watchman. "I do not know where you are from or where you are going, but no person enters this – or any public building – without checking his coat. It is most improper!"

We pushed our way along with the others into the cloak room. "Ai!" sighed the old attendant when she took my coat. "You have no loop inside!" I watched as she hung six coats on one hook, even though half her space stood empty and rows of empty hooks, like so many baby birds, arched hungrily upward. "Now here are wonderful loops!" she said as she took Nick's and Lucia's coats. She pinched my cheeks. "Tell your friend there to do some sewing!"

Later, I saw her and several other Russians examining our coats with great curiosity, rubbing their hands along the fabrics, and discussing them with one-other.

From the cloakroom we walked up one set of stairs and down a series of corridors, almost half-way back to the bus stop, it seemed, for Linguaphonics class.

Dear Kids:

Classes were a whole different thing forty years ago, in the Soviet Union.

They separated us according to our Russian language capabilities. Nick and Lucia, with their nearly-native Russian, were at the top of the group. Thanks to my Navy training, I joined that class, along with two others – Timothy, and Rick.

We met in a room that was barely wide enough to hold a podium, the chairs, and a long table with curves from years of leaning elbows. The professor, an attractive woman about thirty years old, stood on a platform next to the chalky writing board. "Stand up and introduce yourselves," she commanded. "It is my way to meet you, and to learn of your Russian language capabilities, or lack of same." She spoke in a thick, faux British accent. "My task is to give my students a genuine Russian accent," she said, and I thought she was looking directly at me.

As class continued, I noticed that, luckily for me, she picked mostly at the occasional minor mistakes of Lucia and Nick. I sensed that the teacher, Nadezhda Andreevna, resented the presence of these two native speakers in her class. "When you use that peculiar inflection, Nick, you sound like an eighty-year old counter-revolutionary." she said more than once. "It is a language – and an age – which is now a part of the past." Her almond-shaped eyes glared at him although there was something of a smile on her face.

Ah, there was a manifestation of the conflict between old Russia and the Soviet Union, between the West's émigré Russians and those Soviet citizens who had remained in the country and who had survived five horrible decades.

I hoped she would be more tolerant of, and more willing to work with, non-native speakers, like me.

Linguaphonics lasted ninety minutes, and the heat radiating from the ceramic stove nearly put me to sleep. Then the bell rang, and we dashed down the narrow hallways along the worn floor boards to translation, our next class. Tatiana Ivanovna, the translation professor, seemed at least eighty years old. A kind smile lined her baby-smooth face, as she gently cajoled her charges into the most accurate and appropriate translations. She gasped with joy whenever a student provided just the right word or idiom. That first day, we labored an hour over a single phrase in Pushkin's The Captain's Daughter. I made one suggestion, and she shook her head. "Your translation is literal, but it does not have the alliteration that is there in Russian. You do not simply replace words," she insisted. "You transfer ideas, feelings, and values! And you must remain as true as possible to the original." She was so dear, I never wanted to hurt or disappoint her. It was the same feeling I had for my nuns, back in grade school.

Lunch break followed our translation class, and Nick, Lucia and I followed the masses into the student cafeteria. Oddly, a series of poles and ropes set us Americans off from all the others. "Is this something we requested, or is it something the Russian students had requested?" I asked the manager.

She smiled under her ridiculous white paper hat. "You need to eat fast and return to your classes, so we have reserved tables for you in a special section."

"Well, don't the Russians have classes too?" I countered.

She bit her lip. "It is the order of things here. It is the way things are done." With that, she walked away.

"Come on!" I told Nick. "Nothing says we have to eat in this section. Let's go over there and sit with the Russians."

We did. One Russian woman at the table dropped her spoon as we sat down, and the other gasped in horror. "God, I sure am hungry!" said Nick, digging into his soup. I nodded. The last Russian woman at the table gobbled up her bread and left in a hurry.

The soup was hardy and tasty, the bread delicious, and I reached for the high point of the meal – a piece of meat that looked like a ball-park hot dog. At the next table, I noticed how an attractive Russian coed delicately held a wiener on a fork in her left hand, while peeling off the skin with a knife in her right hand. I ate my wiener with a knife and fork – more delicately than I did at home, but I didn't peel the skin. I heard some mumbling behind my back, and maybe even a few giggles.

That night, I got sick to my stomach like I never had before. Olga, the cleaning lady, told me why the next morning. "Sausages are wrapped in plastic these days!" she said, and a smile nearly found its way across her face. "There used to be natural casings, but now, we use plastic." Then her eyes turned steely. "You see, my country has to spend so much of its money on the military – so many countries want to invade us, that we must make sacrifices."

My jaw dropped. I didn't know what to say. "I don't know of any country wanting to invade you," I finally said.

"You have invaded Viet Nam," she countered.

"You have invaded Czechoslovakia," I said.

"We were invited there, by the people," she said.

"So were we, in Viet Nam, I guess," I answered.

"You Americans!" she said, and tears welled up in her eyes. "You know nothing about war, about suffering!" With that, she turned and left the room.

The next day at our class break I told Nick about my argument with Olga. "Oh, give her hell!" he said. "I'm sure she's been trained to spy on us, to argue with us, just like all the other Soviets around here!"

"I'm not so sure," I said. "And I think she's a very kind person under that veneer."

"It's one hell of a veneer!" he said with a laugh. "When the veneer is ten times thicker than what it covers, do you still call it a veneer?" We finished up our cups of double Russian espresso and rushed off to our afternoon classes, Syntax, and Advanced Grammar.

In the late afternoon and evening, we were allowed to attend courses in the university's regular curriculum. It seemed like an opportunity to meet some Russian students finally, since the main point of our days' schedules seemed to have been to prevent us from doing just that. I signed up for contemporary Soviet History and for Poetic Analysis. The renowned seventy-year-old Professor Fillipov taught Poetic Analysis. I had read his books at the University of Minnesota.

The rudeness of the Russian students surprised me. I thought that living in a totalitarian country meant they'd sit up straight in class and pay attention, but some read newspapers, while others dozed or talked among themselves, and not even in whispers. In history class, most of he students slept, and no wonder. The professor droned on, as if reciting from a script he'd recited dozens of times before.

Everyone, however, paid attention to Professor Fillipov. He spoke in hushed tones, and each word mattered.

My Dear Children:

You love homework?

Each professor assigned massive amounts of it. Nadezhda Andreevna made us memorize two or three poems each night, for her correction of our intonation and pronunciation the next morning. "Memorization is good for you!" she added. "It is good exercise for the brain!"

Homework left us very little free time, and maybe that was the reason for it. Still, I managed to sneak out. I gradually, very gradually, found my way around your city's center, although I still felt very much like, say, a Dorothy in the first minutes after the house landed on the witch.

Home for me and the others was that capitalist dormitory, 'Shevchenko Street Twenty-Five.'

"This building was put up fast, in the early fifties," said Olga one morning when she heard us making fun of the slipshod construction. "There was a big shortage of buildings then, housing was very scarce – materials and workers too, because of the Nazi invasion. They surrounded the city, you know, for nine hundred days. Now this building is scheduled to be torn down, and you capitalist students will then move across town, near the other students and the new university."

"It will never happen," said Nick after Olga left the room. "They want us isolated. They don't want us contaminating their virgin Soviet youth with our corrupt capitalist ways."

Friday mornings were reserved for showers, for a reason that got a different explanation each time that I asked. Olga said it was because the shower room leaked and was destroying the foundation. Others said the water overflowed into the boiler room and shut down the furnace, but, wait, that didn't seem right. The city had district heating, with heat coming from giant buildings elsewhere from which shot pipes in all directions. The water was tepid by the time it concluded its trip out to our end of the island.

The water coursed through the dormitory's pipes that usually ran a series of loops in each bathroom. It was warm in there, and clothes hung on the pipe loops dried fairly quickly. On the coldest days, like thirty degrees below zero, the water was not even tepid. Those same pipes provided the 'hot' water you got when you used the hot water faucet in a sink or a tub. That water was not for drinking, as I discovered while making cool instant coffee in the morning.

The building guards made sure students took showers only on that building's weekly 'shower day.' The ladies went first, then we males. By then, the water was barely warm. My skin itched after the first few days of not showering, my capitalist skin no doubt spoiled by so many years in the America. I soon figured out that other dormitories had their shower days too, and I learned which dormitories to sneak into on which days.

As the weeks passed, I lost more and more of my American trappings. My soap ran out first, then my shampoo and toothpaste. I bought a Russian toothpaste called 'Lesnaya,' which meant 'forest' and it tasted like pumice or mud. The strongly-scented, lather-less Russian hand soap tasted better than the toothpaste, and it also worked for washing clothes, I learned. It never lathered –nary a bubble. When my Prell Shampoo ran out, I bought a Bulgarian brand, the only shampoo I could find in the stores.

I was taking a shower one icy Saturday morning in an alien dormitory down the street from Shevchenko Twenty-Five. A comrade sharing the spray from the rusty pipe hung from the ceiling came over to me. "Might I borrow your shampoo for a moment?" he asked in precise English with a no-doubt unintended haughty tone. "I seem to have forgotten mine."

I wasn't surprised. The Russians weren't shy at all about asking for American goods. Lucia told me she and the other women in our group had already given away most of their cosmetics, and she told me how Russian women stared, open-mouthed, as the American women soaped and shaved their legs in the shower.

This Russian comrade thanked me and took my shampoo, looked at the label, and groaned, "Ai, why do you use this stuff?"

"I ran out of my own."

"Don't use this slop!" he groaned. "Even plain soap is better!"

"Why?" I asked.

"This is Bulgarian shampoo. Have you ever seen a Bulgarian over twenty years old with a full head of hair?"

Contrary to the assurances of the lady in customs, toilet paper <u>was</u> in short supply. Whenever it sold at kiosks around the city, people rushed home, racing down the street and jumping onto busses or trolleys, balancing a dozen rolls of their bounty on broomsticks. Other people rushed off in the opposite direction, seeking the source of that booty.

Old issues of 'Pravda' were conveniently left behind in the bathrooms, as were copies of <u>The Collected Works of Vladimir Ilych Lenin</u>. I stole skimpy paper napkins, meticulously cut into two-inch triangles, from the university cafeteria.

Once, while I was using a urinal in the university men's room, my history professor rushed out of a door-less toilet stall, every muscle of his face revealing his physical urgency. "Do you happen to have any extra paper?" he asked. I gave him his notes from that day's history class, which had been a lecture on Western imperialism.

The day-to-day grind of life was hard. If the Russians were trying to impress their first American undergraduate exchange students, they were failing. Yet, prosaic matters became unimportant; there were more compelling, more important things in life in Leningrad in 1970.

Anna, Katya, Alex:

I liked going out on my own and trying to blend in with the crowds, although it never worked. My coat, my boots, my height – everything shouted 'foreigner', and there were so few of us then. Blank stares from people who must have spent years practicing not blinking, met me wherever I went. I was a wanderer in an altogether strange land indeed, yet one that somehow seemed connected to me.

I preferred riding the streetcars, even when it sometimes meant going out of the way. Most of them were wooden, although I rode a few newer metal ones too. The wide, ponderous wooden cars sometimes rode tandem, the nose of the second trolley nudging the leader's tail end. There were sometimes miles between stops, down countless lines of five-story buildings, with ever-so-wide turns at the intersections.

I loved the streetcars. They reminded me of when I was a kid, when I stood on Selby Avenue, holding my Father's hand, staring at those metal matrons. I especially loved to watch them turn corners. With their cow-catchers gracefully nudging forward, with sparking electric lines overhead, with an awesome hum on the rails, ringing of the trolley bell, ticking of the ticket-taking machine, these portly maidens rounded their courtly turns, their matronly bustles elegantly listing to one side – back in Saint Paul, Summit Avenue, in all its studied architectural splendor and excess, never knew as much grace or aged dignity. I bet that when streetcars first came out, they were viewed as awful iron things that destroyed the beauty and appeal of cities. Today they are looked upon with nostalgia. Such is the way we humans adapt to our pasts and our presents.

Before I had wanted to become a priest, I wanted to become a streetcar driver. Is it not ironic that by the time I reached adulthood, streetcars had disappeared from Minneapolis and Saint Paul and most other American cities. In the case of Minneapolis and Saint Paul, the transition was quickened by the payment of bribes, almost in Soviet fashion. I saw a car once, years later, being used as a chicken coop on a small, failing farm.

I stood or sat on the trolleys, watching the passing scene outside, watching the other passengers, and, yes, they stared at me without blinking and so I could stare back at them, which made them turn red and turn to look somewhere else. Why, I wondered? Why could they stare at me as long as they wanted, yet I wasn't supposed to stare back at them? I never discovered the answer.

I loved watching the crowds of people on busy corners – who was carrying what, how the people dressed, how women held other women's hands, how men carried their women's purses.

I liked too the long glides between stops, when all seemed dark, when street lights and store lights, always dim anyway, now disappeared in snow flakes that never stopped falling. Sometimes, for reasons I don't know, sparks flew from the lines overhead -- Leningrad's life in staccato.

The games people play in streetcars, subway cars, and airplanes? The looking at others while pretending not to be looking at others, the moves to mark territory -- a foot there, an arm here. I played such 'dances' often, looking at someone until they looked at me and then turning away at the last moment, and then turning back quickly to see if they were still looking. And why, again, was it that Russians on a streetcar or bus could stare at me, yet one look from me and their eyes would dart away, like frightened baby sparrows?

Not to mention those long escalators down to the subways and back up again – escalators so long that you couldn't see beginning or end when standing in the middle. I'd pick out someone from the escalator running in the opposite direction, catching, for example, the eye of a woman while I went up and she went down. Would she turn back to see me more? Usually not. And how about the couples leaning in to one-another, she often fingering his coat button, he often brushing snow flakes off her scarf? Facing one-another, with the taller one on the lower stair, they had a moment of genuine privacy that they no doubt elsewhere lacked.

Staring. Getting stared at back. Looking, getting looked at. One time I was on a trolley and I noticed a pretty woman looking out the window. Oh, how I wished she would look at me! Surely I would then approach her and we would talk and then I'd have a Russian girlfriend, as did so many of my American counterparts. But this one, so suited for the part, continued to stare through her window, as if reading a teleprompter. Then, as the trolley bumped its way over the top of an arching stone bridge, I saw that she was not just looking out <u>her</u> window, but she was looking at me, indirectly, through her window's reflection, through my window's reflection. Yes, I would approach her. There were so few passengers aboard. How perfect. Just perfect.

But I didn't move. Call it shyness – I don't know. Fear, maybe. Afraid of rejection. She turned away from her window, and maybe I noticed a sudden disgust or giving-up on her part, or maybe I imagined it.

She did not look sideways as she walked in the falling snow along the accelerating streetcar. Sparks flew from the trolley wires overhead and briefly illuminated the storefronts in a white electric light. The streetcar made a wide turn, and the woman vanished into the Leningrad night. I was too stunned to move. The lights from the trolley and the rhythm of the window reflections that flashed by – it was as if I was watching a movie.

"Shit!" I said, under my breath. Why hadn't I gone after her?

Kids:

Your Father was angry at himself. How could he have let that moment slip by, in a world that doesn't allow second chances? During Linguaphonics next day, during Translation, Syntax, Advanced Grammar, and Soviet History, my mind carried me back to the woman with snow on her collar.

Fool and optimist that I was, I made it a point to ride the same streetcar almost every night, at the same time. The conductor even nodded at me once as I boarded. I did not see the woman who had vanished.

Why was I alone? Why didn't I have Russian friends, like all the other Americans?

As Russian-speaking students, we got to go where other tourists didn't. Even though the 'authorities' tried often to isolate us from young Russians, it usually didn't work. We were curious to meet young Russians; they were curious to meet us. Luckily for us, we were away from the tiny Leningrad tourist groove that centered around the Winter Palace and extended a few blocks to the Bronze Horseman statue. Sad to say, but the only Russians who approached those tourists were those Russians speculating in foreign currency or getting Western goodies that they could later sell at a high price. Why was it that, when currency speculation was a crime with serious consequences for the foreigner and the Russian – why was it that so many young Russians followed tourists? I'd see them at various tourist bus stops – on the point of Vasilievsky Island, on Nevsky, near the Bronze Horseman, etc. The same Russian black marketers working different 'stops.'

Why? Surely the Soviet police and the KGB, who knew everything about everybody, knew about these black marketers. How did those guys get by with it? My guess is that many of them worked for the KGB. No, they weren't professional spies or even on the KGB payroll – it was, I figured, a tit-for-tat situation – You spy for us and we will allow you to retain your Leningrad registration card, without which the person would be living elsewhere, out in the Russian boondocks.

And so, then, what about the people who befriended Americans? Were all of our friends working both sides of the fence, as it were? I don't know. I wonder who does know. Russia was open enough a few years ago that it might have been possible to find out. For the past few years, however, the government is doing what Russian governments have always done so well – restricting access to information.

One evening we were at a dance in one of the halls in a large restaurant. Our Russian guests were an exact match in terms of age and gender and number. A few Americans ventured outside the private room and began conversing with a group of curious young Russians in that room. Within seconds, it seemed, men wearing various styles of clothes, coming from various parts of the restaurant – patrons, bus-boys, chefs, waiters – they closed in on those young Russians and whisked them outside, where they stood shivering without coats until a line of black cars whisked them away.

I was often a bit too brave, too foolhardy. I asked the Soviet 'head' of our restaurant party why the police had hauled off the Russians. "Oh, but of course. Those young men and women had too much to drink. We were worried about them hurting themselves or causing incidents on the street or in public transportation. So those cars were making sure the young folks got home safely."

I wonder what kind of 'home' it was that those black cars took them.

Still, with all that stuff going on, Russians approached us everywhere, it seemed, or else they ran. It was a real ego trip, as the popular expression then went. We were probably the first 'capitalist' young persons that Soviet citizens had ever seen, and the fact that a foreigner spoke Russian and was not an émigré – that was a real rarity. I felt like a movie star. I had fans. A few younger female students at the university became sort of groupies of mine.

It was a complicated time, two years after the invasion of Prague and at the height of the Viet Nam War.

In January and February, I watched my fellow American students pair off with Russians or sometimes with other foreigners. Everyone but me seemed to have a partner. Was this not like my phy-ed classes in grade school? No one wanted me on their team.

My roommate, Nick, was in love with a Danish woman who lived on the other end of the floor. Anther roommate, Dmitry, son of an American physics Professor, was in love with another Dane. Lucia loved a Hungarian and Lynn loved a Russian.

I became friends with Tanya and her husband, Yury, after Nick got me invited to one of their parties. I didn't know if they were part of that 'KGB' system where they spied on foreigners in exchange for being allowed to spend time with them or in exchange for something else. Or perhaps there was another possibility — perhaps some families were so well entrenched in the Soviet system that they could see whom they wanted, without fear of reprisal. I suspect this might have been the case with Tanya and Yuri. Tanya's Father was a fairly well-known Soviet writer who towed the party line. I learned later that, as often was the case, he wrote genuine things 'for the drawer,' as it was called – things that could never be published in Soviet times but that could be smuggled out or circulated in 'samizdat,' that non-Soviet, unofficial method of disseminating literature, pages at a time, often in barely legible carbon copy.

Tanya's giggly younger Sister, Elena, followed me around and was interested in all things American and never ran out of questions even though I could understand only about every other word. I gave her a cassette of Simon and Garfunkel's 'Bridge Over Troubled Waters.' I helped her with the lyrics, and she was super-thrilled. It was too bad she spoke so fast that I couldn't understand her, and that her dialogue was peppered with current Soviet slang, which I hadn't ever studied. This failure between me and Katya frustrated both of us. Still, she followed me like a shadow, and oddly, although I had a difficult time understanding what she said, I could always understand what she was singing, either in Russian or in English. Her favorite song was 'I'd Rather Be A Hammer Than A Nail' ('El Condor Pasa')

I went to an evening party hosted by Tanya, in the giant spaces that belonged to her parents – Her Father's importance giving them extra living space, as did the importance of her Mother's sculpture, which merited a large studio for her massive works. Some of her sculptures are still around Leningrad – I mean – Peterburg.

At the party were a few people from my group of visiting American students, and many of the Russian hangers-on who appeared wherever and whenever the Americans appeared – it was like a square dance at times – partners switching partners as the dance continued.

But at this particular party, off in the corner, sitting on a window ledge that opened up only to the darkness of a Soviet winter night, there sat a stunningly lovely woman. Her beauty did not fit any Russian stereotypes with which I had become familiar, nor any American or Western European sterotypes. She was just she, all to her own.

She was the woman I had seen on the streetcar, that magical, snowy, other-worldly night. Or was she?

She seemed shy. Only once in a while did she turn on the sill to look at the party, at the small groups that had formed, with some people switching from one group to another. No one approached her and she approached no one. I asked Tanya about her, and she told me this was Natalya, a grade-school friend who had remained a friend all through their lives. She was generally shy, Tanya reported, but more so this evening, perhaps because this might have been the first time she had been around foreigners. She was a violinist with the Civic Orchestra, Tanya reported.

Drawing up the bravery that I had so lacked with the beautiful woman on the streetcar, I walked up to her. I greeted her, and was relieved to hear my own voice, steady, not cracking. She smiled and nodded, without taking her eyes off whatever it was that she saw in the darkness of the window. I told her my name and I told her how I had come to Leningrad, and how I had ended up at this particular party.

"I have never talked with a foreigner," she said, still not turning her head. It was as if she was watching a movie so riveting that she dare not move her eyes. "I have never been around foreigners before."

"We are not <u>all</u> monsters or spies," I reported.

She turned and smiled. "You are quiet. You don't talk much with anyone here."

I didn't know how to respond. After all, not responding would have kept me in character for the role she imagined for me.

I didn't know how to continue the conversation – someone had cranked up the music so it was nearly impossible to talk – as was typical for young Soviets in those days. The Russians who were somehow fortunate to have access to foreign music boasted of their good fortune to all passers-by and their neighbors by playing the music at full volume. The music was, for the most part, on tinny reel-to-reel tapes, and the sound wasn't very good.

"It's impossible to talk in here," I shouted.

"Yes, it is," she responded. "And there are no quiet places here. It seems that you foreigners and their Russians have filled up the building."

"Let's go for a walk then," I proposed. "It's a beautiful night, with the snow falling so softly, so evenly."

She looked at me, as if surprised by what I had said. "How can I trust a foreigner?"

"I am generally not dangerous. I am unarmed, for instance. I normally don't abduct Russian women, no matter how beautiful they are. And, how can I trust a Russian woman?"

She leaned back on her sill. "You have learned a lot about Russian women?"

"No. Only the ones who seem to follow the Americans around."

"Many of them have their reasons." She paused. "Let us go for that walk."

I helped her on with her coat and as she put on her soft fur hat and her gloves, I put on my own coat, and this time I really regretted that I had brought with me a P-Coat. Something more formal would have helped me fit in better, would have made me less conspicuous.

It was a long walk that we took, down a wide avenue. Snow continued to fall, swirling around the small bridges and the traffic overhead.

"This is a perfect place for a crime," she said, and I began to acknowledge the quiet humor that sometimes emanated from her.

"Yes," I answered, in key with her remark. "I can see the headlines now: 'Leningrad Violinist Murders Innocent Foreign Student.'"

She smiled in a way that seemed a prelude to a laugh, but a laugh was not forthcoming.

The snow now was falling faster and a wind had come up, such that the swirls on the pavement were replaced by mini-blizzards, blowing the snow aside. The wind cut into our faces. "Time to turn around," I said. "My weak American constitution isn't up to facing this blizzard."

Now she laughed. "A blizzard, you say? Some day you will have to see a <u>genuine</u> Russian blizzard."

We returned to the flat, the wind having helped us along while nipping at our ankles – I noted that neither of us was wearing proper boots. Perhaps she, like me, had decided that the day was going to be spring-like, or at least resembling or reminding one of spring. The wind made it otherwise. But even against the wind, we could hear "The Beatles" blaring 'I want to hold your hand."

She asked me for the words to the music and I obliged.

"The theme, of course, is not original, but I have never heard it expressed in such music."

"I am not a fan of such music but I do like 'The Beatles,'" I said.

"And what is your favorite kind of music?" she asked.

"I can't tell you or you will think I am making it up, trying to impress you or to win you over."

"Try it!" she answered coyly.

"Okay," I said. "It's a mix -- eclectic, to say the least."

"Start with the non-Russian composers first, so that I know your love of Russia hasn't affected your opinions."

"Okay," I said. Let's see, there's Mahler's his First, Second, and Fifth Symphonies, but especially, the third movement of his First Symphony – the version where they haven't wedged in that 'other' Second movement, the one that doesn't belong there at all."

"I agree. Please continue."

"I very much like the second movement of his fifth symphony, the third movement of Bizet's Symphony in C –"

"Why these particular pieces?" she asked. "Especially those <u>specific</u> movements of Mahler and Bizet?"

"I've thought about this, and I've reached a conclusion. I believe that at times, composers comes up with something so touching, so intimate, so beautifully fragile, and then it's as if they become ashamed of letting down their guard, and so they finish off the music with a flourish, with noise, with the sounds of a full symphony whereas the heartfelt part might be a solo instrument, or a string section-

"I see that you know music and that you feel it. You favorite Russian pieces, please?"

"Anything by Prokofiev and Rachmaninov, especially that crashing second movement of his Second Piano Concerto."

"These pieces are eerily close to my favorite pieces. Continue, please, with your list of Russian pieces."

"The closing moments of 'Boris Godunov.' There seem to be about five themes competing there, and sometimes the gentle theme is literally crowded out, but it is still there, if you listen for it. The second moment of Tchaikovsky's 'Fourth Symphony,' The second movement of Prokofiev's 'Second Piano Concerto,' although that piece doesn't have the quietness that I describe in the other pieces. Prokofiev's 'Cinderella Suite," Kachaturian's pas de deux' from "Gayne. Shostakovich's 'Romance' from 'The Gadfly."

"You have an ear for music," she said. "Gentle music, sensitive music, pieces with strong emotion but it is held in check. Is that perhaps you?"

Her question stunned me. This, from a woman who, moments ago, was too shy to look at me or to talk with me? "No one else has ever told me that. I must think about it."

We had reached the Kammeny Ostrov Bridge ('Stone Island Bridge), and we turned left, entering the park. Snow settled on the benches, on the ornate lattice work of the fences and gates, and on us. She pulled her collar tight,

"That truly is an eclectic mix," she said. "How odd that I would put many of your pieces on my list. Do you play an instrument?"

"No, I regret it, but the answer is 'no.' I had nine brothers and sisters and we lived in small apartments, so buying an instrument or paying for tutoring or even finding a place to practice-"

"A big family such as yours? We would never see it here, except, perhaps, out on a collective farm, but even there, rarely. You seem to have been – how can I say it delicately – poor. Your coat, for instance. It is not the kind of coat that a wealthy man world wear. I hope that I am not being indelicate."

"No delicacy is required. We were poor."

"Most interesting," she said quietly. "I should think that American officials would choose only their wealthiest students to send to other countries."

"Not so, or I never would have ended up here."

Time passed quickly as we walked, arm-in-arm now, through the park. She told me about her background, about beginning violin lessons at age four and how she knew right then that she had been born to be a violinist. How the State paid her way through school, how she passed the most stringent examinations for entry into the institute and then for acceptance by the Leningrad Civic Orchestra. Her explanation of that orchestra made it sound as if it was a 'farm team' for the Leningrad Philharmonic, and maybe someday she would play with the Philharmonic.

It was time to turn around.

Back in the flat, above the artist's giant studio, the party looked like the type that would go on all night, with the party-goers eventually falling down on the floor to sleep, and with, perhaps, some intercourse of a non-intellectual kind occurring here or there.

Natalya scanned the scene. "And where will you spend the night here?" she asked.

"Nowhere. I am going to walk you to your car or bus or streetcar or whatever, and then I'm going back to the dormitory, the place I have called 'home' now for a couple of months."

She reminded me how the bridges go up at night so that big ships, supplying the city and taking away things of value, could ply the Neva, and that if you ended up in the wrong place, at the wrong end of a bridge, you would be stuck there until morning.

I told her that was all the more reason for leaving shortly, and we put on our coats and hats and mittens, still wet from our walk. We stood at the trolley line, with about ten others looking at their watches.

I looked at mine. Yes, it was near the hour when the bridges would go up. She urged me to leave, but I refused. Luckily, a streetcar came by at that moment, and we both hopped on. I had learned enough about the city's transportation system to know the most direct way home, and luckily, her streetcar would be the fastest way for me to get to Bus Number 47, the aftobus nearest the 'Kapitalist" dormitory.

As the trolley approached us, verily rocking in the swirling snow, I looked into her eyes and she looked into mine.

"Friday?" I asked. We jumped onto the back end of the trolley.

"Concert. I will give you a good ticket, through Tanya, and then you will hear the orchestra. Only I will not meet you after the performance and I do not expect you to wait. Let us meet on a week from Monday."

"We will have dinner at my place," she continued. "And you will meet my parents and you will see what life is like inside a communal apartment that no doubt is not on any Inturist tour. Now hurry along or the bridges will catch you."

We kissed, rather formally. I leapt off the car and headed for the bus stop. Had there been more time, I would have walked her to her parent's apartment and then walked in the snow back to the dormitory, making it sort of a magic snowy night. But the bridges forbade that. I made it over the last one, but barely. A policeman on one side blew his whistle at me, so I picked up the pace of my running. As expected, a policeman was waiting for me at the other end. I feigned that I didn't understand Russian and I didn't know anything about the bridges. He let me go with a look that suggested he knew I wasn't telling the whole truth, nothing but the truth, so help me, Lenin.

I thought of the beautiful woman I had just met. Yes, she was a new acquaintance, but at the same time, I felt as if I had known her longer. Many decades later, I learned that this is a warning sign. A psychologist friend in Honolulu wrote in her book something like, "If you walk into a room and your eyes meet someone and you both feel you've known each-other all your lives, then it's time to run out of that room as fast as you possibly can." Something about paradigms, the repeating of old scripts.

But what about Natalya? This looking into eyes and reading messages therein – was this real, or did I merely project onto her what

I wanted to see? Was she truly intrigued by me, did she like me as a person, or was I to her a mere convenience, a chance to get to know a foreigner, the knowing of which would help her on the orchestra's foreign tours? Was I just an interesting, uncommon specimen for her?

But what about me? Was I really attracted to her, or was I attracted to the idea of being attracted to her? Was I attracted to her because she was so different from other women I had known? Was I attracted to her because she could slip effortlessly into a life plan that would include all I had loved about Russia for the past twenty-five years?

I knew that the gods or fate or whatever it was that spins planets and determines streetcar stops and snow storms and the times for bridges to go up or to come down – they would answer my questions.

Dear Kids:

Eight o'clock Wednesday evening, came finally. I had walked to an embankment, crossed the bridge, and then walked down another embankment, this one in the clutches of a hard winter wind blowing in from the Gulf of Finland. I found Petropavlovskaya Number Eleven. It was a turn of-the-century hulk of a stone building that had more turrets and towers than any building twice that size should have had – such were the excesses of the 1890's in Peterburg.

I stepped into a doorway and found a tangled connection of descending and ascending stairways, hallways, and doors. But then Natalya's explicit directions started making sense. I walked down a long hallway. The gray plaster walls were dirty, and a single bare light bulb hung from the high ceiling, not at all the kind of place you'd expect for a symphony violinist, not to mention her parents. I peeked at the tags, each one written out in a different script, each one nearly as dirty and smudged as the one next to it. I found my way in the darkness, and I rang the doorbell to the right, next to the big metal door that said '9.'

Through the door I heard the tap-tap-tap of footsteps on a wooden floor. Ages passed, then finally the door opened and Natalya appeared. My days of hesitation had evaporated. All my day-dreaming, all that replaying of the mental 'tape' in my mind about that evening on the trolley and the evening at the party – I had not exaggerated her beauty. "Natalya, I was thinking that-"

She made a quick gesture, indicating I should keep quiet. I shrugged. We walked down another long narrow corridor with a series of shut doors on both sides, a single bare light bulb overhead again, and we approached another metal door directly ahead, at the end of the corridor. She swung the door open, towards herself, with some effort. Then we walked down another long corridor, also lined with shut doors. The walls in this part of the incredibly intricate maze had been painted more recently than the walls in the outer corridor, but they were nonetheless blotchy and streaked.

One door was open on the left; it led into a large communal kitchen, I saw. I noticed a giant cast iron sink, almost like a laundry tub, and several old stoves with long, charred, knobs that had numerous chips and cracks, and that pointed in different directions. The knobs were probably ceramic, and they probably had been white at one time or another, probably during the reign of Nicholas Romanov the Second. I also spotted some aged primus stoves – the Rube Goldberg-type contraptions that worked as kerosene stoves back in the days when metal was too rare for stove and oven-making, and when oil was scarce.

The sounds of a scratchy radio filtered through a closed door on the right. Loud voices came from behind another shut door.

We came up to a thick wooden door at the end of that second corridor. She used a clunky key to unlatch the door. "This is a communal apartment," she whispered, indicating that it was now proper to talk. "Our spaces begin here. We could have a larger apartment in the suburbs, but we prefer to live here, in the heart of the city. You and I shall have dinner here, in my room, off to the left. Then we will meet my parents."

She led me into a narrow room with a ceiling that must have been at least fifteen-feet high. A giant window at the far end looked out at the gritty stone wall of another wing of the same contorted building, and a dead violet stood on the window sill. Poor plant. Winter, as well as neglect probably, had done it in – no flowers, not even a leaf.

We sat at a long table covered with an oil-cloth that smelled like all oil-cloths smell, with wear holes at the points where it stretched over the table's edges. Beyond the far end of the table stood two imposing, mismatched armoires, with the ends of dresses or skirts sticking through the cracks. A mound of shoes and boots lay piled up in front of the armoires. This princess was not too neat. Oh, well, one shortcoming could be accepted.

I heard a tenuous tap at the door. Natalya stood up and opened the door just a crack. A hand appeared, and Natalya quickly brought in a decanter and two glasses, then two plates loaded with hot cabbage salad. "You will meet my parents tonight," she said, as she poured the liquid from the decanter into two flat-bottomed glasses. "This is compot – a combination of juices," she said.

I knew compot from my meals at the university.

"My Father works in the Ministry of Justice," she said. "My Grandmother, my Father's Mother – lives here too. My Brother lived just through this wall, before he went into the army. My Father will convert the room into a study maybe, but my Mother wants the room for a painting and sewing area. We will see who wins the competition, but I am betting on my Mother."

We ate and drank in self-conscious silence. We opened a bottle of red Georgian wine. In between bites, we caught ourselves staring at one-another, and we laughed self-consciously each time. There was another tap at the door. Natalya slipped the empty salad plates through the opening. I heard whispering, and I caught a glimpse of a woman's brown-gray head. Then footsteps echoed down the hallway, while Natalya stood at the door. Soon, two plates of fish passed through the doorway.

Natalya ate like she talked, in a way. She took small morsels into her mouth, chewing slowly and decisively, pausing between bites. Her hands seemed strangely shaky – so unlike the poise I had witnessed on the trolley. How could a violinist have shaky hands, I wondered? She knocked over her goblet, and dark red wine rushed across the oil cloth in a long, insistent line, towards her. I couldn't react fast enough. Drops started spilling onto her skirt.

She jumped up. "Damn!" she said, rushing to the first armoire while holding her skirt. She brought back a rag and a cardboard container of salt. "I have spoiled my skirt. This salt will lift out the stain." She poured a pyramid of salt over the three purple spots on the gray woolen skirt. "I am clumsy sometimes," she said. "It is odd for a musician."

I didn't know whether to help her with the spot on a, um, delicate part of her skirt, and so I didn't. It seemed as if she sensed my situation and that my decision pleased her. We made small talk or else we sat in silence, looking at one-another every once in a while and then turning away, red in the face.

"We will meet my Parents now," she said after our main course. We walked down the hallway and turned left into a large, high-ceilinged room, in the middle of which stood a giant mahogany table. An old chandelier with weak, exposed bulbs hung from the ceiling. A harsh white light came from a tall goose-necked lamp resting on the far edge of the table.

I spotted a middle-aged man and woman in the shadows, as my eyes slowly adjusted to the darkness that the lamp and he chandelier were unable to dispel. Her Mother sat on the far end of a long, high-backed sofa, a book and a pair of glasses resting on her lap. Natalya's Father sat in the shadows in the other corner of the room, in a large high-backed leather chair. He stood up when we entered. "I am Pyotor Pavlovich," the man said in a deep voice. "I am pleased to meet you, and I welcome you to our apartment. This is my Wife, Inna Ivanovna."

He set his book on the table, swiveled the kinked arm of the goose-necked lamp over towards the window, and resumed his seat. He wore a white shirt, a narrow black tie and an official-looking uniform – a black jacket with white epaulets, a gold star on each epaulet.

Natalya's Mother leaned forward in her chair. "We are very pleased to meet you, and we hope your dinner was adequate."

"It was more than adequate," I said. "And, in fact, it was delicious, especially when considering the cafeteria food I usually eat."

"Neither I nor Natalya are very good cooks," she said.

Natalya's Mother was about fifty years old. She was thick, but not fat, and had a grace in her movements that was indicated even by the gestures she made while sitting. She was kindly-looking, as if somewhat concerned, possibly very tired. "You are the first person Natalya likes who is not in music," she said. "I think it is a good sign. She is expanding her horizons."

I saw Natalya cringe at the word 'likes,' but the word sent joy into my heart. Her Mother, sensing Natalya's discomfort no doubt, shrugged her shoulders and sighed, grasping the book in her lap.

"Are you from Leningrad, Inna Ivanovna?" I asked, hoping to replace the uncomfortable silence with a serviceable conversation.

Inna seemed pleased that she was to be included in the conversation. "Why, yes, both I and my Husband were born here. I have never lived anywhere else. Pyotor Pavlovich has traveled around the world, but I prefer to stay here. I could not thrive in a foreign existence. Are you thriving here?"

"Yes, I am. I haven't traveled much, not nearly as much as your Husband, probably, but here I am comfortable."

"I did not know Americans studied at our university," she said. "We are hospitable to our visitors?"

"Yes. Very hospitable!" I answered.

"You are the first American I have ever met," said Inna, and I could see her staring at me like a specimen. She turned towards her husband. "Pyotor, is he a typical American?"

"I do not think so," he said from across the room. "He speaks Russian."

I was anxious to draw him out in a conversation. "Have you been to America, Pyotor Pavlovich?" I asked.

"I have been to Washington twice and to New York twice, but in each place they tell me it is not typically American. Where is a typically American place then? Where are you from?"

"Saint Paul," I said. "It's in Minnesota, but they say that's not so typical either."

"Saint Paul. A city named for a saint?" asked Natalya's Mother.

"Yes, like Saint Peterburg," I said, glancing at Natalya, who was tight-lipped, sitting at the edge of her chair, but smiling unconvincingly. She was nervous about my first meeting with her parents, I could tell. Yet somehow I had the feeling she was disturbed by the easy way that I got along with them. I didn't know what all that was about, and still don't.

"Is it as beautiful as this city?" Inna asked.

"No city is as beautiful as Leningrad, but Saint Paul has its beauty too, especially in winter."

"I will show you some of the beauty of this city you maybe have not seen," said Inna.

"Be careful," said Pyotor. "My Wife is a painter – a frustrated artist. She has sketched every building in this city. She will walk you to death!"

"What have you not seen that you should see in Leningrad?" Inna asked, paying her husband no mind.

"Well, I haven't visited the Cathedral of Saints Peter and Paul."

"Why, shame on you!" she replied. "And it is so close to the university! It is the heart of the city, and named for the Saints Peter and Paul. You are from a city named after Saint Paul, how coincidental! For shame! You must go there. Natalya rehearses all day Saturday. You and I will go to the fortress at noon!"

Natalya's Father laughed. "You are in trouble, young man. You now have two women to contend with – Natalya and Inna. And I will bother you too."

What a way to be bothered! Here I was, sitting near an absolutely beautiful woman who liked me, and here were her parents, who seemed to like me too. "And how will you bother me, Pyotor Pavlovich?"

"I want to talk over certain things with you, but we will reserve those discussions for another time."

"Give me an idea of the subjects, so that I can research and prepare brilliant responses."

"There is no brilliance required from either of us. I have questions about American politics. You know, our country supports the antiwar movement in America. It is natural, but we see pictures of the riots and disturbances in your universities and even in front of your capital. I do not understand why your government tolerates such disorder."

"It's difficult to make comparisons between the two countries, but-"

"We will discuss this another time," interrupted Pyotor Pavlovich. "Natalya is jealous because we are stealing you from her. You two go back to her room for dessert, and Inna Ivanovna and I will resume our reading."

Natalya winced at her Father, who did not balk. She stood up and walked through the hallway to her room, with me in tow. "You have a way of charming people," she said once we sat back down – me on the chair near the table, her on the edge of her bed. "It is an infectious charm you have."

I could not have heard better words. My heart raced. "Has it infected you?"

"Well, yes."

"You've infected me too," I said. Our hands met. She flinched. It felt like electric current charging through me.

"Well, you have charmed me!" I said, drawing her closer. "Enchanted me even!"

I bent low to kiss her, but she broke away. "I will play some music, softly," she said. "It is getting late. Maybe you will add this one to your list of favorite pieces." She walked across the room and lifted an old fabric-covered phonograph from the floor onto a stack of books on the far end of the table. "This record is Marcello's 'Concerto for Oboe and Orchestra,'" she said.

A solitary oboe played a slow, plaintive, melancholy tune against a backdrop of gentle strings. She sat down on the bed and motioned for me to sit beside her. The phonograph needle hit a scratch and caught in a groove, protracting the oboe's tune. She pursed her lips and winced slightly, but didn't speak and motioned for me not to speak or move. The needle somehow found its way out of the groove and brought the movement to its conclusion. "That is my favorite part," she whispered as the piece continued. "I play it so often I have scratched the record. I am not patient enough to hear the whole piece – I just want that part. The scratch is punishment for my impatience."

It was strange, sitting on the edge of the bed of a woman I hardly knew, sitting alongside one-another like students listening to a lecture. I had never found myself in the company of such a beautiful woman, particularly one who seemed attracted to me and didn't appear to be trying not to express it. And, she didn't play games, the kind that men and women play when meeting or courting. She spoke directly. I felt hypnotized, yet somehow super-alert. Or was I attracted to the idea of being attracted to her? That labyrinth of questions tugged at me all evening.

Damn, I hate the first moves of 'enchanted' people getting to know one-another. What to do? What not to do? How to read her signals? Put it in 'drive' and step on the gas? Slam on the brakes and put it in reverse? I hated that indecision, that not knowing. It made me feel out of control.

I leaned her way, but she stood up and walked to the armoire, returning with a small decanter and two goblets. "We will drink this cognac, and then you will be on your way."

Marcello became livelier, making me feel bold. "You're intriguing, Natalya," I said, inching towards her. "I've never met a woman like you."

"I have met men like you, you suppose?" she asked, laughing. She moved away from me an inch or two. "There are many attractive women in America."

"Sure there are, but attraction is strange. It follows its own laws, and I'm attracted to you." I inched towards her again.

"Maybe your attraction is merely because I am a foreigner to you?" she asked, inching away from me again. We were running out of bed space.

Her logic had me, of course, because it was exactly what I had been thinking. How to answer? Too much honesty might dispel the spell, the magic of the moment, yet lying would serve no good. God, how I hated these indecisive moments. Get on with it or get over it – one or the other!

"Well," I began. "Then why would I pick you, when there are so many other Russian women to pick from?" It made enough sense to convince me. The more I thought about it, the more convinced, in fact, I became. "You are the one I'm attracted to. It's you – the person, not the nationality!"

"I rarely meet a man who attracts me," she said, deflecting my response. "I bury myself in my work, but I miss that attraction, that chemical thing. You know, when it happens, it is terrifying."

"Yes, it's terrifying," I repeated. I felt like awe-struck high school sophomore at a prom.

"It is terrifying!" she said. Then she picked up my right hand as if it were an unknown creature and examined my palm and the underside of my forearm, as if looking for clues in the run of the veins. "I got very excited when you touched my arm," she said. "You don't know what it does to me, just to be touched so softly on the arm like that. I have heard that you Americans are kind to women. Be careful. I could lose control."

I swallowed hard. "Well, maybe if we lose control, it won't be so bad?"

"Not now!" she said. "Not so soon. It frightens me. Let us get to know one-another first. Let us control ourselves in the meantime."

"It won't be easy for me," I confessed.

"We <u>will</u> be controlled," she said. "My schedule – and maybe your schedule too – will keep us apart enough to stay cool. There are rehearsals daily, for me."

"I have classes during the day," I sighed.

We stood at her bed. We hugged. "I am terrified," she whispered.

We took off our shoes and crept down the hallway, through the series of doors leading to the exit. At the third doorway, she took my hand, kissed it across the back of my fingers, then stared into my eyes with a look that made sure I wouldn't forget her, as if I had any intention or any ability to forget any of it.

Dear Children:

It is odd that even though I live in a trailer park, I have more 'luxuries' than did Natalya and her parents. I understand they sacrificed some things by deciding to live close-in rather that out in a newer and bigger apartment, such as where you lived perhaps. They would have had a private kitchen there and possibly their own refrigerator and a clothes-washing machine. But even that standard, in a new apartment, would not equal mine, in the trailer park, where most people who drive by shudder and then make sure their car or SUV doors are locked.

I know that the standard of living has risen sharply in Russia the past few decades. Still, they have a long way to go before Khrushchev's "We will bury you" (a lousy translation of a phrase that really meant "We will surpass you") remark becomes reality.

Dear Young Adults:

Anna and Katya, you are young but in a few years you will have boyfriends and girlfriends. You will be tormented by things. You will spend hours on the phone with other girls, discussing your love, asking how you can tell he loves you – the questions and answers are endless. Your girlfriends will tell you girls how to act, how to kiss, how to let him know you like him, how to ward him off if he becomes too arduous. They will talk about the secrets of kissing, of touching, and of making love.

Alex, your male friends will tell you how to score, how to know when to move in for a goal, how to get her to notice you, and a thousand other things about which they know practically nothing.

Me? I got engaged to a Russian violinist in Leningrad, the city where you three were born. This was the generation, no doubt, of your grandparents – thus are the advantages and disadvantages of having such an old father.

Yes, I was excited by the chance to marry a beautiful Russian woman, to travel freely from the USSR to the USA, and to see the whole world, the two of us together. And, to push things along, at a high and dangerous speed, there was the attraction thing that I will never understand.

You children will learn soon enough that there is no logic to attraction. You cannot predict it or escape from it. You will see handsome men with ugly women, and ugly men with beautiful women. You will dash off with a handsome prince, girls, while all others believe you are running off with a frog.

The attraction comes from something deep inside. You will see an attractive person of the opposite sex and feel nothing. You will see a common-looking or even ugly-looking person, and your heart will jump. Why?

Yes, this attraction thing with Natalya, and hers with me, was strong, like a mighty river's current. Looking back now, as I have looked back so many times, I see that we hardly knew one-another. Today I have just a few photos of her, and only one does her appearance any justice. A video clip, so easy to obtain today, was nearly impossible then.

There was 'something in the way she moved,' as the Beatles' song of that same time said. I wish I could have preserved more than just a pale memory of the way she moved, capturing the grace of her movements.

There was another captivating aspect about Natalya. I think she embodied a certain trait that I have perceived in just a few people, all of them Russian. It's in the face. In your faces too.

Standing in those incredibly long escalators that led to and from the subway, I had ample opportunity to study Russian faces. On the busses and trolleys too, with crowds of people jammed into contained spaces, their bodies jammed up next to mine, I had ample opportunity to study faces. In public, they are stone-like, unchanging, but in a private setting, where there is no danger, their faces, as it were, awaken. What life! What animation! I have noticed that in you three children. Yes, you are Russians through and through, "High School Musical II" and Scooby-Do and Barbie notwithstanding.

Back to 1970.

Another way to observe Russian faces and gestures and postures, at least when your city was called 'Leningrad' and the country was Communist? Go shopping. You will end up in crushes of people, and you can watch how they act and react, what happens in a crowd.

You want an example? Let's say that canned cucumbers are for sale at one 'univemarg' that somehow received a rare delivery. Why? Bribes probably paid, a good 'middle man' working the system to the advantage of his store, the inefficiency of the Soviet delivery of essential goods once again being proved. Lines flow down the block. Inside the store, there is pure chaos. All shelves are empty except for the pallet of jars stuffed with sorrowful specimens of cucumbers.

Although the shelves are bare, the crowd is oppressive; it seems that not one more person can get inside the store without a wall or a showcase collapsing. Once inside, after others have pushed their way ahead of you, you have to push yourself through to the counter to get the clerk's attention, while her job is really not at all to serve customers but to examine her nails and confer with her fellow workers or chat on the phone or look into her pitted, dim pocket mirror.

Once you have managed to get her attention, she gives you a slip with the number of the cucumber 'group' that will soon belong to you. But first, you have to push yourself all way through this massive crowd to the cashier's box, on the other side of the store, of course.

There, high on a stool, behind a scratched plastic window, the cashier seems to be having a problem with her nails that demands immediate attention, but at last you do manage to get her attention. A little bit of work on the abacus -- click, click, CLICK, then click-click, and then she collects your money and hands you a flimsy piece of paper that might easily self-destruct in your sweaty palm.

But, hey, there is only one commodity for sale in the whole store, and there is a limit of one jar per person. The price, then, should remain the same, so why does she have to tally each sale on her abacus and grumble about people not having enough change?

You didn't ask questions then, or if you did, you didn't get served. You push your way through the thick crowd, contending with people who are experts at cutting in front of you. This was, after all, The Soviet Union. The clerk behind the counter stares at your receipt, as if it might be something you forged. Once she decides it might be genuine, then she must match the number on the receipt with the number pasted on each jar on the mountain of jars, while talking to other clerks and minding her hair and nails.

But there was a reward in all that effort too. You got to see Russians in public. Crammed into a small place, they will make eye contact with no one. They are experts at pushing. There is an art in it. They hardly ever actually 'push' anyone. Instead, they concentrate on slipping through the spaces between bodies, the spaces that last only a second or two.

Heaven forbid that you should be afraid of crowds. Stay away from Russia if you suffer from agoraphobia. Even if you don't suffer from it on your way into the country, you may easily get it after you arrive.

Okay. The USSR is history. How much has Russia changed? I am not sure. Sometimes I think it's changed a lot, sometimes I think it's hardly changed at all – the same bureaucratic offices but with different titles on all the doors. And sometimes I think that Russia now is the 'reverse' of what the Soviet Union was then. By that, I mean that things once great (free medical care, low-cost apartments) are now awful, and that things once awful (empty stores, fear of speaking out) are now great.

Back to the USSR. The benefit of all this work and pushing and wasting of time? Well, first of all, you have acquired a real trophy – a jar of cucumbers that will be the envy of all your friends, relatives, and colleagues. You will open the jar with great reverence, and then you will share your good fortune with people you love. Or you might trade it for something you really want, and which you will then share.

Such a treasure might be anything – a roll of toilet paper, a newly-published book, an antiquarian book. I even saw one sweating guy trying to jam a refrigerator onto a trolley.

On the sidewalk, in the stores, on the long subway escalators, on any public conveyance, you will get to see the 'public face' of a Russian – their stony mask that's worn in public.

Your friendship becomes real, once the stone mask is removed, in the privacy, say, of their parents' kitchen. Then they will smile like no one else can smile, and they will be so hospitable that they won't let you leave without, say, taking their sofa or anything else you made the mistake of admiring.

Dear Young Adults:

The Russian tale continues. You don't need to read all this at one time, in linear fashion. I didn't write this to be read that way. But when you want to know more about Natalya and about 1970, you have come to the right place. Too bad I haven't figured out a way to append an index to this manuscript.

I spent little time with Natalya, because of her practice schedule, not to mention her solitary hours of practices and her practicum with a retired violinist. As if that weren't enough to keep us apart, factor in my class schedule, not to mention homework.

On some evenings we arranged things so that I'd walk up Nevsky to the concert hall and catching her leaving when rehearsals ended. Then she started asking me to meet her three blocks away. I agreed, wondering why the extra caution all of a sudden.

To make matters in this fairy-tale even worse, she was leaving the city soon, with the orchestra, on a Russian tour.

We decided that I'd come back in the summer of 1971 and we'd get married. It would take at least a year to get the Soviet and the American papers in order. Plus, I needed to make some money, to tide us over once we get to the U.S. Right then, I was broke. As a Soviet citizen caught up in that country's love-hate/loathe-envy dichotomy concerning America, she couldn't imagine that an American could be short of money.

How would we manage after the marriage? I would spend some time in Leningrad, I figured – getting a visa would not be a problem now, with a dual-citizenship wife. I'd find a job interpreting, translating, or perhaps teaching English – the USSR definitely needed teachers of American English, since they all learned antiquated British English.

Back in the United States, I figured that I'd get my graduate degrees in a few years and then I'd get a job teaching Russian in a college. Meanwhile, Natalya could get a slot in an orchestra or, if not, she could tutor or teach violin.

It all would work itself out.

Her parents approved of us, but they appeared relieved that we would wait a year to get married. I believed they wanted to be sure that

I truly loved their daughter, and that she truly loved me. And, I admitted to a deep crevice inside myself, that I needed time to sort this all out -- things had happened so fast. One dinner, a couple of walks, some problems in communication because of language difficulties – and all of a sudden I am pledging my life? Infatuated as I was, I knew I needed to make sure this was for real.

So how did all this happen? We decided to marry, I remember, as we were leaning on the Neva River wall, with the frozen river before us, and the Winter Palace behind us. I proposed. She leaned into me and said, "Yes." That was it. The famous ship Aurora, the one that fired the shot 'heard around the world' in 1917? It stood on the other side of the river, to the right a bit. It didn't fire any shots.

"We will be good for one-another," she said as we walked back to her apartment. "Now, let me kiss you again," she said, "And then we will go wake up my parents."

But her Mother and Father were in the sitting room when we walked in. "Mother, Father," Natalya said. "Bill and I are getting married next year."

Inna took off her glasses, stood up, grabbed the bottom of her apron, and broke into tears. Pyotor set down his book, took off his reading glasses, walked up to me, and shook my hand somberly. "I am very happy for both of you. And why are we waiting a year?"

"It will take much time to get all the paperwork in order, both from your side and from the American side. And I need time to make money."

Her Father looked me in the eyes. "You do not have adequate money to care for my daughter?"

"Russians think all Americans are rich. but it is not so. I am far from rich. Maybe I'll take a year off my studies to make some money." I added the possibilities for Natalya in the U.S. and for me in the USSR, and he seemed satisfied.

"It is not a bad thing to wait," Inna said. "You and Natalya are so emotionally involved, it is better to wait until it fades-"

She paused, just for a second, but I knew what she was thinking and she knew that I knew what she was thinking. What mother or father would want their daughter to move to another country, perhaps losing her ability to return, and all this after spending a brief time with a foreigner? There was no doubt for any of us in that room that relations between the USSR and USA had for decades behaved like a roller coaster gone mad like the devil, and things had not changed.

It was now time to ask the question I didn't want to ask. "When I come back, there will be no problems with – with your daughter marrying a foreigner, an American?"

Pyotor laughed. "Contrary to what they might tell you sometimes, this is a free country, and Natalya can marry whom she pleases!"

"My Father has a very important position, with much authority," Natalya whispered. "There will be no problem."

Dear Children:

I begin another story before the fairy tale concludes.

The next evening, Natalya and I took a walk along the Moika Canal. On the street. I saw one young man with long hair being escorted out of a café by two uniformed guards. I recalled all those times that Russians who had merely approached us foreigners were whisked away in unmarked sedans. "Are you sure this is alright with your parents?" I asked Natalya.

"It is okay with my parents," she assured me. "They have nothing to fear. My Father is important enough. He does not have to worry about his daughter marrying a capitalist."

We kissed several times, but we never got more physically intimate than that. A few days later, she left on tour. She didn't want me accompanying her to the airport. How strange. Here she was, ready to marry a foreigner and leave the country, and yet she feared being seen with me in front of her orchestra colleagues. She had her Father drop me off on the road close to the last subway stop leading back to the city. He took our picture with my camera. I still have that picture, and I believe you kids have seen it. I looked alright, but the photo did no justice to her.

At the car, with its doors open like two wings, we all said good-bye.

The car drove off. I saw Natalya in the back seat. Oddly, she didn't turn around. I made up a silly game for myself. If she turned around, then that meant she was truly in love with me. She didn't turn around.

Oh, well, so much for getting involved in superstitious games. I headed for the station, hopped on the next train, and soon I was back on Vasilievsky Island.

1970, all this was. What a high-horsepower fantasy. The combination of her and me. America and Leningrad combined, Saint Paul and Saint Peter. Perfect.

I was equally enamored of your Mother, kids, when we met in 2000. That time was no fantasy, however. I was a widower, in my early fifties, and I was looking for reality, not fantasy, if I was looking at all and I wasn't. Your Mother had sterling qualities. She was beautiful in a most individual way and smart and quick and stubborn and charming – a treat, a beauty, and a real challenge as well. You three are lucky to have such a Mother.

Dearest Anna, Katya, and Alex:

It is time for more of the 'back story.' On my way to class one morning, I decided to walk through Peter the Great's Hall of the Twelve Colleges, the heart of the University. The building is so long that they used to hold races inside its long corridor.

I spotted a statue of a world famous mathematics graduate, Pavnuti (what a great first name!) Chebyshov. I don't know anything about math except how to turn on my calculator. I have hunted around, but I have never been able to grasp anything at all about what made Mister Chebyshov famous in mathematics circles.

This Pavnuti was the ancestor of Olga and Nina Chebyshowa, my Russian teacher in Pacific Grove, and her Mother. How far away California seemed. How long ago did Navy language school seem.

I decided it best not to mail the photo. I had learned that Soviet émigrés often didn't receive mail from the USSR. Luckily, my roll of film later made it through customs with me.

Once I got back home, I mailed out a bunch of things, including the photo of Chebyshov to his daughter and grand daughter. "Countries may come and go," I wrote on the back of the photo. "But the deeds of great men remain." Or something like that.

That photo later changed my life.

Anna Anna Anna –

I fail you as a Father. Forgive me, or, better, show me how to treat you. You'd think I'd know, having been the second-oldest of ten children and the oldest male child.

You are two years older than your Sister, who is barely one year older than her Brother.

This means you are the one who must stand by and smile while people gush over the cuteness of your younger Brother and Sister. You are the responsible one. You should know better. You must be a good example for your cute younger Brother and Sister.

But in those murky months before you three ended up in a Peterburg orphanage, you were the sole caregiver – you, three and a half years old at the time.

It's been hard for you to relinquish control, I know. And still, even though you are the oldest one who always should know better and who always should be a good example – yet, you have your own childhood needs.

I recall that on nights when your Mother was working, I might leave the house for a moment – to get the mail up by the road, to stop off at a neighbor's to return or take something. Of course, in the winter it is dark by 5:00 PM. As I walked, I'd catch a shadow moving behind an arbor vitae, or I'd see the shadow of a person stalking me while working her way around the trees and buckthorn in the gully. I could hear the crack of buckthorn branches.

Sometimes I caught you or you let yourself get caught. Then you smiled and your face turned red. You were following me because Katya had told you she was afraid that I might get lost in the dark. Yeah. Right.

At age nine, you are already a sullen teen-ager. You come to the trailer, your open up Harry Potter and read two hundred pages by bedtime, or you put on earphones and play on the computer or watch a DVD movie.

Which came first? Your withdrawing from me? My ignoring you? Why don't I have more pictures drawn by you on my walls that are covered with the drawings of Katya and Alex?

We try to make personal time for the two of us. We shut the

door to your room and begin a game of Scrabble. Every minute there's a timid knock on the door. Alex reports that the computer won't work. Katya tells me she can't find her reading book. There are enough reasons so that one of those two siblings of yours knock on your door every two minutes. Opening the door, I see the anguish on their faces. Their Father has abandoned them.

Last weekend, you and I decided to take a walk along the State trail that's on the other side of the highway. We checked first with Katya and Alex to make sure they'd be alright in our brief absence. I wrote down for them my cell phone number, and I told them that Pudge, the neighbor could help, if needed.

Our walk took longer than planned. I was winded at the end — the combination of walking and talking being difficult for me. And approaching the last hill leading to the trailer park, I had to stop again and rest.

My cell phone rang. It was an anxious voice whom I hardly recognized as Alex. They were terrified. Where were we? We had been gone a total of fifty minutes, just as I had told them – "Start watching a movie and we'll be back long before the movie is over." We had at least a half hour to spare.

Pudge said the two kids ran out to him as soon as he got out of his pickup. Their faces were red and they were sobbing and out of breath. Pudge is the one who dialed my number for them.

Getting home, I noticed that the two kids had for some reason constructed a 'fort' to hide Lulu the dachshund, and that fort was a stack of pillows jammed into the tiny area under my computer desk. I wonder what forces or decisions led to them constructing that fortress.

I confess, dear Anna, that as much as I loved spending time alone with you, I still felt terrible about abandoning your brother and sister.

Those kids were so grateful to see us, and they were so loveable in their need, so validating my value as a Father and as a person looking for love in all the right places.

But what about you, dear Anna? You stood at my side, shrugged in a teenage girl way, and headed into your bedroom to read Harry Potter.

Later, at least, you and I had a moment alone and we smiled secretly at one-another, not winking but knowing it was an appropriate time for winking -- both of us realizing the infant-like needs of Alex and Katya.

You asked me why Pudge was called 'Pudge' even though he wasn't fat. Had he been fat before? I told you that I had asked him those very questions, and he reported that his real first name was Darwin, but when his Mother re-married, this time to a Roman Catholic, they needed to come up fast with a nick-name. Pudge.

Oh, Anna, I so hope that when you read this, you will be an inquisitive, confident, and sensitive young lady.

I love you so. I work with you on being a tom-boy, and we make clothing choices together. Then we are friends, not father and daughter.

I bet that some day you'll realize how difficult it was for me to be father to three when there was just one of me. That rhymes. We could write a song.

Dear Katya, you who are the lover of bugs:

In the spring of 1970, I developed trouble sleeping at Shevchenko Twenty-Five. Small red lumps appeared on my arms, legs, and back. They itched through the night and in the morning I discovered new lumps, then my arms and legs started to swell. One morning, I showed the lumps to Olga, the dormitory cleaning lady.

"Ah, bedbug bites, and they are making you sick!" she screamed. "Go off to a polyclinic immediately!"

She waited for me to shave and dress and wouldn't let me smoke my morning cigarette. She pushed me out of the room, down the stairs, and out the front door. I took a phrase book with me. My Russian vocabulary didn't include medical terminology beyond the most essential things like, 'I have diarrhea. Please direct me to the nearest bathroom.'

Olga and I walked four blocks to the polyclinic, near the so oddly-named Skipperskaya Street, and I read the phrase book along the way. By the time I checked in, I was able to say, in Russian, "I have an allergic reaction to bedbug bites." But I didn't need to. Olga did all the talking.

The nurses turned red when they saw me. "You are a foreigner?" they asked.

I nodded.

They straightened up their desks and their counters and then adjusted their hair and their tall paper hats. "We will take you to the doctor in charge!" said the head nurse.

Doctor Grushenko wore thick-rimmed glasses set in square brown plastic frames. "What is the nature of your complaint?" he asked in a formal, clipped speech.

"I have an allergic reaction to bedbug bites," I replied confidently. Olga nodded.

"Where are you from?" the doctor barked.

"America."

"You have brought bed bugs with you!"

"I have never seen a bed bug before in my life!" I protested. "If it weren't for Mayakovsky's play by that name, I would have had to look up the word in a dictionary!"

The doctor slammed his fist down on the desk, and the young nurses at his side flinched. "We do not have bedbugs in the Soviet Union! We used to have them. The Nazis brought them in. But today, we do not have bedbugs!"

I showed him the bites on my arm.

"How do you know they are from bed bugs?" he asked.

"Olga, the cleaning lady, told me."

Olga nodded. "Those are bed bug bites."

The doctor glared at Olga, then at me. The nurses stared at me too, as if it all were my fault. I stared back, occasionally scratching a lump.

"Do not itch those bedbug bites!" commanded the doctor. "They will get infected!" He squirmed in his seat. "Where are you staying?"

"Shevchenko Twenty-Five, four blocks from here."

He sprung up from his chair, "Is that the foreigners' dormitory?"

"Yes, it is."

"Aha! Are there Hindus living on your floor – Indians, Pakistanis?"

"Yes, there are two Pakistanis on the floor."

The doctor was pleased; the puzzle was solved. "They brought the bed bugs with them! You see, Hindus never, never kill anything!" He smiled, and both nurses sighed while he scribbled out two prescriptions and directed me to a room down the corridor.

"I will wait out here," said Olga in the hall.

A young woman in a lab attendant's coat met me at the door. She was almost as tall as I. She had big hands, large shoulders, and no indentation at the waist. "Take off your clothes!" she commanded in a guttural Russian I hardly understood. "Off with your clothes! I am busy! Do you think you are the only person in this clinic?"

I stripped to my shorts. She studied my legs and my arms and shook her head. "Not enough nutrition in those capitalist countries, I see."

I didn't tell her that I had lost at least twenty pounds since coming to Leningrad.

"Now, lie down on this table, supine, chin in, toes up!" she commanded. "Arms to the side, elbows straight!"

I lay down on the icy cold gurney. She wheeled over a clumsy-looking lamp suspended on a metal cable, and handed me a pair of goggles and barked another set of orders.

I wished Olga was with me. "I'm sorry," I said. "I didn't understand what you just said."

She grabbed me by the ankles with her left hand and by the shoulder with her right hand, flipping me over like a sausage on griddle. It was a sunlamp. I got my treatment both front and back.

Doctor Grushenko ordered me to return to the clinic three times weekly for a month. Liuba, the laboratory attending, became less hostile each time. "I am studying medicine in night school," she told me on the third visit. Two weeks later, she called me her 'tan Hawaiian bachelor' when I turned brown from the lights, except for the conspicuous white band running lengthwise around my head, where the goggle strings blocked the sunlamp rays.

"You know, I lived in Hawaii once!" I told her. It seemed a world and decades away.

She clasped her hands at her chest and looked upward. "Oi, I thought Hawaii was a place that did not exist – it was just made up!"

During visits, she begged me for information about Gavaii and Kalifornia and she scolded me for not having brought pictures.

One of the other students had brought a coffee table book on California – all pictures. I traded that for a carton of Tarreyton American cigarettes. Liuba clutched the book to her chest. I could tell she was just itching to open it, and so I told her I'd wait for my treatment – she could look at the book. She shook her head many times and thanked me many times. I knew that if she got tired of the book, she could trade it for something valuable.

After that first visit, I walked out of the Polyclinic with two prescription slips. Liuba directed me and Olga to a pharmacy two block away.

"Nyet! We do not have these," snapped the pharmacist. "We usually have them, but today we are out. There is another pharmacy two blocks that way."

Olga and I walked two blocks.

"Nyet, we do not have these," the pharmacist reported. "We usually do, but today we are out. There is another pharmacy two blocks that way."

"We've already been there," I answered. "They sent us here."

The man sighed. "What is the matter with those people over there? They cannot manage their inventories? Try Pharmacy Thirty-Four, three blocks that way."

"This is an outrage!" Olga told him. "Here is a foreigner. What must he think of us!"

The pharmacist shrugged.

By mid-afternoon, Olga and I had walked most of Vasilievsky Island. I was cold and tired and itching like crazy. I hadn't managed to get any prescription filled. At each stop, we heard "Nyet, we do not have these. We usually do, but not today."

The last pharmacist on our 'tour' of the city directed us to the 'duty' pharmacy on Nevsky Prospekt. "They have everything," she said.

I parted with poor Olga. She was clearly tired, the dear, from all the walking we had done. I jumped on a bus headed for Nevsky.

This 'duty' pharmacy filled one of my prescriptions. Concerning the second prescription, well, they usually stocked it, I discovered, but on that particular day, unfortunately, they were out.

I brought my treasured prescription back to the dorm. I peered into the smoky-orange ointment bottle, with a slender glass tube inside the cap, that was not unlike the mercurochrome bottles I recalled from years ago back home.

The itching and burning were getting worse, and it was getting hard to concentrate or study, so I painted every possible bump with the dark purple medicine. The label, and the doctor as well, failed to warn that it was a permanent dye. Even Soviet soap could not remove it; even Bulgarian shampoo didn't help.

I was at times glad Natalya was on tour. How would she have reacted if she saw me covered with Howdy-Doody freckles, as if she would know who Howdy-Doody was, as if you kids would know who Howdy-Doody was.

Olga somehow obtained the second prescription weeks later, and she held it out for me as if it were a treasure. It was a round, fragile, cardboard container of plain vitamins, containing no minimum daily requirements, I discovered, when I got home.

Alex, Katya, Anna:

Kids, those Soviet days of 1970 will no doubt never return. I mean, imagine a country cut off from the outside world for fifty-five years, and all of a sudden, a trickle of foreign student visitors arrive. We were like celebrities. I certainly felt like one, and I didn't always like it.

"Pride goeth before the fall," it is said. It sure as hell did in my case.

Perhaps you will identify more with the process of learning a language.

On a Monday in March, I was the only student in Linguaphonics class. Unlike other professors in the university, Nadezhda Andreevna took it as a personal affront when students missed classes. "I cannot help them if they will not come to class!" she said. "They will go back to America with bad pronunciation, and I will have failed."

She turned her attention to me. "You have acquired a very good vocabulary, William, and your grammar is quite good. You make yourself understood in Russian."

I blushed, trying to look humble and not like a celebrity.

"But," she continued. "You have a horrible accent. You cannot speak Russian well until you start all over, from the beginning. To speak a foreign language, you must abandon your native tongue, forget all the categories you have constructed in your brain since childhood. Your whole thinking and your perceptions are based on language. You must abandon your premises. Otherwise, you will not progress further. I wanted to tell you this for a long time."

My blush had disappeared, as had any attempt, or need, to appear humble.

"You have no feeling for the language at all," she continued, and each word cut deeply. How many years had I studied her blasted language?

"I have been told I do alright," I said, measuring my words. I was angry, and maybe because I knew she was right.

"Your spoken Russian is far from alright," she said, not

looking up. "Your Russian is coldly precise and correct, but it is not living Russian. Your intonation is horrible."

I switched to English. "Look, you tell me how terrible my accent is, but you criticize it in your own stilted, old-fashioned, out-dated, clipped British pronunciation that you probably picked up from some old professor who studied at Oxford!" It was the first time I had talked back to a Soviet professor.

She flinched, and her eyes flashed. "Ah, but the difference between me and you is that you have the opportunity to visit the country of your second language and improve. I don't."

I felt like a heel.

We made peace of sorts, and we made a pact. I would help her with her English, and she would help me with my Russian. We started meeting in the language laboratory during lunch break and for an hour after afternoon classes. We worked with a spectroscope, a machine that showed voice patterns on its tiny, oval screen. She recited a series of vowel and consonant pairs, and then I repeated them until the patterns that I made on the screen matched hers. Then it was her turn. Both of us had seen the movie "My Fair Lady," and we joked about Liza Doolittle. I had a hard time with Russian intonation, which is inordinately high at the end of sentences if you were from Leningrad.

"You are afraid to raise the pitch of your voice!" she urged. "You only have a few tones, all of them low. For emphasis, you stretch out your vowels. You say 'I don't w_a_a_a_nt to do this.' In Russian, you must keep all your vowels the same length. You emphasize by changing your pitch, like this."

She demonstrated, and I began to perceive the essence of that Leningrad intonation I heard all around me. Her voice raised in pitch at pauses she placed in the middle of her statements, and her voice lowered at the end of each statement.

"You can go high like that, Nadezhda Andreevna," I said. "You're a woman."

The next day she carried in an antiquated reel-to-reel tape recorder that must have weighed thirty pounds. I noticed it had been made in Germany. She played tapes of several male voices she had just recorded. All exhibited the same wide range of pitch, although, of course, lower than hers. "You are a man, but you need not be wooden and inflexible," she said.

Dear Children:

A week-long spring break was scheduled in March, 1970, during the time that Natalya was on tour. As part of the program, we Americans in Shevchenko Twenty-Five would visit Moscow. "I will be one of two professors going with you," said my linguaphonics teacher, Nadezhda Andreevna.

On a windy evening, our group gathered in the train station and we boarded 'The Red Arrow Express' for Moscow. The train was wider than any I had seen. An attendant poured us steaming water from a giant 'kipitok' and steeped it in a samovar in her compartment. She served her tea in glasses that were stuck into ornately-decorated pewter holders, and she passed out long chunks of hard sugar.

The train pulled out from the city and gently rocked back-and-forth on its night-long journey to Moscow. At ten o'clock, the attendant came by and unlatched the upper berths. She brought fresh linens to each cabin, and rolled out mattresses. The Russian passengers changed into baggy cotton pants and long-sleeved cotton tops. I stood in the hallway, leaning on the wide window frame. A small Russian girl peered at me from the doorway of her compartment. I smiled, and she quickly slid her compartment door shut.

The train rocked back and forth, ever so gently, ever so sturdily. Every once in a while, I heard the sound of the train's engine accelerating or the sound of the train's whistle as we approached a crossing. I looked out the window. Darkness. A few illuminated windows flashed past, then fewer and fewer, as the train headed out into the darkness, across the countryside, towards Moscow. I saw reflections from the interior lights of the train flickering on the low black-and-white fence-posts outside, as we passed over gradings. It was hard to see anything outside because of the glare from the interior lights. I stepped into the enclosed space between cars. It was refreshingly cold there, after the hot and stuffy cabins, and, in those tiny spaces, it was possible to smoke.

All trains have their particular rhythms, I have learned. Russian trains, with their unusual width and with the unusual spacing of railway ties, have a special rhythm, a sustained staccato, a 'double anapest with its tertiary foot absent,' I said to myself, recalling my classes with Professor Fillipov.

I stood, balancing myself on the sliding gratings joining the cars. The upper slab connected to the rearward car, the lower slab to the forward car.

The next morning we checked in to the Rossiya Hotel, a gigantic slab of concrete and glass across from the Kremlin and Red Square. (This, children, is the hotel where we stayed as you three were being processed for emigration. It was torn down within a year of our stay. I hope that whatever replaces it will be okay; it could hardly be worse.)

The hotel was for sure the ugliest hotel in the world. It clashed with its surroundings in a way that its architects must have intended.

Saint Basil's Cathedral stood, unfairly dwarfed, directly across the street, and from my hotel window, I spotted a series of elevated driveways that, like octopi strangled two ancient churches. I decided that I did not like Moscow nearly as much as Leningrad.

That night the group was scheduled to see the Moscow Circus. Nadezhda encouraged us to go. "It is the largest and best circus in the world. It is famous in your country, as it is all over the world. It performs in a gigantic new building. It is impressive!"

I declined the ticket she offered. "I hate circuses. I had a bad circus experience once which turned me off forever."

"Did you try to run off with a circus?" she asked.

"No, nothing that romantic. When I was about four years old, I saw the Barnum and Bailey Circus at the Saint Paul Auditorium. I sat with my Mother and Father in the front row of the balcony. A woman was swinging on a trapeze over our heads. She wore purple tights, a pink tutu, a white, frilly top, and a smile for the crowd. She yelled at someone down below in the ring, "God damn it, get me off this fucking thing now!' It ruined the circus forever for me."

Nadezhda smiled and put the ticket back into her handbag. "I will help you expand your vocabulary. There's a Russian adjective that describes you – 'yehidny.'"

"I've never heard the word," I said. "But if it describes me, I suppose I should know it, and it's probably a pejorative anyway."

"Well, it could be a pejorative!" she said, smiling. "It has a strange derivation. Centuries ago, when canvas-makers shaped sails for ships, they needed a way to made sure the material was strong. A 'yechidnik' was the person who took a long knife and plied the canvas until he found a weak spot. Then he poked the knife through the weak spot and ripped out as much as he could. You are a 'yechidnik.'"

I laughed. "Thanks a lot!" She took the circus ticket out of her handbag and offered it again. I refused. "Look! Here I am in Moscow, home of the Bolshoi Ballet and Opera, the Mali Theater, the Taganka Theater, the Moscow Philharmonic, the Borodin String Quartet, and you want me to waste a night watching bears in tutus ride a bicycle!"

"We would never get tickets for any of those things!" she said.

I noticed the 'we' in her response. "We could try," I said.

The group left on the Sputnik bus to watch the bears in tutu's ride bicycles. Nadezhda and I walked across Red Square to the Bolshoi Theater. The fat lady with red, round cheeks in the ticket kiosk laughed when I asked if there were any tickets available. "Young man, when Plesetskaya dances in 'Swan Lake,' even her own grandmother would have trouble getting tickets!"

Nadezhda seemed strangely pleased with the lady's response. "I told you so," she said. "Now what do we do, young Professor Higgins?"

"We'll keep trying!" I said. We stood outside the theater as the lucky ticket-holders passed by. Several people stood around the Bolshoi entrance, like me and Nadezhda, politely asking those passing by if they had any extra tickets. There was a special intonation in the uniformly-phrased request. "<u>Yest</u> u vas lishniye billety?' The word 'yest' was raised significantly in pitch, quite unlike what Nadezhda had been teaching me in the laboratory. I tried to imitate this Moscow accent. "<u>Yest</u> u vas lishniye billety?"

"Nyet!" was the response.

"I am sorry I do not," said one woman, about sixty years old, in Russian. "You are from Leningrad, aren't you?"

I grinned as Nadezhda stood next to me.

The woman was puzzled. "Are you not from Leningrad, then?"

"No, I'm from America."

"You have come all the way from America to see Plesetskaya

and you are standing out here in the cold?" She grabbed me by the arm and motioned for Nadezhda to follow. She marched into the theater, directly up to the closed door marked 'Administratsiya.' A sign on the door, like many signs on many doors in the Soviet Union, said 'Do not disturb.' The woman pounded until a secretary opened the door, and she bounded past her with me in tow. Nadezhda followed closely behind. "I demand to see the administrator!" said the woman.

A man in a uniform walked in from an adjacent room. "What is the reason for this disturbance?"

The woman pointed. "This young man came all the way from America to see Plesetskaya dance, and I catch him standing out in the cold. This is an outrage!"

He reached into a drawer, the kind that all Russian bureaucrats have, and handed Nadezhda and me two tickets. We sat in the center box. Plesetskaya danced "Swan Lake." I later learned that theater managers usually save a few tickets, just in case some important personages show up.

The audience broke into wild applause when the orchestra's last note sounded, and the applause gradually turned into a nearly deafening, rhythmic, unison clapping. Plesetskaya made a dozen curtain calls.

Dear Children:

1970 marched on.

I was no longer a celebrity, more just a common and mediocre student. That seemed to be the transformation that had taken place by late March. In addition, my world seemed less bright, without Natalya. It's strange how I missed her; yes, I mean I did miss her and think about her almost daily, but I was not falling apart or in the throes of romantic despair or unable to focus on other things. Did that prove I really didn't love her? Or was it the opposite?

Dearest Kids:

I didn't have a lot of time to brood after Natalya's departure. Other things kept intruding.

The esteemed Professor Fillipov handed back his students' midterm papers the day classes resumed after the break.

"I have made comments in your margins," he told us as he handed out the papers. "I am, in general, pleased with your work."

But on my paper I found just one comment, on the top, in thick blue pencil, "You are all wrong. See me immediately!"

I was shocked. I thought I had been doing so well. Then I was angry. After that, I became miserable. What a rotten bit of luck I'd had! My fiancée was out of town, and now a crusty old Soviet professor had become insistent on making my life even more miserable. I made an appointment with the professor at the end of the class, and went to see him the next day.

His office stood off from the long corridor of the university's oldest building. A young, serious graduate student with gigantic glasses, short hair, and a gray skirt led me into the anteroom. She looked like she hadn't seen sunlight in five years or so, and didn't want to, and she smelled like she didn't believe in deodorants, drycleaners, or regular baths. She sighed, walked into another room, then reappeared and ushered me into the professor's study. The look on her face suggested she was corrupting everything sacred by letting a slob like me into the hallowed inner offices. I adjusted my tie and pushed my pale blue dress shirt into my jeans.

It was a tiny room with bookcases built into all four walls and above the windows and doorway. The desk was piled high with books and manuscripts. The professor's head was barely visible. "Did you bring your paper with you?" he asked from behind his manuscripts. "Sit down! Give it to me!"

I handed it over. The only sound was that of his slow, regular breathing. "Simply stated," he began finally. "You are all wrong. This is trash." He tossed the paper across the table and then stood up and glared at me.

My fists clenched. I had written about one of my favorite poems, and I knew I had done it justice. I had analyzed a section of a long poem by Mikhail Lermontov, the most Romantic of the Russian Romantic poets. The poem was called 'Mtsyri,' a Georgian word meaning 'novice,' and it was about a young boy whose Father leaves him at a mountain monastery while making his way towards battle along the Georgian Military Highway. The Father never returns, and the boy is raised inside the monastery.

Years later, the young novice escapes over the monastery wall and spends a stormy evening climbing down the steep mountain towards the Aragva River. One of my favorite passages in Russian poetry follows. The sun rises, and the novice sees a woman for the first time in his life, a young Georgian woman, carrying a water jug on her head, skipping along the rocks in a stream, carefree and laughing.

At this point in the poem, my favorite part, the poet replicates in verse the light, graceful movements of the woman skipping so lightly over the stones. For my paper, I looked at that stanza within the context of the whole poem, trying to show what techniques, what literary devices, distinguished it from the rest of the text.

"What you have written is, simply stated, trash!" the professor repeated. "It is worse than trash! It is a sin! You, by your dissection – you have killed a living thing! This is not zoology! You do not dissect things – picking at them until they're motionless and dead. You must not take the life out of things!"

"How does one analyze a poem, then, professor?" I asked, trying to sound like I wasn't pissed.

"Exactly the opposite from the way you did!" was the reply. "You twisted it out of shape, until it fit into your categories."

"How does one analyze a poem, then, professor?" I repeated.

"You come to the poem empty and open. It will tell you how it wants to be read. Listen!" He shut his eyes and recited by heart the stanza preceding the one in question, while his hand moved, as if he were conducting the string section of the Leningrad Philharmonic. "Now, what did my voice do?" he demanded afterwards. "What did the poem force it to do?"

I had no idea what he was talking about, but I was determined not to give in to him, not to sound like a fool. "Well, you paused, um, many times. There were breaks in the syntax, and there were some difficult consonant clusters too."

"Right!" He then recited the stanza in question. "Now!" he thundered, "What did my voice do? What was it forced to do?"

"There was no pause in the first line of the stanza, but then-"

"Right!" he roared. "Show me the first line of any other stanza in that blasted poem that does not have a pause! And what happens then?"

I was catching on. "There is a pause at the end of the first line. Let's see, the second line lacks a pause, then in the third line-"

"Right!" was the reply from behind the stack of monographs.

I was on to him. "And then, there is a pause in the penultimate foot of the third line."

"What else about that third line?" the professor demanded.

I was silent. "What else?" I finally asked.

"Look at the meter, for God's sake!" the professor commanded.

I grabbed a piece of paper and mapped out the meter just as the nuns had taught me in grade school. "It's – uh – iambic tetrameter, but there's an extra accented foot at the end of the third line."

"Right!" came the thundering reply. "And tell me about accents in Russian words."

"What do you mean?" Again I was lost. How damned frustrating it was, to feel I was on to something one minute and to be floundering the next.

"Tell me about accents, what you learn the first day of studying Russian, for God's sake!" His forehead turned red, and blue veins stood out on its contours. "Russian words have only one accented syllable, no matter how long they are! Correct? And there are no secondary accents. Correct?"

"Right!" I said. "What difference does that make?"

"Ai, I am wasting my time with an imbecile!" the professor continued. "Look at the length of words and where their accents are! That just might be the organizing principle of the whole poem! He dashed around the desk and tapped my term paper with a stubby pencil, the kind that U.S. carpenters stick behind their ear. "Look at that stanza, for God's sake. Use your eyes! Use your brain!"

I tried. "Let's see, the first line has four words, and the first two words are two syllables long, accented on the last syllable, so – yes, the word boundaries correspond with the metric pattern."

"Right!"

"The pattern is established, then, at the beginning of the stanza, but the pattern is violated in the second half of the first line already. The third word in the line is one syllable long. The fourth word is three syllables long, accent on the third syllable, but the metric pattern forces an accent on the first syllable as well."

"Right! There is tension, then, is there not?"

"Yes, professor, between accents, word boundaries, and the metric pattern."

"Right, but you forget the most important thing, the living component!"

"What's that?" My head was pounding from this rapid succession of victories and failures. Yet I had to be careful. This guy was one of the university's most famous; his works were published in Russia and abroad. If I crossed him, he could get me thrown out of the university.

"Intonation!" he thundered. "You must never overlook intonation! How is the poem read out loud? How must it be read out loud? That is the most important! In Russian poetry, it is all-important!" He walked back to his chair and wiped his forehead. "Write me a paper on this very same stanza. Examine metric pattern, word-length, word boundaries, pauses, phrasing, and intonation. Explain how they all interact, and then discuss your findings in light of the sense or import of the stanza. Two days."

"Excuse me, professor. I didn't hear the last part," I said, but I was afraid that I had heard it exactly.

"You have two days to bring me a suitable paper! Now go away! I have more productive things to do than to coddle foreign students whose heads are steeped in rubbish!"

"Shit!" I said under my breath.

I worked through the night and skipped grammar class the next day, as well as my two daily sessions in the language laboratory with

Nadezhda. I handed in the paper on Wednesday, and the professor handed it back during Friday's class. There was one notation on it, written with the same thick blue pencil: "Meet me at five o'clock this evening. My office. With overcoat and necktie." It sounded queerly formal.

At five o'clock, I was standing in the professor's anteroom. The serious graduate student glared at me – I don't know why. In a minute, the professor stepped out of his office with a worn leather portfolio under his arm. "We will go for a walk," he said. "Then we will go to dinner."

We walked down the long corridor of the Hall of Twelve Colleges, and out through the front door of the university, onto the embankment. "I will show you some things about this city before we eat," he said, the wind nearly taking the words from his mouth. We headed along the embankment and up to the Palace Bridge. The professor walked in very short steps, covering no more than a foot at a time. It was as if he was an angel, floating right above the ground and, like a Russian icon, his feet never touching the ground. We walked across the Palace Bridge.

"We are leaving Vasilievsky Island," huffed the Professor. "It has always been a workers' area and a place of intellectual ferment too, an interesting combination. Your name is 'Vasili' in Russian, you know."

"Yes, Professor," I answered.

"And your Father – he is an important political figure? That is how you came to Leningrad?"

I laughed. "My Father is a blue-collar worker. He repairs water meters for the city."

"Did he finish college?"

"He didn't even finish grade school – it was during the depression."

"Then you have come a long way on your own, and that is good." He waved at the sight before us. "Now, open your ears and eyes, and they will reveal secrets."

"The Admiralty, of course – you know this building," said the Professor. "Read the poets Mandelstam and Akhmatova. And over there is the spire of the Cathedral of Saints Peter and Paul. You must visit that cathedral. It will reveal many secrets to you."

I recalled how Natalya's Mother had promised to take me there, but we hadn't done it yet.

The professor and I crossed the bridge and then jumped on a bus that took us up Nevsky to the Cathedral of Our Lady of Kazan. An oval row of columns extended outward from each side of the cathedral, like two outstretched, curving arms. The professor nodded towards the colonnade. "In winter, which is the only suitable season for this city, the sun appears evenly between all the columns on this side."

He pointed towards two statues standing on pedestals, on opposite sides of the colonnade. "Now, I will show you something few people know. These statues are of the two generals who fought Napoleon. On the left, that is General Kutuzov. He saved Russia although Moscow burned, and won the Battle of Borodino. He was the son of a serf, and he came up from ranks. Notice how he holds a scroll in his outstretched right had. It is elegant."

We walked to the other side of the cathedral, near the second statue. "This is General Barclay De Tolly," he said. "He was not Russian, as you can tell from his name. He lost at the Battle of Austerlitz, but because he was an ally, the czar commanded the Russian sculptors to make a statue of him too. Barclay De Tolly holds a scroll too, you notice, but his is down, close to his side, whereas Kutuzov's scroll is at the end of his outstretched arm.

"Kutuzov is much more impressive," I said.

"Right!" he said automatically, in a tone with which I was now familiar. "You are right as far as you go, but now I will tell you the secret. When you look at the statue of Barclay de Tolly and his scroll, from many angles it will look like he is – how do you say it delicately – fondling himself." He chuckled. "That is your first lesson for the evening. Always be careful of the hidden meaning of things."

We walked out of the embrace of the cathedral's arms, onto the sidewalk on Nevsky. "Now, look across the street, the building which is the 'House of Books,' he said. "It used to be the Singer Sewing Machine Company. They wanted to build a skyscraper, but the city followed Peter's plan and refused. No building can rise higher than the angel at the top of the Cathedral of Saints Peter and Paul. Now look at that round atlas on the top of the building. It is one meter shorter than the angel. The atlas was the emblem for the Singer Company. The illuminated word 'Singer' used to spin around at its equator. Now you must read the poet Nikolai Zabolotsky. No one has done that poet justice yet. Read him and see what he does with that Singer emblem in the poem 'Red Bavaria.' And now, we eat."

We walked a few blocks down Nevsky towards the river, then stepped into a basement-level restaurant under a sign that said 'Kavkazkaya.'

"We have come here for two reasons," said the professor after the maitre d' bowed low and brought us to a table. "This is a Georgian restaurant, and we will pay honor to your love of Lermontov and his 'Mtsyri' poem. Secondly, this basement establishment will remind you of the 'Red Bavaria' bar that used to be on this street, and that is the title of one Zabolotsky poem you must examine. He is one of this century's most interesting poets, but hardly anyone understands him, here or abroad, and many of his works are inaccessible. Even though he was rehabilitated in the 1950s, the mark was never removed from his records."

He drew near and jabbed his finger at my chest. "I want you to study Zabolotsky!" he whispered. "As a foreigner, you can say things that Soviet critics cannot, but you must first learn his city well. The city and its poetry are inseparable."

For appetizers, we ate cold chicken with a spicy sauce. An old waiter in a dinner jacket slapped long flat loaves of hot unleavened Georgian bread across the table. The main course, which arrived after eleven o'clock, I think, consisted of shish-kabob. Tall carafes of white wine and champagne accompanied each course. We made vodka toasts to poets and poems, and then we drank cognac to wash down the vodka. The cognac too came in carafes.

I had never drunk as much alcohol in my life, or remained as lucid. This frail old professor seemed well-adjusted to the art of Georgian-style feasts. "Some of this new poetry, I cannot stomach it," he said over dessert. "It is too free-form. It lacks the tension of classical verse, so to me it is uninteresting. I do not like this Voznesenski person, for example. People rave about his 'Goya' poem. It leaves me empty. Do you know it?"

"Yes, I've read it," I confessed. Luckily, Nadezhda Andreevna, my Linguaphonics professor, had made us memorize the poem.

"And you like it?" the professor asked.

"Yes, I do. As a matter of fact, I like it very much."

"Then, let us hear your understanding of it."

Had I been sober, I might have been too intimidated to try. "In 'Goya,' Voznesenski resurrects his earliest childhood memories, the horrors of World War II. His Father had small prints of Goya's 'Horrors of War,' and hence the name of the poem. 'Ya,' of course, is also the first-person singular pronoun in Russian. The first line of the poem exploits the similarity, 'Ya – Goya.'"

"I know all that!" said the professor, downing his cognac. "It is interesting, but too simplistic!"

"There's more," I said. "The poem includes many words with 'g' sounds, 'gore' ('grief'), 'golod' ('hunger'), 'goly' ('naked'). So we see that the poet is sounding out the word 'Goya.'"

"Ah, it is still flat. Flat! It needs more tension!"

"There is more," I said, emboldened by the cognac and vodka. "You see, in the first half of the poem, the predominant sounds are 'ya' and 'go.' In the second half of the poem, there's a cascade of consonant clusters. Listen!" I recited parts of the poem. "You see, professor?" I asked, when I had finished. "The poet spells out his own name too. There's a third level to the poem then – 'Ya,' 'Goya,' and 'Voznesenski!'"

"Right!" proclaimed the professor. "I must remember to look for the hidden meaning! And you – ai, you must turn your talents and energy to Zabolotsky" He leaned in closer and whispered again. "We can discuss things by mail. I will give you an address where envelopes are dispatched immediately, as opposed to the usual way of letting them pile up until a shovel is required."

I laughed.

The professor leaned forward again in his chair, his head and hands close to the table, as if he was making a move in chess. There was silence. The evening had crested, it was clear. And then I remembered the bridges! All the bridges spanning the Neva River lifted at night; you were stuck until morning on whatever island you were on when the bridges went up. And I didn't know what time the subway system shut down.

I was determined to tell the professor this. I leaned back in my chair, and then all of a sudden my head started spinning. "Excuse me one moment Professor Fippilov – I mean, Professor Fillipov," I said. I pushed my chair back. It took a whole chain of decisions and execution of those decisions to manage just standing up, and I walked through a series of rooms towards the men's rest room.

I didn't have to go to the bathroom. All the Georgian bread I consumed had soaked up the liquids in me, but a strange phenomenon had come over me at the table, something that had never happened to me before: My 'vertical hold' went out. Reality blinked before me like on an out-of-tune Soviet television. First, the table stood on top of the professor, then things returned to their normal positions, a black line separating the two images. 'I've never drunk this much before! I might throw up,' I said to myself. 'I have to make it to the men's room,' I told myself, in that state of super sobriety that comes only to those who are flat-ass drunk.

The walls and floor of the restaurant commenced dipping at sickening, precarious angles, but I made it. I sat down on a toilet in the men's room – rather, I stooped down over a toilet – it was the old-fashioned Russian kind, low to the ground, with metal foot rests. I sat in the uncomfortable position for several minutes. I waited to start throwing up, and I felt those first, repulsive signs – the watering of the throat, tightening in the stomach. I noted that someone was throwing up in another stall, as if we would soon be playing a duet. But with me, nothing happened. I wended my way back to the professor.

Again, the room dipped and swayed. I was not prepared for what I saw once I found my way back to the table. The professor sat slumped in his chair, sound asleep, with a placid smile pasted across his lower face. His rimless, gold-framed glasses hung precariously off one ear.

I had to take charge. I asked the waiter to order a cab. In a few minutes, surprisingly, one appeared. I roused the professor into semi-consciousness, and steered him up the steps to the waiting cab. "Take this man home please," I told the cabby.

"Where does he live?" the driver asked gruffly, an unlit cigarette glued to his lower lip.

"Professor, where do you live?" I asked. It looked like he hadn't heard and so I said it again, this time nearly shouting. "Where do you live? Your address?"

"Right!" said the professor.

"Give me your card, please, professor!" I asked, and repeated it louder when he didn't answer.

He stretched back in the seat, fumbled in his coat pocket, and handed me his wallet. I took out a card, put the wallet back into the professor's pocket, and handed the card to the driver. "Right!" said the driver, and the cab spun off into the night.

The bridges were no doubt up already. I walked up Nevsky, wondering when I was going to throw up, and I made it into the long passageway leading to the subway. I rode the long escalator down into the maze of tunnels and passageways that connect the lines at the 'Gostinny Dvor' Station.

A uniformed matron stared suspiciously at me as I stepped off the escalator. She was one of the numberless stern-looking ladies who stood at the bottom of all of those incredibly steep and long subway escalators. Their main job seemed to be keeping drunks out of the system, removing the possibility of them falling onto the tracks or of passing out and knocking someone else onto the tracks – I had heard such stories. This lady glared, but her eyes remained glued on the escalators. She did not call out after me. A few second later, I heard her call out for a guard to take another passenger off to the drunk tank.

I sat down in the car, it soon became clear that someone had vomited. It was not a pleasant aroma at all, in a city that cries out for clean air, and this smell was smelled by me. a passenger who was nearly ready to vomit.

I somehow made it back to the dorm and climbed through a first-floor window although I remember none of it. I woke up at ten-thirty the next evening wondering who had put a sledge hammer to my head.

Dear Children:

The Saturday after my dinner with the Professor, I met Natalya's Mother at the main entrance of the Peter and Paul Fortress. "It is sunny and cool!" her Mother said as she met me at the door. "Perfect for our visit." She grinned, almost as if embarrassed, as she pushed against the wind, her right hand holding her hat to her head. The wind calmed as soon as we passed through the walls into the fortress proper. "My daughter is quite taken with you," she said.

"And I with her."

"It is good for her. She's always been a serious girl – brooding, reading. She was born quiet. She did not cry. She moved very little even as a baby, even when I unwrapped her. She has always been so inward – so 'brooding' – I think that is the word. But even though she is so inward, she observes everything around her. She is highly sensitive. She misses nothing. Others have not appreciated that sensitivity or have not liked that inwardness. You must bring her out of that inwardness."

She turned her attention to the fortress. "Look, the contours of the walls follow the contours of the city," she said. "These walls were built in 1703, the first structure in the city. Dostoevsky and Lenin were in prison, over there," she said, pointing to the left. "We will ignore the usual boring prison tour and go directly to the cathedral. That is what I must show you!"

We joined the end of a long line threading its way towards the church entrance although, as usual, I noticed groups of foreigners allowed to enter at the head of the line. "Guests first!" she said.

The line hardly moved as we spoke, and sometimes because of a busload or two of tourists, we moved backwards.

"The church was built by Tresini from 1712 to 1732," Natalya's Mother said. "The spire – see up there, with the angel on top – it is the tallest point in the city. The angel does not hold out a cross, as most people think – rather, he is holding onto the cross. The cross, not the angel, is anchored to the spire. That is significant, I think."

Our line of compliant Russian citizens barely moved. The wind was now blasting over the fortress walls and was cutting into my face. My eyes watered. How could anyone have built a city here, I wondered? Even in the spring! How many people had died in building it?

"All Sankt Peterburg churches performed a special function," she said. "Princes and princesses were baptized in Saint Isaac's Cathedral. They were married at our Lady of Kazan Cathedral, and they were buried here, in the Cathedral of Saints Peter and Paul. It was the first church in the city. It is appropriate, then, that the czars and czarinas should be buried here."

We peered ahead at the slender spire rising from the building. "From here the church looks entirely baroque," I said. "I see no Russian features. But, you know, it somehow seems Russian anyway."

"Ah, now you are getting towards the heart – at the heart of this city!" said Inna, "Wait until we get inside!"

We finally made it into the Cathedral. Stern ladies in gray dresses and green stockings held onto the massive doors. "Stand back!" they commanded the Russians, folding their arms at their chests. "Do not push! Foreign guests first! There must be order here!"

Inna smiled. "'Order' is a favorite word in this country, Bill. You will hear it everywhere. What is the 'order' to follow in accomplishing this? What is the 'order' for reserving this section or performing this operation? You will hear that word and its opposite – 'disorder' – all over the country. My husband? 'Order' should be his middle name." She laughed for a second at her own joke.

Finally we walked into the main part of the cathedral, barely squeezing through the narrow slit of the door before an onslaught of Japanese tourists rushed by. "Bystro, bystro!" the door-ladies yelled at the tourists, shooing them in through the passageway. People crammed the church's interior, huddling in groups clustered around guides waving their pointers. Russian pupils clung to their teachers, occasionally sneaking a peek at the foreigners huddling in other groups. When they discovered a particularly unusual specimen, they jabbed their comrades for a look too.

We maneuvered ourselves forward in the crush of pushing and shoving bodies, but it was nearly hopeless. Groups located in the front of the church were pushing their way to the back, and groups located in the rear of the church were trying to push forward. "Such disorder!" Inna said, almost with pride. "They have never devised a way to organize the crowds in here, in the very heart of the city. That is significant!"

Wrought iron railings penned the crowds into the central part of the cathedral. Massive chunks of marble, headstones for the Romanovs, stood on the other side of those railings. "Those headstones are solid marble!" said Inna. "The czars and czarinas are buried underneath the floor, under the markers. All the rulers, from Peter the Great through Alexander the Third, are buried in here."

She bent up to whisper in my ear. "They say 'all the czars since Peter,' but Nicholas the Second is not buried here. And under the bell tower, Peter the Great's son is buried. Peter had him killed for participating in the palace uprising, you know."

She maneuvered through the crowd with a minimum of shoving, without using her elbows or arms. I had to push and shove hard to keep up with her. "Just follow the flow of the current," she advised. "And look for the breaks in the stream. Stay with me, and we will visit the marker of each czar and czarina in chronological order. It will take extra time, but it is, as we might say, the proper <u>order</u>."

Our maneuvers eventually brought us to the front of the church, to the carved, wooden, gold-leafed iconostasis that blocked off a view of the holy altar from the congregation. The elaborately sculpted, gilded tip of the iconostasis poked into the narrow steeple opening. Statues and paintings adorned all its multi-shaped crevices.

"Bill, look!" said Inna, her face shining bright. "This is Baroque, Lutheran, Roman Catholic, Russian Orthodox! Here it is! Harmony in disharmony! Combination of the un-combinable. Look! Baroque to the extreme! This is the heart of the city!"

It was the heart of the city, and for a moment, I stood in awe as my mind turned away momentarily from thoughts of Natalya. I was at the heart of it. My heart was with <u>its</u> heart then, I think.

All the hassle and pushing and all the dreary parts of the day for someone leading a dreary life – it was all well worth it, just to feel the beating of the heart of that city.

My Dear children:

Lacking Natalya in my life, my life became boring. Things that used to grip me now bugged me. Maybe that magical moment inside the Cathedral of Saints Peter and Paul was so special because it marked the end of my enchantment with the city.

Nothing was going right. Tatiana Ivanovna, my kindly old translation professor, had given up on me. She took my 'withdrawal,' as she called it, personally. "Maybe I fail as a teacher sometimes in my old age, but please, let us learn the art of translation!" she begged just that day as I stumbled through the end of Turgenev's <u>Fathers and Sons</u>.

"Bazarov and Odintsova – it is their last meeting!" she pleaded. "He is dying of typhus! And cold Odintsova – she caresses him with her hand in a glove."

Inna shook her head, as if she knew both of them personally. "Such an important, telling moment in the story, one of the best in all Russian literature. Can not <u>one</u> of you do it justice?"

And Nadezhda and Linguaphonics, the language laboratory and the spectroscope? "Bill, you become impatient with me at the same time that your own progress slows," she said. "You fell asleep yesterday during class. What is the matter? Are you sick? Have you met someone?"

"I've met someone," I said in my haze. We were sitting in the darkened laboratory, and the spectroscope itself was dark and dead. The machine was not plugged in; its cord sat lazily coiled on the table.

"Is she beautiful?" she asked.

"Yes," I said.

"Is she young?"

"Yes."

I could see her eyes water. "I am happy for you," she said, pushing the lever that turned off the clunky tape recorder that was hissing in the background.

"Thank you for your good wishes, Nadezhda Andreevna," I said. "I'm not happy for myself."

"Well then!" she said, smiling. "Let us improve your Russian so you two can communicate better!" The spectroscope flashed on, but she terminated the lesson early that afternoon. She had an appointment, she said.

I felt like a heel, as if I had broken an unspoken promise to her, which I had.

And Professor Fillipov had become crankier and more demanding in his old age. "You should stick to Fofanov, a third-rate poet whom no one reads!" he told me during one session, in front of the other students. "Alexander Blok is too much for you! You are certainly no match for Mayakovsky either!"

"I'm sorry, professor." It was all I could think of to say.

"Right! You are very sorry! So am I! How much time I have wasted with you? For nothing!"

"I'll try harder, professor."

"You cannot even express yourself properly in written Russian. How can you hope to write valid criticism? In <u>English</u>? That is impossible!"

"How are you doing at the university?" Inna repeated her question at dinner, a look of concern on her face. "My, look at you! How thin you have become. What is wrong? You have changed your mind about my daughter?"

"No, not at all."

"Well, then, what is it?"

I scrambled for an answer to a question I did not know how to answer, even though it was a question I had asked myself a number of times, each time without an answer appearing. "I'm tired, I guess. Just tired. I've been living at a fast pace, burning up my stores of energy, ever since I came here –that's why I've lost weight. I have literally burnt it up. I have some problems at the university. It's demanding work. I have to write a long paper on Nikolai Zabolotsky. The professor complains about my syntax and punctuation, not just the content."

"Bring your paper here, and I will help you," she said. "We will have early dinners after your classes and then we will work. Surely you cannot fail your university program!"

I met her and her husband for dinner three days later. After we had eaten, mostly in silence except for polite verbiage that the setting required. "Please pass me the salt dish, Bill," said Pyotor. This engendered a long dialog on Inna's cooking that had obviously been voiced before and was played out for my entertainment or to conceal what we could not conceal – that not one of us knew what to say.

Pyotor replaced his goose-necked lamp on the edge of the table, then sat down and pulled out his papyrosy. "We have not had our discussion, Bill. Give me one of your cigarettes and take this papyrosa." We lit up, he striking his match-stick in the usual Russian way, holding the match and the box with its scratched flint surface in one hand while cupping his other hand around the cigarette. I could not master the trick and didn't embarrass myself by trying in front of him. He puffed on his cigarette, then took it out of his mouth and studied it. "My work in Moscow was connected with the discussion we did not have. Unpleasant business. In the United States, I understand, people oppose the war. How can that be?"

"And how can it be that no one here opposes anything the government does?" I asked. Was I in for a long diatribe on the USA that could sour our personal relations?

Pyotor continued. "As you know from your press, I am sure, we do not allow opposition here. People can grumble to themselves, if they want, but that is as far as it goes."

"In the United States, people try to change government policy. When they are unable to change it, they resist it."

"By wearing dirty clothes and looking like apes?" he asked.

"I suppose that's part of the process of opposition. In the beginning it was hippies – and students, but the antiwar movement has spread to the middle class now. Many people, in regular clothes, are opposed to the war now too."

"And your government tolerates these riots and strikes and parades?"

"Sometimes, to a limit. You have heard about Kent State?"

"Of course! We all have! Yevtushenko wrote a poem about it, and it was on the front page of 'Pravda' a day or two after the incident. Let me ask a different question. Why do some Americans <u>not</u> oppose the war in Vietnam?"

"They say that if you don't stop Communism today in Viet Nam, it'll be in California tomorrow."

"Hah!" he cried out. "Inna, did you hear that! They must stop Communism today in Viet Nam, or it will be in California tomorrow. It is hilarious! We hear that very same thing here, but to the opposite! Two years ago, it was Czechoslovakia; we had to stop capitalism, before it got to Kiev! Inna, see what sad shape the world is in today!"

Then his face turned serious. "But your government should be more careful. Anarchy is dangerous. It serves no one. When I look at our newscasts and read our papers about your country, I think of Russia under Nicholas the Second, or under Kerensky, when government – and order – was disintegrating. It is dangerous. It is playing with fire to let those young people loose like that."

"Yes, no one can trust those young people!" It was my turn to laugh. "You know, in America, we hear that young people are innocent dupes of the Communists, who corrupt their minds and hearts. And here, your young people are innocent dupes of the capitalists, who corrupt their minds and hearts. See what sad shape the world is in today!"

"The world is indeed in sad shape today," said Pyotor. "But laws are what provide order. A government must have laws, and people must be made to follow them." He gestured towards his bookcases and journals. "A government must command respect from its people, or there is chaos – the abyss, cavemen rubbing sticks together to make fire. There must be order."

"Order – 'poryadok'!" Inna said. "I told you that you would hear that word much. Bill, I want you to meet Mister 'Poryadok' himself!"

That dinner was one bright light in an otherwise dark and smoky blackness that had become my life. I made it through those days in a mechanical sort of way; my spirit and all my heart were elsewhere. Most of the time, I just missed Natalya and longed for her, and other times I wondered if it was all over between us – it had been a bubble of illusion that had burst when exposed to colder air. Time barely passed.

On Thursday evening I brought my miserable research paper, into which I put very little effort or spirit but an awful lot of time, to Natalya's Mother for editing. Inna put on her thick, brown-framed glasses which vanity normally forbade her to wear. The white, opaque edges of her thick lenses stuck out from both sides of the frame. "American handwriting!" she said. "It is so strange! We write more straight up-and-down, our letters not connected this way."

"It's hard for you to read, Inna Ivanovna?"

"Sometimes." She took off her glasses, blew on each lens, and wiped them with the tip of her apron. A speckled film covered the lenses, suggesting she had fried something for dinner that evening in the communal kitchen. "There!" she said, putting her glasses back on and smoothing down her hair. "When you write a word in Russian with a series of letters like 'p,' 't,' and 'sh,' it can look like this. It is very confusing to see which is what letter." She drew a series of garlands and handed the paper across the table to me. "So," she continued, grabbing her glasses by the temples and adjusting them on her nose, "We add lines like this over the p's and the m's and the t's and under the sh's, like this. Now you can tell the letters apart, yes?"

Her blue pencil lines speckled the first page of my composition book. "See, now it is more legible." She turned over the page and read, holding her glasses on her face with her left hand. She shook her head with bewilderment, and smiled, as if trying to hold back the laugh that would inevitably follow. "Do you have comma's in English?"

"Why, of course we do, Inna Ivanovna!"

She bit her lip, then laughed. "Do you know when to use them in English?"

It was my turn to smile. "No one knows when to use commas in English. There used to be fixed rules, the ones I learned in grade school, but now they've abandoned the rules and they say that a comma belongs where you would take a breath if you were reading the sentence out loud. I follow the old rules."

She shook her head, still smiling. "In Russian we have strict rules, but not like yours, obviously. From my perspective, I would say that you put commas where they are not needed, and you leave them out where they are needed. Look!" She took a piece of scratch paper from a stack on the table and wrote something, then passed it across the table to me. "You need a comma there, Bill." she said.

I read what she had written: "I know, that she will wait for you." For a moment I didn't know why she had such an earnest expression on her face. I looked at her lines of cursive again, and this time I read it for content.

"She took back the paper and wrote, "Her moods come, from the deep feelings she has for you. She is afraid."

When it was my turn next, I wrote, "I will wait for her. I hope she waits for me. I will cope with her moods." I passed the paper back across the table. "I'm not sure about where the commas go," I said. "But I'm sure about what I wrote."

Inna wiped her eyes, then folded the paper and stuck it into her apron pocket. She smiled valiantly. "And now for style, William. You write simply and directly, using short sentences – that is good. The damage can be repaired."

We worked until ten-thirty. She left to make tea while I studied her corrections, and she returned with two glasses in tarnished silver holders, and with a platter of rolls and malina jam. "Eat!" she commanded. "You are too thin. You know, the Russian words for 'thin' and 'evil' are not that far apart!"

"And Shakespeare's Julius Caesar said 'Let me have men about me who are fat,'" I added, coating my roll with the sticky jam.

"I am glad you came," she said. "Pyotor Pavlovich was called back to Moscow again, on the same dirty business."

There was a crash behind the wall lined with bookcases. "Excuse me," she said. "It is Pyotor Pavlovich's Mother."

Inna hurried out of the room. I heard shouting but I could not make out the words. Inna returned, red in the face, adjusting her housedress and apron. "I am sorry. Pyotor Pavlovich's Mother wants to meet you. She is old and feeble and her mind is not right. Will you come and meet her? It will only take a moment, and it will quiet her down."

"Of course!" I said. "I have a Grandfather, eighty-six years old. He's feeble too."

We walked into a tiny room jammed with furniture and possessions. "Ekaterina Petrovna! You have a guest!" Inna screamed right into the old lady's ear.

Ekaterina Petrovna sat dwarfed in the middle of a large, overstuffed chair. She suddenly stiffened her arms against the sides of the chair and pushed her body forward and upward until she was standing. Then she took three halting steps towards a round table, picking up a wooden rectangle about a six inches wide and twelve inches long. She turned and stepped towards me, her jaw hanging open, the wooden rectangle shaking and trembling before her. "Look!" she commanded. "Icon! Virgin Mother!"

Inna's face turned a dark red. She steered the old woman back to her armchair, guiding her by tugging at the tip of the icon. "We know, Ekaterina Petrovna, we know!" Inna said. She managed to maneuver the old woman back to the chair and turn her around, so that she stood facing me. Inna pushed at the old woman's stomach and jabbed at her sides, but Grandma refused to sit down.

"Natalya is baptized!" shouted the old lady in a hollow voice. "She is a Christian! I baptized her myself, right in the Neva!" Her bony left arm gestured towards the window. With that pronouncement, the old lady's body relaxed and Inna was able to seat her. Then Grandma took out her dentures, placed them on the table, closed her eyes, and fell fast asleep. The conversation was clearly over. Ekaterina Petrovna had spoken her piece.

Inna patted the old woman on her nearly-bald head and put the icon back on the table. Back in the sitting room, Inna apologized for the 'disturbing scene.'

"There's no need for an apology, Inna Ivanovna. If you'd really like a scene, you must meet my Grandfather when he's been drinking."

She smiled, then bit her lip. "Are you baptized?" she asked suddenly.

"Yes. I was baptized, they tell me, at Saint Paul Cathedral, in 1945, the year I was born."

"Did you have religious instruction?"

"Too much!" I said. "I had a solid Catholic education – eight years of grade school with nuns, which I liked, and four years of Catholic military high school with Christian Brothers, which I hated."

"No Jesuits?" she asked.

"No Jesuits," I said.

"Good!" she said, with some relief. "The word 'Jesuit' is a pejorative here."

I laughed, "I know. It is in many places."

"Are you a believer?" she asked suddenly.

The question made me squirm, like it always does. "I believe in something – I don't know what. I believe that people are rewarded and punished for what they do, somewhere, some way."

"That is exactly what I believe," she replied. "Pyotor Pavlovich would like to see all the rewarding and punishing in this life!" Her smile suddenly dissipated. "Do you love my daughter?"

"Yes, I love her."

"If you love one-another – as I love Pyotor Pavlovich – things can work out. What worries me is that you two are so infatuated. It is not healthy. It is such a strong attraction, it can lead to strong, long-lasting, genuine love, or it can lead to disaster."

"I know," I said, and I only needed to recall the despair that had followed me around the past three days.

"I never thought my daughter was capable of it," she said. "You know, I never believed she would marry – such a solitary, brooding girl she always was!" She removed her glasses. "Be kind and patient with her. After you left the apartment the last time, she cried most of the night – I heard her through the walls. She loves you. Be kind and understanding with her. She does not make friends easily."

I left that night feeling better than I had in a week. Being with Natalya's Mother helped keep the fire in my heart burning. Besides, the woman had been kind and endearing in her own right. Further, it was encouraging to be around her. Here was a woman, Natalya's flesh and blood, and she had a husband and a marriage filled with love and respect, and a life. Natalya and I could do it too, I told myself over as I headed back to the dorm. It was a cold night, with few people out. I decided to walk across the bridge. I pulled my hat down and my scarf up.

In Leningrad, my navy P-Coat soon hung from my shoulders – I'd lost 25 pounds. I traded it with another American for a trench coat that fit but was too short in the sleeves. Natalya's Mother was appalled at the way it looked. She took it, let out the hems for the arms, and carefully sewed in a new lining for the insides of the sleeves.

"To protect and to keep you," she said. "Go in peace and in love!" She kissed me on the cheek.

That was the last time I saw her.

Dear Children:

The fairy tale ended. This departure from my normal, boring, American life was over.

The plane that took me back to the United States was brightly painted and the flight attendants smiled; this was not the Soviet Union.

And I missed it. I recall rather absent-mindedly opening my parents' refrigerator a week or so after my return. I saw apples and oranges and lettuce and milk and eggs and meat and whatever.

I started to shake; I hadn't seen such a variety of food in one place for a very long time. And fruit? I had nearly forgotten what it was.

I recalled those winter days when one thin slice of cucumber tasted sweeter and better than any fruit of any size.

Dear Young Adults:

Do not follow my example when it comes to education.

When I got back from Leningrad State University in 1970, I needed to get credit from the University of Minnesota for my work there, so I walked to the records office in Morrill Hall, off the main quadrangle of the East Campus of the University of Minnesota. The clerk, I remember, wore yellow polyester pedal-pushers and black cats-eye glasses. She looked over my prized Leningrad 'Foreign Student Program Certificate of Completion,' and she held it away from her face, by one finger. "What's all this hieroglyphics?" she asked.

"It's a certificate of completion," I said.

"From what? From where? Where does it show your hours, your credits, your subjects?"

"It's from Leningrad State University. I'm sorry, but this is what they give you. It doesn't show any of the things you asked for, Ma'am."

She shook her head. "Where's your transcript from this place?"

"They don't have transcripts."

"I need an official copy of your transcript!"

"I'm sorry," I said, finding myself apologizing for the Soviet Union, feeling sorry for its supposed backwardness. "They don't have copy machines."

"Well, you can't come in here waving one piece of paper and expect to get university credits for it! You need at least two pieces of paper!"

So I went back to my apartment and dug through the rubble still cluttering the bottom of my suitcase. I found my 'Leningrad Transportation Pass.' It was a card, about two-by-four inches and it said, in Russian, of course, 'Good for Transport on Subway, Bus, Trolleybus, and Streetcar.' Two official-looking red stripes ran diagonally across the card, and black letters on the lower left-hand corner said 'March 1970.'

I presented my streetcar pass to the lady with the cats-eye glasses in Morrill Hall the next day. She slapped it faced down on a glass plate on a machine that flashed a bright green light and then spit out a fuzzy, thin brown paper with faint blue letters.

I got my university quarter credits by virtue of the streetcar pass. I framed the pass along with my Certificate of Completion.

I graduated from the University of Minnesota in the spring of 1971, with a major in Russian, and it was time to think of graduate school. There was no question about it – my field of study would be Russian, even though so many warned me that there were few jobs available, particularly for a non-native speaker who wanted to teach language and literature. I ignored the well-meaning advice, believing that fate would take good care of me.

Russian it had to be. I knew it. I just knew it. Life would take care of me. I ignored the people who warned me how I wouldn't be able to use my education to get a job.

Dear Alex, Anna, and Katya:

It was spring of 1971. I was all set to go back to graduate school in Russian studies at the University of Hawaii, and I was going to be their first graduate student. Then I got a phone call from Professor George Mooney from the University of Michigan. "Why haven't you accepted our scholarship offer?" he asked.

"It wouldn't be enough to live on," I said politely. "And I have a full scholarship, including living expenses, at the University of Hawaii."

"That place has no reputation at all in the field," he said. "It's a new department, and our is well-established as one of the best, if not the best. What if we double our offer?"

"I'll have to think about it," I said, leaning on my parents' refrigerator.

"I need your answer now."

I had never needed to make such an important decision so fast,

I sometimes wonder how my life have ended up, had I gone to the University of Hawaii. Maybe I would have stayed in Hawaii after getting my Master's Degree. Maybe I'd be their next Russian teacher, because the present one was nearing retirement age.

Would I have somehow adopted you three Russian children? It is difficult sometimes to distinguish sometimes between choices freely made and that which is preordained.

Dear Anna, Katya, and Alex:

Your Papa was now a graduate student at the University of Michigan, with Slavic Languages and Literature as his field of study.

It was a strange place. Professor Danilova was into some Indian guru named Mahara Ji or something, and she practiced swallowing her tongue and reciting mantras in her office, sometimes with students present.

She lived in some sphere other than earth, I think. If her literature class was supposed to start at nine and go until ten-thirty, she might show up at nine-forty-five and go until noon. She was on my dissertation committee and she missed my first meeting because she was having a personal vision of Jesus Christ in her office, and it wasn't even during regular office hours.

There was Mark Kirkonen, whom I picked as my dissertation adviser, even though he wasn't very popular in the department. He was a plain and brilliant Finn from Michigan's Upper Peninsula, and he liked to play Yukor. He could translate a poem from Russian to English like nobody, but his plaid shirts made him an outsider, as did his demeanor and his Yukor and his preference for large quantities of beer.

There was Professor Waterman, who taught Polish literature and who did most of his classes by tutorial. He was a quiet, gay man who was brilliant and drank way too much way too often, right in his office even, and he had the face and nose to prove it. Gradually, all the athletic team members found out they could get three easy 'language and culture' credits, taking Polish literature by tutorial. When these students checked into the department office, the secretary handed them a blank piece of paper and said, "Here, sign this."

She took the signed papers home, and her son had his bedroom walls lined with pictures of Wolverine athletes, each 'autographed' by a slip of paper attached to the photo.

I am sure that Professor Waterman engaged in no improprieties. He was much too shy for that. Looking at young men was probably all he wanted, or needed.

The months passed, and I waited, and dreaded, the arrival of summer. Would Natalya even remember me? To return to Leningrad, I had organized a student summer study tour to the Soviet Union, for the University of Minnesota.

Gradually, letters from Natalya tapered off. I didn't know why. Was she forgetting about me? Had the censors gotten busier? Was someone intercepting her letters? Was she receiving my letters?

Those were the questions that a person had to ask about the Soviet Union in the 1970's.

I arranged to meet my students in Frankfurt for our train ride into Russia. I had left the U.S. a month earlier with my University salary and Eurail Pass, and I spent the time in the Danish hinterlands of Jutland with those crazy and wonderful Danes who had occupied much of the dormitory in Leningrad the year before. (The Soviets liked to put all the capitalists in one dormitory; it cut down on surveillance costs.) I was in a remote part of Denmark, on the dunes, and I didn't keep up with the news.

1971 was the summer of the Leningrad sky-jackers' case. Some Jewish dissidents from Leningrad had hijacked a plane to Denmark. The hijackers were returned to Leningrad and were sentenced to death. There was an outcry in the West over the sentence, and the Soviet Court reversed its decision.

I didn't know this. I also didn't know that Natalya Makarova had just defected from Leningrad's Kirov Ballet, and that the government was cracking down hard on contacts between capitalists and Soviet citizens, particularly in the cultural spheres.

Our study group visited Moscow, then Leningrad. Only a few students in the group knew why I had arranged this study tour. And now, in Leningrad, on that day, or at least on the next day, I would see Natalya. She would be wearing the engagement ring that Gretta, one of my best Danish friends, had snuck into Leningrad for me during the winter. I was so excited or nervous or whatever – I had trouble signing my name, trouble breathing even. What would transpire? What would it be for me to see her again, those first critical seconds? What would it be like for her?

"These are the rooms for your students," said the hotel clerk as we filed into the Leningradskaya Hotel. "You can divide them up as you want. Just make sure that there are no males and females staying together." This was standard procedure for Soviet hotels.

Then the clerk handed me a key. "This is <u>your</u> room."

This was not at all a standard procedure, and it set me to wondering. Then I relaxed. 'Great, I'm getting a special room,' I thought. 'Maybe it's a suite.'

I helped my students cram their luggage into the tiny, jerky elevators that took forever, and then I went to my room. I was disappointed. It was an ordinary Soviet hotel room, with a functional but unbeautiful bathroom – the typical Soviet kind, where the whole room was tiled, where the shower sprout hung high in a corner, where a drain in the center of the floor caught the water. In the main room stood a tiny, sagging cot, a small desk made out of Soviet fake wood, the kind that made 'engineered' wood back home look like real wood. On the desk was a gooseneck lamp without, naturally, a light bulb and without an on/off switch. There was no doubt that the burnt-out light bulb part was the result of a common Soviet trick. Workers brought their burnt-out bulbs from home to their office or factory, and they slid the good bulbs into their net bags, after screwing in their burnt-out bulbs. Light bulbs with a low intensity were hard to get. Most rooms scorched my eyeballs.

The room phone rang. "Hello, William!" said a man in Russian. "This is Boris."

Boris? I didn't remember any Boris, and besides, no one in Leningrad but Natalya and her family knew when I was returning or where I was staying. Or, that is, anyone who had been reading Natalya's mail would know. I got nervous. I couldn't lie. "I'm sorry. I don't remember you."

"No problem!" he said. "I will come to your room and you will recognize me immediately."

I hung up the phone. Within seconds, there was a knock on my door. It was Boris, a middle-aged man with a puffy face. He shut the door softly behind him and sat down in the tiny chair next to the desk, motioning me to sit at the edge of the bed. "Natalya is not here," he said.

"What?" I felt myself growing numb, starting at the edges and spreading inward, where it ran into a tall wall of panic.

"She is in Sochi, in a tuberculosis asylum."

"She's sick?" Worry now replaced numbness.

"No," Boris said, as if fatigued. "She is out of the city. You cannot see her."

"Why?" I demanded.

Boris adjusted himself on the tiny chair, and then he leaned in towards me. "It is not a good time. You must not see her or try to contact her family. Just go about your business of being an American group leader, and there will be no unpleasant consequences."

"What kind of consequences?"

He shrugged, stood up, and left my room. I was at first numbed but angry and defiant and sad and remorseful, all together.

Why the ruse of his calling me on the phone? Oh, of course! That was easy to figure out. He didn't want to blow his cover to anyone else in the hotel; I had opened my room door for him; he didn't have to kick it in or announce his arrival. No one would know he was KGB if, in fact, he was KGB or just someone who knew their tricks.

Numbness. Memory. I was shutting down. I went along with my students on their introductory bus tour of the city. They were restless. They wanted to get off the stuffy bus filled with American tourists, and meet Russians. They hadn't come all the way to Russia to meet Americans. They could have done that at home. I smelled a rebellion.

Me? I didn't know who I was or what I was, but I realized I had a job to do. It would serve no good purpose to do my job poorly. Perhaps things would calm down, even during that five-day visit, or maybe in a few weeks or a month – I'd figure out a way to get back, and then I could meet up with Natalya.

I busied myself, helping the other American students as much as I could. When they managed to meet Russians, I translated for them. Despite the anesthesia that coursed through my veins, despite the freezing of my memory, thoughts of Natalya rarely left me. They might have been blurry, but they were there.

The tour bus drove right by Natalya's parents' apartment, and the driver took the students to the places and monuments I had already seen many times – the Fortress of Saints Peter and Paul, which I had visited with Natalya's Mother, the Hermitage, the Russian Museum.

How different the city was this time. I had become a temporary guest of that strange 'Potomkin Village,' that country within a country, that part of the Soviet Union that was open to tourists. It was an unreal place, a place without a sense of place. For me, it was a cruel exile.

"What is a 'Potomkin Village?" You might ask. The phrase is used a lot in reference to Russia and the Soviet Union. Here goes.

Catherine the Great was convinced that her 'empire,' after she had conquered parts of Crimea, would be the messianic 'Third Rome' of religious belief. She even had coins minted with the bust of the last emperor of Byzantium (Emperor of the 'Second Rome') on one side, and a bust of her son, Constantin (Future Emperor of the 'Third Rome') on the other side.

This was all so important to her that she sent Potomkin, her best lover, down to the Crimea, to construct her new empire. Well, Potomkin spent most of his time doing to Crimean women what he had been doing to Catherine the Great back in Saint Peterburg.

She wrote to let him know she was coming down to check on all the progress about which he had written in glowing detail.

In panic, probably, Potomkin had a bunch of 'fake' villages built. They might look like a town, but they were really more like a movie set – two dimensional, unreal.

So that's a Potomkin Village, and the tourist spots of Leningrad on the soviet itinerary comprised such a village. From a distance, it looked great. Don't look for any depth.

What if I accidentally ran into Natalya? I could hang around the symphony hall. No, that Boris guy had said that Natalya was out of the city. There would be no encounters, accidentally or otherwise. She was lost to me. I was lost. Lost. Lost. Lost.

I was lost.

I peered through bus windows and saw no one I knew. Natalya was cut off from me, certainly. Russian students were cut off from me too – I don't know why. I walked up to them and they turned away or passed by, as if I was some madman walking the streets. I took an afternoon off and wandered around the university. Even the cheek-pinching coat-check lady acted as if she didn't know me, but I saw her dash behind a row of coats as soon as I began turning away. Yes, she remembered me. Natalya's friends and, it seemed, all 'non-official' Russians were cut off from me.

I went though the motions required of tour guides, but I was dead inside. Rather, I had no 'inside.' What you saw is what you got.

My Dear Children:

Everything I have written is true. Whether or not it 'really' happened is another matter – These letters are what I remember, and I swear on the three things that I love the most, you, children, that I have worked at writing what I remember. Period. No attempts to make me look good or to make someone else look bad, or even to make this series of letters more 'interesting.'

But in this letter, I am telling you a story that I am not sure happened. Many times, I fictionalized my romance with the non-violinist Natalya, whose name was not really 'Natalya.'

Is this letter 'real,' or is it part of my imagination? Some might say that this story is too contrived, too literary to be true. Perhaps. But I have had other experiences that have been more literary, and seemingly more contrived. Meeting Elena later – that was a giant coincidence, and no fiction editor would have allowed it.

Here, the dimming bulbs in my brains won't let me know. I do know, however, that by the time I left Leningrad in 1971, I knew exactly why they had yanked Natalya out of her city. I can't recall any other way that I could have discovered this, other than the story I tell you here.

I don't like looking back at that time. I understood then why people sometimes grow numb after a loss, why I, for instance, grew numb after my Brother Jimmy drowned in 1965.

But this time, in Leningrad, in 1971, I was not numb, but I would have wished for it.

I was lost. My hand was not my hand – it belonged to someone else. I had never felt so disconnected, so like a pile of old bent metal chunks, like the charred shell of my Father's burnt-up truck.

I caught myself looking for myself through bus windows, through reflections from bus windows, in the crowds of passengers jamming my bus and other busses.

What the hell was going on, I had no idea. I was in her city, but she was not. and I couldn't see her. This confounded me. I began dearly to obsess over this, and I continued to obsess for a long time, adding more sticks to a fire that needed to go out.

What had gone wrong? From December on, she and I had ended our letters with the same phrase, 'Nothing has changed.' She wrote that in early May, soon before I flew to Copenhagen to meet up with the crazy Danes and spend days wandering their heath, climbing their mounds of sand leading to the sea and then laughing as we stood in the water and tried to get the sand off our bodies and out of our hair.

But what had gone wrong? Her secure position in the orchestra, her reputation, her Father's high position in government, her Mother's confidence--what had gone wrong?

I needed time alone, time to begin to sort things through, or at least to realize what was happening. I was jumping inside my skin – I needed to work off some of my frenetic, flammable energy.

I met my group in the crowded hotel foyer so our Soviet guide could give us her 'seety' orientation tour, as she called it. We drove down Kirov Prospekt and stopped at the mooring of the Aurora cruiser, the boat that in 1917 fired 'the shot heard around the world.' We crossed the Kirov Bridge, and followed Chalturin street along the side of the Winter Palace. I could see the steeple of the Cathedral of Saints Peter and Paul across the river, and I could see the beginning of Petropavlovskaya Street. I had walked every inch of pavement that the bus now followed, and each square meter seemed to hold out to me a specific memory, in mockery, as if saying, "Here it is, but you can't have it."

I had to stay with my group. It was my job. I would not give in. The next morning, we went to the Peter and Paul Fortress. The bus went right down her street, and I, an agnostic, prayed that she would step out of the building and look at me, give me some signal, grant me some hope or command me to give up hope. No one walked out of her building or up the street or down the street.

Inside the fortress, we, of course, got to go to the head of the line, and so within ten minutes, we were inside the jammed cathedral, as packed as it had been my first visit. Our Soviet tour guide was good, but she couldn't hold a candle to Natalya's Mothers' ability to work her way through a crowd.

It happened near the grave of Peter the Great, I think. It was hard to tell, because the place was so crowded and there was jostling and shoving all over. But it was near Peter's grave. I felt three sharp, rhythmic jabs in my side, then a hand reaching into my pocket. I reacted to none of it – I had spent too much time in the Soviet Union or had watched too many spy films. I forced myself to look forward, as if hanging on every word of the Soviet excursion guide, yet wanting more than anything to turn around and find out what had just happened and who had made it happen.

In the bus, I made sure to sit in the rear sea, a polite thing to do, a sign to the Soviet guide that I was not interfering with her spiel. I slipped the piece of paper from my pocket. It was about two inches square, and it said, in terse block Cyrillic letters, "Walk up the left side of Nevsky 8:00-8:30 this evening. I'd rather be a hammer than a nail."

"Elena." I wanted to call out, but I didn't.

That evening, I skipped dinner and told Irina, our guide, that I was jet-lagged and needed a long walk. She nodded. It was not at all uncommon for American tour guides to have 'second agendas' and to slip away from their groups, dumping them all upon the shoulders of the Soviet guide while they went about their 'real' business.

I wondered how I could I get to Nevsky without being followed. I should have watched more spy movies. I walked quickly out of the hotel, three blocks up Kirov Prospekt, and then at the last minute I jumped on a Number 80 bus that took me to Bolshoi Prospekt on Vasilievsky Island. The bus was packed, of course, but I hadn't seen anyone get on after me at that stop. At the corner of Maly Prospekt and the Ninth Line, I made my move. I pushed my way through six or seven people, making sure I was the last to jump off. Then at the last possible minute, I jumped onto a Number 47 bus that took me to Mayakovsky Square, up Nevsky from where I had to be. Commuters jammed the busses and trolley busses.

My heart pounded. I was not cut out for this type of juvenile bullshit. I looked at my watch and calculated. Yes, I still had time for extra precautions. I walked into the subway station at Mayakovsky Square, and put five twenty-kopeck pieces into the automatic change-machine. I waited, looking around for familiar faces or anyone paying attention to me. Everyone looked suspicious of me -- the young kids huddled together, the old ladies clutching their net bags. I buried myself in the push of the crowd jamming through the turnstiles, and I descended the long escalators, staying to the slow-moving right side most of the time, but occasionally darting out into the fast lane. I looked up the incredibly long escalator. No one seemed to be staying with me, darting ahead as I darted ahead. I was sure no one was following me; yet, <u>they</u> were the experts. I was not.

I picked my way through the maze of tunnels connecting the Kirov-Vyborg line with the Neva-Vasileostrovskaya line under Mayakovsky Square, and I got onto the Vyborg line. The train was jammed with commuters, some dozing, some reading. I was the last one to push my way onto the car as the unseen attendant announced over the scratchy speakers, "Be careful! The doors are closing. Next stop, Chernyshevskaya."

At Lenin Square, I took a subway in the opposite direction to Leninsky Prospekt. On the way back, I exited at Ploshchad Mira ('Peace Square'), went up the long escalators to the station itself, and abruptly turned back down on the opposite escalator. People stared-- like the always do at foreigners -- wild-eyed, desperate ones like myself, especially, I suppose, but I was getting a little more confident. No one seemed to be following me.

A subsequent series of rides, which included the Number 3 streetcar on Sadovaya, a Number 2 streetcar along Mars Field, and another subway ride, brought me finally to the Gorky Subway station. Commuters swarmed the station, funneling from a widening mass of humanity onto the narrow escalators, and then fanning out below again, un-dammed, towards the departing and arriving trains. I squeezed onto the train at the last moment. A young man's elbow dug painfully into my side. The young man and his female companion were deeply involved in a private conversation, oblivious to the world and the crush of humanity around them.

I exited at the Gostinny Dvor Station and looked at the digital clock on the wall. It was eight-ten. I walked out of the station and followed the flow of the crowd up the left side of Nevsky Prospekt. It was so crowded you could never see the pavement.

The light changed, and the crowd surged forward.

"Ayd Rather Be A Khammer Dan a Nail." It was a female voice, high-pitched, soft-spoken, coming from behind. Elena. "Go into the record store, one block ahead," she commanded in a low voice, her face buried in the collar of her coat that she had pulled up, along with other pedestrians, because of the wind blowing off the river, ahead. I couldn't see her face, but as she walked, her right arm nearly touched mine – not uncommon at all on Nevsky. "Ask for Shostakovich's Seventh Symphony, and a listening room."

I stepped down the rounded stone steps, into the record shop. Customers jammed the store, naturally. Jostled around, my height gave me some advantage as I studied the long lists pasted onto the wall. I pushed my way over to the counter and I stood before a clerk. "I would like to listen to Shostakovich's Symphony Number Seven, Leningrad Philharmonic Orchestra, please."

The clerk didn't look up. She was trying to re-assemble a pair of scissors that somehow had separated. Her hair was orange with purple highlights – the combination that I saw all over the city, and that I first saw when going through customs one year earlier, a lifetime earlier, yes?

"Our listening rooms are full, and the line won't get through before closing," she said, still not looking up and still working on the scissors, trying to figure out how to re-assemble them. "And besides, the record it sold out. It is always sold out. Why do you want to listen to it anyway?" she demanded. "You don't know how it sounds? You don't have the symphony in your country?" She looked up, no doubt trying to figure out which country I had come from.

"I know how it sounds," I said. "Many American orchestras have performed it, and, in fact, the work was <u>first</u> performed in America because Leningrad was under siege." I tried to say this in a way that would not offend her.

The woman's eyes softened.

"So, yes, I have heard the symphony," I continued. "The Boston Symphony, the New York Philharmonic, the Cleveland Orchestra -- But I wanted to hear it performed by the orchestra of the city of its birth. How disappointing for me that I will return home without it."

Then she did what all Soviets seemed to do, no matter their job or profession – She reached into her 'secret stash.'

She smiled. "You <u>must</u> have the Leningrad Philharmonic Performance. It is the best!" She reached under a long table running the length of the wall facing Nevsky. "And I will personally take you to a listening booth!"

She walked around the counter and led me by the arm through the packed store. We stepped down into a narrow corridor lined with closely-spaced doors on each side. She knocked hard on the third door on the right. "Katenka, time's up! Get back on the floor!" She turned to me. "They will be out shortly, then you can have the listening booth." She turned and left.

In a few moments, a red-faced Katenka stepped out of the room. She smoothed down her hair and straightened her skirt at the front of her hips. A young man with a red face and bad complexion followed her out.

I entered the booth, and soon the sounds of the first movement of Shostakovich's Seventh Symphony filled the room. The sound system was monophonic and poorly-wired -- there was a lot of static. As compensation, the clerk turned up the volume high at her control panel behind the counter, at the other end of the store.

There was a tap on the opaque window glass, then the door opened. It was Elena. She shut the door fast behind her and whispered right into my ear, "Listen! We do not have much time! This is very dangerous, for both of us! We must hug because that is what people do here in these booths. Okay?"

I nodded. She took me by the waist and pressed her body tightly against mine, resting her head on my shoulder so that her mouth was close to my ear.

"What in God's name is happening?" I pleaded.

"Shhh! Whisper! Whisper! You did nothing! We did not think you would come. Have you not you read the newspapers?"

"I was at a cabin in Denmark. It was isolated. Then we went by train, with my group, to Warsaw, Moscow, and Odessa. I could find no news papers in English or Russian, and I didn't know Polish or German well enough.

"Natalya Makarova, prima ballerina at the Kirov?" Elena asked. "She defected from in London, two weeks ago. Did you know that?"

"No!"

"It is a very big scandal for the Kirov, as you can imagine! And the government has tightened up all connections with foreigners, particularly connections that involve <u>any</u> artist."

I was, as usual, having a hard time understanding Elena. "How's Natalya? Where is she?"

"She is in a tuberculosis asylum in Sochi, on the Black Sea." This information coincided with what 'Boris' had told me in my hotel room.

A shadow passed by outside the opaque window. Elena shifted so that now her other cheek rested on my other shoulder. "We must hurry. Natalya is not sick. She will return soon, as soon as you leave. But listen. Makarova is only part of the story. Natalya's Brother, did you meet him?"

"No, he was away in the Army."

"Yes, and now he is in a secret army institute. They are teaching him English. He will work in intelligence. Did you know that?"

"No," I said, wondering how so many things could happen around me and yet I, the fool, caught none of them. Here it was – Natalya's Brother would end up in the kind of job I might have had in the U.S. Navy.

As if to prove my ignorance, even though it needed no more proving, Elena continued. "There is more. The Leningrad sky-jackers -- you have heard of them?"

"Yes." That much I had heard of.

"There were protests and threats in the West. The Soviet Supreme Court reversed their convictions."

"I didn't know," I said, not catching the full import of her words.

"Natalya's Father was one of the assistant prosecutors in that case. Did you know that?"

"No."

"They reversed the Court's decision because of international pressures," she whispered. "Legal technicalities. He is out-of-favor in the ministry and in the party. He may lose his position. And you, Bill, did they arrest you?"

"They detained me. That's all. They warned me not to contact anybody here."

"That is not so bad," she said. "It could have been worse. It will be, too, if you contact anyone. For your sake -- for Natalya's sake more -- do not contact anyone!"

"Will you see her?" I pleaded.

"Yes, probably. When they allow her to return."

"Would you give her a message from me?"

"A written message? That would be too dangerous."

"An oral message, a short one. Tell her, 'Nothing has changed.'"

"I will tell her. And I have a message from her for you."

"Yes?" I asked.

"Nothing has changed."

Dear Children:

I think I saw Natalya once, for the briefest of moments on a streetcar, years later, when her eyes told me not to approach her. Or maybe I just thought it was Natalya. Maybe I was projecting a mountain of often-contradictory feelings upon an entirely innocent young Russian woman of approximately the same age and stature.

Years later, I tried to locate her via Russian and American friends from 1970 with whom I kept communications. One friend told me that Natalya had been married for three years, was happy with her life and profession and husband and child and did not want to see me.

It is odd how I accepted that without questioning it, without slipping into a deep depression over the loss.

I guess romantic love, particularly passionate love, can come and go, and thus is so different from a Father's love for his children, which is a constant. It never diminishes.

Novels could be written about such events, no?

Did any of these 1971 things with Elena really happen? I think they did. My heart tells me so, and the heart speaks more strongly than the brain.

One New York literary agent told me in 1987 that my novels would sell great, if only this wasn't 1980's America but 1890's Russia.

Katya, Anna, Alex:

Did I go into a long depression with mourning and grieving after I got out of Leningrad? One might expect that of a disappointed lover. No. I was like a notebook computer that goes into hibernation. Inside, I locked down, shut windows, locked doors, barricaded entrances, closed down programs, eliminated lights. Ever the soldier. Ever the fighter. Hardly ever the winner.

Have you ever heard the way a jet engine whines down after the plane pulls up to its gate? That was me. I became a different person, or, rather, no person at all. I went through the necessary motions, dead inside. I helped the American students catch their flight back to Minnesota.

I hopped a train to Denmark, back to those fun, crazy Danes. Gretta, my best Danish friend, was staying with her family at their summer cabin on the shore in Jutland. I tried to get directions there when I was in Frankfort. The German railroad clerk insisted there was no such place on his official map; therefore, it didn't exist. So I took the train as far as it went. I got off at the end of the line in Denmark, in utter, deep darkness. I slept in a cow field and awoke to find a mammoth, dumb beast drooling down on me, no doubt wondering why I was trespassing on his property. I hitch-hiked, getting rides on horse-drawn carts mostly, going towards the sea all the time. I walked when the road became deserted. My optimism was wearing thin. Then out of nowhere, a bright red VW convertible was coming towards me.

She was on her way to the store and to the post office, hoping there would be a letter from me. In those days, you never went into the Soviet Union without alerting friends when you'd be coming out and promising to confirm in writing that you were, in fact, out. Otherwise, they knew to start looking for you. Gretta was preparing to send out a general alarm around the Russian student community, which was small. They would start looking for me in the Soviet Union and would pass out that information to their counterparts in the West.

I spent a week with Gretta and her delightful family at their cabin, and then I was shuttled back and forth between friends and their families. I stayed mostly with Gretta, who was hopelessly in love with a Russian-American in our exchange group in 1970, who wanted to become an orthodox priest and didn't want anything more to do with

Gretta or any other non-Orthodox woman.

"You must forget Natalya," Gretta told me six months later. She had seen Natalya when she dropped off the engagement ring in January. "It was a fantasy love for both of you. You do not know one-another at all."

"That is all part of the past now," I told her, with a smile and with great assurance to all but me. "It is a closed book."

Then I went to Paris, to meet some of exchange students from Leningrad who were staying in Western Europe then. I didn't have any money, and so I had to go back home almost directly. I didn't tell my story about Natalya to anyone, and no one asked. A lot of the American students in the dorm didn't know about my romance, or if they did, they probably figured it was all a fantasy thing anyway, and it was probably best not to bring it up.

That first evening, I remember, we ate a dinner of filet of sole and we drank far too much wine. Many in the restaurant, I remember, were impressed with the way I could fillet a sole. This was something I had learned as a waiter. Something I could be proud of, perhaps the only thing I could be proud of.

Many of the guests went on to another party. They invited me, but I didn't feel up to it – my head was spinning. I think there might have been something in the wine.

Through one of the women in the American exchange group, I met Michelle, a French student. I honestly don't recall how it happened or who first came up with the idea. She came to America in my first year of graduate school in Ann Arbor.

I can't decide whether she learned to hate me or America first. But it was a disaster. Besides, she had just broken up with a helpless and needy French guy whom she had cared for and nurtured too many years, and she was writing her thesis on Graham Greene, not the jolliest of people when it comes to depicting human relationships.

I think she was taken with me because I was the opposite of the man in her last relationship, and I was taken with her because she was, well, French. In Ann Arbor, she soon came to hate the way Americans drive, then the way they arrange their houses, then how they eat, then how they pursue their educations – and finally it all came down to her hating me and anything in the world that was not French.

She left me in November and I was heart-broken, processing, perhaps, my grief over her leaving, and perhaps stored-up grief over Natalia as well. After Michelle left, we wrote long letters to one-another almost daily, alternating between how much we hated one-another and how much we wanted to remain 'friends,' which I think is either an easy way to end a love relationship, or an attempt to keep it going, over the rough spots that are, you hope, only temporary. Well, you don't write a 'friend' long letters daily. Gradually the letters between Michelle and me tapered off, and I lost contact with her.

I hope she found her place. May all of us find our places.

Dear Children:

By the winter of 1972, I had learned there was one way to make good money in the summer. I'd organize student study tours of Eastern Europe and of the Soviet Union. I'd receive my slot on the tour, including transportation from Minneapolis to Russia, for free, and also a little spending money, as well as a Eurail Pass for Western Europe. With that pass, I could go anywhere I wanted on just about any Western European train for thirty days after coming out of Russia. The salary was not bad either, I figured, and the job was a bit more exciting than waiting tables in Saint Paul.

I was nervous about being allowed back into the Soviet Union.

I saw Michelle in Paris, on my way East. Our meeting was cordial and cold, as if we had engaged in some childish mischief that we now regretted.

Poor Michelle. She had found that her American experience had changed her so much that she no longer liked Paris a lot, and she certainly hadn't developed any love for the United States. She moved to Montreal where, I hope, she found a happy compromise.

I took the train to Frankfurt, where I would meet up with my group, and where our adventure would begin. Soon, I developed a crush on one of them, Julie. Apparently I had used up all my 'foreign fiancé passes,' and it was now time for an American woman. Julie was cute and intelligent and full of hope and promise, wise beyond her twenty years, and she had a sharp, quiet sense of humor.

And even better, Julie was the opposite of the exotic foreigners I had been falling in love with. She was a Minneapolis girl. My Father worked for the Saint Paul Water Department. Her Father worked for Northern States Power Company.

It was a union of utilities.

Kids:

That 1972 study trip was a pile of disasters heaped upon other disasters. We began in Frankfurt and had an awful train ride across Poland to Warsaw. Geese, chickens, and a smelly goat (a redundancy, I know) occupied our car, and there were two couples arguing and screaming at one-another, each at one end of the car.

I hadn't noticed that the itinerary said 'Arrive Warsaw Gl, depart Warsaw Gd.' Funny language, that Polish. The sounds of the language just don't correspond with the Roman alphabet that the Catholic Church had thrust upon them. Too bad. I could write a book about that.

The difference between 'Gl' and 'Gd' was wide, I soon discovered, one being 'Warsaw Main Station' and the other being 'Warsaw Gdansk Station.' We had twenty minutes to get to the Gdansk Station, just about all the way across Warsaw from the main station. I spoke a few words of my weak Polish. and a few American dollars passed around, and then we all rode a long line of hospital ambulances, with sirens blaring and lights blinking, from one station to the other.

I had scheduled the group for a four-day stay at a youth camp in Sochi, near the Black Sea in Crimea. I figured it would be a restful visit and a great way for American students to mingle with Soviet students – the very thing that the Sputnik Youth Travel Agency worked hard at preventing, and the very thing that visiting American students wanted most of all. They soon would get tired of palaces and of being told how many columns it had and who lived there and who was murdered there, and they were tired of visiting dark churches and being lectured about the excesses of religion and about how many workers died while coating the dome with a gold paint that included vast amounts of lead.

But the camp visit turned out to be not at all a good idea. It was like a prison. Every moment was planned, and everything was timed, and there were giant loudspeakers on poles all over the place, telling you all the time where you should be and what you should be doing.

There was a truly juvenile costume contest on the first afternoon, and I was appointed one of the judges. My students felt like second-graders, and I couldn't blame them. Two of them agreed to join in the contest, with great reluctance. I was grateful.

Whenever someone paraded by on the stage in a god-awful costume, we judges had to hold up a number, just like they do at the Olympics. The first contestant was a Polish young lady dressed up as a milk maid. The other judges gave her a seven. I gave her an eight. The judges frowned at me. One leaned over to me and whispered, "We all must give the same number, you see, or it will look, well, subjective."

"But I think she deserves an eight," I answered.

Then the next contestant came up on stage, a Bulgarian dressed as a hobo. I gave him a seven. Everyone else gave him a six. Then something magical happened. One of the judges set down her six and gave him a seven too.

The next contestant was a young Russian male dressed as a Greek god. Each judge gave him a different number.

Wow! I had pierced the Soviet veil of conformity. I was proud. The master of ceremonies shrugged, looking as if he'd be exiled for our rebellion.

That night Julie and I visited the tiny room of the master of ceremonies, and six or seven of us all drank vodka. It turned out that the master of ceremonies was hopelessly gay, and he apologized for being harsh with us Americans, but he said he had to, in public, or he would surely lose his job and end up working on a factory assembly line. I felt sorry for him, but I had been somewhat hardened by hearing too many similar apologies after too many anti-western tirades?

The next day I was called into a meeting with the camp director and our Soviet escort. It turned out that the whole purpose of the camp that season was to perform a 'dry run' of a youth solidarity event to be held in East Berlin for all the 'brotherly communist countries' the next summer. There was going to be a 'practice rally' that night.

"It is not important at all," said the director, not looking at me. "But a petition will be read, and all attending will sign it. As the group leader, you will sign for the Americans."

"Well, I'd like to read it before signing it," I said.

"It is in Russian."

"My Russian isn't great, but I can read it."

"We don't have a copy. Anyway, it just states that we do not like war, and nobody likes war, correct?"

"Well, we don't like war," I answered. This was 1972, and Viet Nam was a hot topic. "But I still want to read the petition before I sign it, and I won't sign it unless I see it in advance."

Somehow a copy appeared after waiting for an hour or so in a windowless office with yellow furniture and no air to speak of. I read the manifesto. It was a prototypical Soviet anti-American diatribe. "We oppose the imperialist, capitalist aggression on the peoples of South Viet Nam and Southeast Asia...."

I was conflicted. Here I was, strongly anti-war, but the petition nonetheless pissed me off. "Let me show it to my group," I requested. "In an hour I'll bring it back and let you know what we'll do."

I read the petition to the group and to our Soviet escort, translating it on the fly as best I could. "You must sign the petition," our Soviet escort told us. "Or there will be unpleasantness."

I asked the group what we should do, telling them I had no idea what might happen if we refused to sign. I put it to a vote.

"Let's not sign it, and let's write our own," they said, unanimously, I believe, or almost so.

So they did. They did it all – I am so proud. I merely translated it into Russian and handed it to the director.

"Of course, you can read your petition at the rally," said the director. "There is freedom of speech in the Soviet Union. I believe it is one of the personal freedoms that is 'tacked on' to the end of your Constitution, in the Bill of Rights." He continued smugly. "Whereas the Soviet Constitution begins with a list of the personal freedoms."

Whatever.

At the torch-lit rally began that evening, the Russians read their petition, and then representatives from Ukraine, Poland, Hungary, Russia, Bulgaria, and Czechoslovakia marched up one-by-one, and with much posturing, like kids playing grown-up, they signed it.

Then it was our turn. I walked to the podium. "We are not going to sign your petition," I said. "Instead, we would like to read our own."

Silence like I had never heard before. I began to read. The microphone went dead. "I will stand here until the microphone gets turned back on!" I shouted. I turned to the director, who was standing behind me, off to the side. "You said you have freedom of speech in the Soviet Union, so I want the freedom to read what my students have written."

After a long time, the microphone came back on. I read our petition. "We too are opposed to war," I began. "Many of us here have participated in anti-war demonstrations in America."

There were nods and smiles from the crowd.

"But reading your petition," I continued. "One could assume that the only big country that tries to impose its will on a smaller country is the United States."

No one moved. Not the Czechs, who had been invaded three years before, not the Poles, who'd been invaded twice, not the Hungarians, who'd been invaded too. Not the Russians, who had done the invading.

I finished reading. "It is our hope that someday the world will no longer allow any large country to impose its will on any smaller country."

Silence. The ceremony was over, I guessed. No one knew what to do or say, it seemed.

We Americans walked around the camp grounds for the rest of the evening, not knowing what would happen next. We walked down to the beach. Eyes averted our gazes whenever we passed. We stayed together; we were scared.

After our surreal walk around the camp, we Americans headed back to our assigned dormitory at about ten o'clock and eventually went to bed.

Hours later, long past midnight, we heard noises outside, off in the distance. Then shouting. And it was getting closer and closer. "This is it," I thought. "A riot, arrest – who knows what?" Many of the American students crammed into my room.

Then we heard singing. It sounded something like "The Battle Hymn of the Republic," sung in different languages, all of them off-key. From somewhere, I recalled the Laurel and Hardy movie, "Chumps at Oxford":

Fee Fie Fo Fum!

We want the blood of an American!

The singers were getting closer. Was this a lynch mob, peopled by Communist goons? I didn't know what to make of it. Was this derisive, scornful? I would soon find out. My heart pounded. Into what kind of danger had I plunged my students? Had I the right to do it? Was I just working out my own personal grudge against the country?

Then there was no longer any time to think of such things. The group of rioters broke down the door of the dormitory and rushed through the halls, towards our rooms, or they climbed over balconies or ran up fire escapes. Now we were really scared. The Soviet press could call it a fire or else they could ignore it completely—No one would know how or why we were killed.

"Zheleznyie Amerikantzy!" ("Iron Americans!") these invaders were yelling, over and over.

Good Grief! We were heroes!

They pushed into our rooms through the doors and windows, carrying Russian and Polish vodka bottles and glasses and Hungarian champagne and Russian champagne and Bulgarian wine. There was much crying and shouting and kissing on the cheeks and on the lips and even on the legs and feet. Two guys hauled up a heavy tape recorder, and someone else held on high a copy of Simon & Garfunkel's "Bridge over Troubled Waters."

I don't know why that album and that song have followed me.

I'd rather be a hammer than a nail.

Yes, I would, if I only could…

A man gets tied up to the ground

He gives the world its saddest sound.

Its saddest sound.

I would write out all the lyrics but I can't without violating copyright laws, without perhaps offending the performers, which is far more important than any copyright law, despite all the warnings you see on DVDs and CDs and at the beginning of movies.

I'd rather be a hammer than a nail.

Each person in those rooms on that night was a nail.

The party went long, into morning's light, and people were still crying and toasting and hugging and, by now, shouting at one-another how much they loved one-another. Drinking makes people shout.

There were some Russians there too, including the camp master of ceremonies.

The next morning we were scheduled to take the train to Leningrad. It was the custom at this piss-hole of a camp to play the national anthem of whatever country's students were leaving that day, as the group's leader took down the respective flag from the row of flags lining the camp's entrance.

There's a photograph of me, taken from the back, as I was taking down that American flag. I am glad the photo was taken from the back. I was crying. So were people on the bus and people on the ground.

From whence came all the patriotism in me? I, who opposed the war, who hated Nixon and Agnew? I, who hated so many things about the country of my birth?

I cried again, like a damned baby, when they played the American National Anthem over their lousy loudspeakers. People were crying inside the bus and outside the bus too. Americans and East Europeans and even some Russians.

Right before the bus door closed, a thin, young man jumped on board. "You must come to Hungary!" he shouted. "We have beautiful beaches there! Better than this one!"

Two men in uniforms yanked him off the bus, as a woman with medals on her chest looked on. I wonder what happened to him. He, who was a nail.

But guess what, kids? (Alex loves to say, 'Guess what, Papa?')

Well, guess what?

We arrived in Leningrad by train the next day. All those Russians who avoided me on my previous visit? They seemed elated to see me this time, and they took great pains to make our whole American group feel welcome.

Guess what, kids? All of them had heard about 'The Sochi Incident'—the 'sluchai v Sochi,' as they called it. (Try saying that five times in a row, fast.)

Guess what? We were heroes already, a thousand or so miles from Sochi.

Julie and I ran out of money after we left Leningrad, including the advance the University of Minnesota had given me. It happened in Kiev, in the office of the Sputnik Travel Office, populated with the usual snarling Soviet bureaucrats and clerks and minions.

It turned out that the specifics of our Sputnik tour package, printed in an admirably small font in those days, long before computers, included the train ride out of Russia only as far as the Soviet border. It did not include the portion of the ride from the Soviet border, through Czechoslovakia to Vienna.

What a fool I had been not to check into that before we left on the damned tour (yes, it was truly damned).

Great. We were near the Pripet Marshes. Mostly uninhabited. A few seventeenth-century villages, mostly abandoned. Lots of swamps. Giant, man-eating mosquitoes. Chernobyl nearby would soon be famous. Not a heck of a lot to do.

I had to pay seven hundred dollars or my students wouldn't have been able to stay on our train as it ran from the Soviet border to Vienna. I forked over all I had, including the 'emergency' money the university hade given me, and Julie forked over what she had. Other tour members chipped in. Julie and I were left with about twenty dollars between us, and our charter flight didn't leave Frankfurt for a month. Gone were our plans for seeing Venice and Rome and Munich and Paris. So soon it all had become a question of surviving. How would we do it?

The end of our adventures that summer, kids? Nope. Hardly. All that had happened already was merely the overture before the curtain went up. It was just the beginning. Read on, dear Kids.

By early afternoon of the next day, the train stopped at the border checkpoint, between Ukraine and Czechoslovakia. A stern Soviet matron checked each passport, especially the photograph, and took back our Soviet visas, the last proof that we had been there.

Soviet customs inspectors followed the lady who checked passports. Golly, she looked pretty much like that first customs lady I had seen in Leningrad in my first visit there, in 1970. I had come full circle, perhaps.

There were no 'incidents' involving my group. No anti-Soviet material, no 'samizdat' prose or poetry, no contraband except for some questionable seeds in the bottom of one suitcase. Luckily, one the customs agents had grown up on a collective farm. "Ah, those are pear seeds!" he said.

So were we home free? Hardly.

The train jerked forward. I was leaving the Soviet Union and damned glad of it this time, but just as the train seemed to gather steam, it stopped again. "Czech entry point," the car attendant told me. Okay, we had just 'checked out' of Russia, and now we were 'checking in' to Czechoslovakia (cute pun, no?) for our one-stop express ride to Vienna.

A tall, stern-looking man in a green uniform talked a bit with the car attendant, then started walking towards me. I had a strong sense of foreboding. Perhaps by then I had learned to smell it. 'What the hell's going to happen now?' I asked myself, for no reason I knew of. "This is Czechoslovakia, after all. Not the Soviet Union," I reminded myself.

"But how much of a difference is there now, really?" I wondered, remembering Dubcek's Prague Spring barely three years earlier. The officer walked down the passageway, towards my compartment. He stopped at my doorway. "You are the group leader?"

"Yes, Sir, I am."

"You speak Czech?"

"No. I understand a little."

"But you speak Russian?" he asked, without looking up.

"Yes, I studied it in school."

The officer looked at the stack of Czech transit visas I handed him. I have since learned that the smaller the country, or the more paranoid the country, the larger are their passport stamps. Paper currency follows the same rule. The Czech transit visa took up an entire American passport page.

"How many people in your group?" he asked.

"Thirty, including myself."

"That will be three hundred and sixty dollars, American currency."

"For what?" I asked.

"You have visitors' visas. Visitors are required to spend six dollars a day for each day they are in Czechoslovakia. You will be here today and tomorrow. That is twelve dollars apiece for thirty visitors."

"We're not visitors," I said slowly, politely, in Czech. "We are in transit, sir."

"You are visitors. It says so right on your visas."

"The visas say 'transit,' right at the top!" I said, damned glad that I could read enough Czech to make out the words.

He seemed unconvinced. "It says you will be in Czechoslovakia for two days. That is not transit!"

"That is transit, Sir. We'll be in Czechoslovakia for less than twenty-four hours, even though it happens to fall on two dates, and we're on an international train! That's transit!"

"Where did you get these visas?" he asked, still unconvinced.

"From the Czech Embassy in Washington, in the United States."

"They don't know what they are doing! You and your group are visitors, and you must pay twelve dollars apiece."

"We're transit!"

"You refuse to pay?" he said, not looking up.

"Look, sir, it's not even a transit tariff. It's just a requirement for tourists to spend a minimum amount of official Czech currency inside Czechoslovakia, as a safeguard against black marketeering. We won't even be leaving the train. We won't exchange any currency. We won't subvert your precious socialist economy."

The officer shrugged. "I will return, with others! You will pay!" He left, taking my passport and the transit visa with him. From the way people were loafing around outside, it looked like we would be at the tiny station for a while.

We Americans stepped off the train, and we witnessed a strange occurrence. The train was about twenty cars long, and our car was about seven cars back from the locomotive. Starting at the front of the train, workers had jacked up each car while teams of other workers crawled underneath. They unfastened the heavy assembly of axles and train wheels, and slid another assembly underneath, fastening it to the car.

Trying to figure out what was going on, I looked at the tracks. Ah, there were two sets of rails under our train, one running inside the other.

Why?

The wider rail stretched backwards, under the train, towards Kiev. The narrow rails extended forward, into Czechoslovakia. Then I figured it out. Eastern Europe and Western Europe had different track gauges! No wonder Soviet trains seemed so wide and sturdy. Now, at the border between East Europe and West Europe, the workers had to jack up each train car to change axles before the Soviet train could ride on into Czechoslovakia and beyond.

Two or three hours later, workers motioned for my group and me to get back into the car. "The coast is clear, and we're ready to roll," I told myself.

Not quite.

The tall, thin officer returned, this time accompanied by two other men, the heaviest of whom wore red stars on his epaulets.

"This is all a misunderstanding, Meester Jack," said the officer with the red stars. "You must exchange money only, not pay it." He smiled. "It is a formality only. You can exchange it back in the morning, at Bratislava. You see, there is no problem!" The fat man smiled broadly. "Just give this officer, if you please, your money."

But I had spent too much time in railway stations and airports, and too much time in general in Eastern Europe and the Soviet Union to take any comfort from his words. "There <u>are</u> problems!" I said. "First of all, we don't have the money to give you. Secondly, we have transit visas, not visitors' visas."

"Alright, but let us not create a problem or an incident," the fat man said, working hard to hold the smile on his face. "Exchange your money now, and reconvert it back in the morning! It is simple!"

"Thirdly," I continued, gathering steam. "I have looked at a visitor's visa here that belongs to a Canadian on this train. It says right on top, in your own Czech language, that the minimum currency exchange amount is <u>not</u> refundable."

The smile left the man's face.

"Fourthly," I continued. "As if all that wasn't enough, we'll be in Bratislava at six o'clock in the morning, and I don't believe a bank will be open then. Fifth, even if a bank was open, thirty people couldn't exchange money during the half hour allowed for the stopover."

"You refuse to pay?" the fat man asked incredulously.

"Yes!"

"Then you must leave the train and come with us. We will take you to the police station."

"I'll not leave this train until you have representatives from the American and Soviet Embassy here! We're Americans, and this is a Soviet, not a Czech, train!"

The man's eyes turned steely. "Then we will uncouple the train and leave you and your group sitting here."

I thought of the tracks, the axles and the wheels, and the fact that our car stood seven cars back from the locomotive, with a long chain of cars behind us. How could they ever back up the train to uncouple us without changing all the axles twice? Hell, they'd have to back up all the way to Kiev! "Go ahead!" I said. "Uncouple our car!"

The Czechs conferred on the platform, occasionally sending menacing glances our way. The fat man and his two cohorts returned to me, in the narrow hallway of the car. "We will remove your group from the train."

I turned to my students, who were peeking out from their compartment doors, enjoying the nasty argument and wondering what it was all about. "Hey, everybody!" I shouted. "They want to kick us off the train, but they don't have the right. Lock your compartments! Open your luggage and spread your things around! Strip down to your underwear, women especially! Make it as hard and as time-consuming as you can for them to get you and your belongings off the train!"

"I am a lieutenant general in the Czech border guard," the fat man said.

"I am an American citizen!" I replied. Yes, once again it was funny how the Soviet Union and Eastern Europe forced out of me an American patriotism that I thought I no longer had.

The lieutenant general ordered his two assistants to open the first compartment door. It was locked. "Tell them to open the door!" he said.

"No. This is a Soviet train, not a Czech train," I answered. "If the conductor tells them to open the door, I'll tell them to open the door!"

The guards tried the next compartment door. There was a tug of war, almost comedy-like. Four females squealed. The guards pulled hard at the door. It jerked open eventually, revealing four nearly nude, screaming American 'coeds,' as they were called then, shamefully. The red-faced guards quickly shut the door.

"Get the conductor!" the lieutenant general yelled to his subordinate.

The conductor, whom I had met, and with whom I had shared a love of the sorrowful, twisted world of writer Nikolai Gogol the night before, returned with the Czech guard within a few minutes.

"Bill, they want money -- foreign currency," he said in Russian, shrugging his shoulders. "It happens all the time."

"It's not happening this time!" I said.

The conductor turned to the lieutenant general. "Our train is ready to depart." He looked at his watch and checked it against the big clock on the station wall. "We must leave on time. I suggest that you telegraph Czech authorities, and I will telegraph Soviet authorities.

The train will proceed onward, as scheduled. The Americans, of course, will not leave the train. You can arrest them later."

The fat man conferred with his two assistant. All looked at their watches, then at the schedule fastened to the depot wall. "We will leave you now, Meester Jack," said the fat man, jabbing his finger at my chest, "But you will be arrested in the morning, in Bratislava."

The train jerked, then groaned forward, gradually picking up speed. The students dressed. "That's the greatest adventure ever!" said one woman. "We didn't understand a word of it, but we loved it!"

I explained what had happened, and they liked it even more.

Later that night, I sat with Julie and the conductor and the car attendant in the little compartment forward of the car that my group occupied. "You Americans are so independent!" said the attendant. "So fearless! I have never seen anyone stand up to those Czechs! Here! Vodka and tomatoes!"

The conductor quietly cut out the bad chunks of his tomato with a penknife. He did it with all his attention, as if it were surgery. "People make stands," he said slowly, still working at his tomato. "Some incident, some event touches it off. But why such a big risk over three hundred and sixty American dollars, with some scheming Czechs?"

"Sometimes," I said, biting into my tomato and catching the dribble of juice and seeds with my left hand. "Sometimes, a person can't take a stand where he wants, so he takes it somewhere else." I told him about Natalya. I felt my eyes watering. Yes, I had memories.

"I see," said the conductor. "Well, I will try to help you through this one. I won't call Moscow."

"Thank you!" I said. We opened another bottle of vodka, a bottle of champagne, and a jar of pickled fish.

Early the next morning, the conductor stashed me between four musty-smelling crates in the window-less, stuffy mail car. An hour later, the train slowed, then stopped. I peered out through a narrow slit between the crates, and I saw the conductor walk into the car. He paused at the spot where I was concealed. "First stop, Bratislava, suburbs!" he sang out. "Next stop, Main Station, Bratislava, thirteen minutes!"

My heart beat fast. The train jerked forward. Exactly thirteen minutes later, it stopped again. The minutes ticked by.

I could honestly hear my heart pounding, and I feared the Czechs might hear it too. It was beating so hard I swear it caused the crates to reverberate.

The train began to move and soon it picked up speed. Once again the conductor walked into the mail car. "Let us have one of those American cigarettes," he called out.

We stood on the platform between cars, that windy, dirty space with two rocking floors competing with one-another, the movement that I so much liked. "What happened?" I asked.

"Nothing. At the main station two police officers came on board and asked for 'William Francis Jack.'"

"And?"

"I told them that two uniformed officials boarded the train at the first Bratislava stop and took William Francis Jack off the train. They shrugged, they left, the train moved on."

"Thank you!" I said.

We rode on to Vienna and at the station, I hugged the conductor and the attendant. The Austrians looked upon us with disgust as we ran into the station hugging and kissing and shouting at one-another and at the Russian crew, and then we Americans ran outside and touched the dirt of Western Europe.

So Julie and I and all the others were 'free' in Austria, but Julie and I had twenty dollars between us. Frank, my oldest living Brother, was stationed at the army base at Bomholder. He lent us a hundred dollars that he couldn't spare.

Luckily, Julie and I both had Eurail passes. So even though we couldn't eat, we could travel. Breakfast one morning consisted of a jar of Norwegian smoked fish, given to us by a Dutch passenger who knew no English but surmised that we were starving. It wouldn't have taken much to reach such a conclusion – just the way I stared at the articles on the breakfast cart, as a smiling woman wheeled it through the car.

But where to go? Denmark. Of course. I'd hook up with Gretta and the other friends I had made there. Would it be, well, uncomfortable, my being there not alone this time, but with an American girlfriend?

The small group of Danes and Russians whom I knew in Copenhagen and Aarhus and Horsens had somehow already heard all about the 'Iron Americans,' the 'sluchay v Sochi.' I don't know how.

We were heroes. People bought us Carlsberg Beers and Tuborg beers and even some food once in a while, and Gretta lent us a big chunk of money.

"There's no way we can repay you for saving our lives like this," I said.

"There's one way," Julie told Gretta "You must come to America!"

Dear Anna, Katya, and Alex:

For once, it felt good to be home. I had had enough foreign adventures for a while, and I enjoyed the anonymity of staying at my parents' house.

I wondered if I had gotten over my 'Russophilia.' I didn't look forward to going back to graduate school.

Then one afternoon the phone rang. "Are you William Francis Jack?" asked a male voice.

"Yes, I am," I answered.

"I wonder if you are the same William Francis Jack that has an arrest warrant out for him in Czechoslovakia."

"I probably am," I said, wondering where the conversation would lead. I was surprised, of course, about the arrest warrant.

"My name is Ron Harvey," said the voice. "And I'm a reporter for 'The Minneapolis Star and Tribune.' I'd like to hear your story, if I may."

"It's not just my story," I answered. "A lot of other Minnesotans were involved."

"But there are no international arrest warrants out for them," he said.

"Okay, but I'd feel better if other group members were with me when you interview me. I don't want to have the story center on just me."

So a meeting was arranged in a tiny room on the second floor of Coffman Union at the University. More than half the tour members showed up. The reporter introduced himself and then started asking his questions. He was good at drawing information out of people, I could see.

"This train thing wasn't our only adventure on that tour," said one of the students (I wish I could remember who) after an hour talking about the train ride.

"What do you mean?" Ron asked, grabbing for his notebook.

"Well, we almost caused a riot at a student youth camp in

Sochi," said the student.

So the reporter, hand shaking, flipped a page in his notebook and asked to hear all about Sochi and the speech and the jumps over the wall and the Star Spangled Banner and the flag.

An article on all that appeared the next week, August thirteenth, 1972, on Page One of the Minneapolis Sunday paper.

I was famous, or infamous. Even my young nephew cried out, "Unca Billy!" when he saw the Sunday paper lying on the coffee table and after he spotted my picture.

The newspaper account was later translated into Russian and became a part of an exercise book for Russian language students.

Dear Anna, Katya, and Alex:

I did not have long to wallow in my fame and greatness. Gretta came to America that summer. She stayed with Julie and me in the attic of Julie's parents' house. The first day, Gretta came downstairs wearing a bikini in order to get some sun. The bikini was the smallest I had ever seen, and Gretta was just about the most 'endowed' woman I had ever seen. Julie's parents were shocked and worried what the neighbors must think. Julie's teenage Brother's jaw dropped, and it remained in that position until we left.

Gretta joined me and Julie on our cross-country 'honeymoon' trip in my 1965 Ford station wagon that hauled her Father's pop-up tent/trailer. The Ford had really bad rear suspension, so the car bottomed out on even tiny bumps. I had bought a cheap 'air shock absorber' kit. When it was inflated all the way, to the point of blowing out one of the lines, the car almost looked level, and it didn't scrape across the pavement after hitting a small bump.

When a mechanic in Arizona was replacing a dead muffler, a spark from his torch hit one of the air hoses. There was a loud hissing, and from then on, we had to be careful or else the back end of the station wagon would bottom out.

This bottoming-out makes a fitting metaphor for our honeymoon trip. Gretta had brought along a pair of brown-tinted sunglasses, and she needed to remind us every ten minutes how beautiful it made everything, <u>even</u> in America. Thanks. We were an untidy, impulsive, uncultured people. This did not sit so well with Julie, or with me. During the next two hours, then days, of this incredibly unpleasant trip, the two women began to dig at one-another, first in indirect ways, and then less subtly. In Wyoming, I gave up trying to make peace. I was getting tired of the tinted sunglasses too.

A few miserable weeks later, weeks that included a drive in a low-riding station wagon with a bumpy camping trailer, through an Arizona summer without air-conditioning, but with a passenger who remarked every few miles how pretty the desert landscape looked through her brown glasses. Julie and I dropped Gretta off at the Los Angeles Airport. None of us said a word. Then Julie and I shouted for joy.

All was great for the rest of the trip – at least for the first three hours. Julie and I got into an argument over something, and it continued through all the states between California and Minnesota. There were many such fights during our four years together.

Our marriage can be seen either as a continuation of one long fight, or as an ongoing series of separate fights. Either way, it was a disaster. Two people who shared so many interests and who liked one-another so much? We should have remained friends and not become spouses.

Dear Anna, Katya, and Alex:

Married? Julie and I married in 1973, over spring break. She wanted a Catholic wedding, to please her parents, and to have beautiful ritual and music, but no priest wanted to marry us. We had been living together 'in sin,' as they say.

Then magically, the old Polish pastor of her parents' former church relented, and we were married there.

I found out later that Julie's Father, years before, had switched over to another parish because of differences with this pastor and her father led the resulting 'schism.' Half the parishioners followed Julie's Father, jumping this particular ship for another Catholic church, of which there are many in Northeast Minneapolis.

It turned out that the pastor at the old church had struck a secret bargain with Julie's Father, "If you pay me all the money you would have put into the collection plate each Sunday for each year that you were at that other church," said the priest. "Then I will consider marrying the couple."

We didn't know about this agreement until much later, but for some reason we didn't like this church anyway. Julie made sure that we took all our floral arrangements with us after the Mass; we paid for them, not the church.

I didn't find out about the 'deal' between Julie's Father and the pastor until much later. I am sure that, had I known at the time, I would have refused the pastor's offer. I think Julie would have felt the same way.

We had a fun wedding reception in an old house on Summit Avenue that rented out for such occasions. Mary Ann, Julie's best friend, was proud that she had found a six-member Ukrainian band who would play for an extremely low price.

Well, it wasn't exactly a six-member band, but a one-man band, and that one man played six instruments, some of them at the same time, but none of them very well. His skinny wife sat at the edge of the stage and blew smoke rings the whole time. I think she went through about six ashtrays.

The next fall, Julie and I drove to Ann Arbor, and I crammed for my Masters exams. She, who had never lived away from her family, now shared a dinky, musty basement room in Ann Arbor with a graduate student who was way too busy taking classes and teaching classes and doing research. Worse, we had no money.

Julie wasn't accepted at the University of Michigan, but we couldn't have afforded the tuition anyway. She worked a couple of really ugly jobs in a college town that didn't offer any jobs except ugly ones.

She worked in a dark downtown bar where Mark Kirkonen, one of my professors and a department outcast, went to drink beer and play Yukor. The first day on the job, a woman marched in with a laundry basket filled with dirty clothes and dumped its contents on top of the head of one of Julie's customers.

Julie didn't make many friends in my department; she wasn't 'academic enough,' but Joseph Brodsky liked her and sought her company. He considered her 'real people,' and he advised both of us to get out of academia. "You are not cut out for it," he said. "It will suck the life right out of you."

We were so poor that one day the only thing we had in our refrigerator was a jar of pickles. We ate all of them and we got sick.

Anna, Katya, Alex:

Relax. We are almost done with graduate school stories.

Things improved a bit after I got my Masters Degree and started working on my doctorate. We found, by chance, a beautiful house on the Huron River, east of the University, in an area which is probably now all built-up. We had five rooms with two fireplaces and a view of the Huron River through big picture windows, all for one hundred and sixty dollars a month.

We had some good times, and created a circle of close friends. David, a manic depressive who was a fuming alcoholic genius and a Russian doctoral student, and his wife, Betsy, came over every Saturday. We watched "Mary Tyler Moore" and "Bob Newhart" and then awful late-night horror movies hosted by a local TV hero called 'The Ghoul.' Julie, bless her, got me interested Woody Allen, Mel Brooks, and in old movies.

I had never seen "Sunset Boulevard" or "All About Eve," for instance, or any number of other pre-1940 classics. Detroit TV had a local announcer who hosted old matinees each afternoon. He was a former actor named Bill Kennedy, who liked to remind everyone at least once each show that he had played the policeman in the remake of "High Sierra" and that he had talked personally to Ida Lupino, on a real movie set. He showed old movies and we watched them all, classes and research be damned. I skipped some classes with the professor who had visions of Jesus Christ and who swallowed her tongue while mumbling.

In 1972, Leningrad poet Joseph Brodsky was taken before the KGB and told he'd either have to leave the country or go back to the Gulag. Carl Proffer, a professor at the University of Michigan, was in Leningrad at the time, and he knew Brodsky. It was said that Proffer helped get Brodsky a position as writer-in-residence at the University of Michigan.

I took two, maybe three (I don't remember the number), poetry seminars from Brodsky. In each one, he railed against academics and universities, against the 'fatal dissection' of poetry, against social-based and literary-based criticism, particularly Formalism and Structuralism – that were both fighting for domination during those years. Formalism was on the way out. Everyone knew it except for the professors who had devoted to it a lifetime of research, writing, and teaching.

Structuralism was just beginning to replace it. I sensed that early on, and I decided to use a Structuralist approach in my thesis, using Russian literary critic Yury Lotman, exiled to Tartu, as my guide. Unfortunately, my dissertation was written a few years too early, and I paid for it.

Hang in, and you shall see how. Nowadays, Formalism and Structuralism are like two old guys sitting on a park bench as the world whizzes past them. I think that 'Deconstruction' is still all the rage now, but I may be wrong. I have been out of the field for almost thirty years.

Brodsky eschewed all such labels. He made us memorize long poems before each class. He said that in memorizing a poem and in thus making it a part of our mind, our heart, and our bodily rhythms, we were coming as close as we could to the experience the poet had had while writing the piece.

He spotted me emptying my department mailbox one day, and he was most impressed that I was looking at the latest issue of "Car and Driver" magazine. Joseph took a liking to me and to Julie, perhaps because we were the least academic people around, and because we didn't come to him for favors or to arrange speaking engagements that typically became political showcases.

We talked cars a lot. I was interested in all the changes in automobiles those years – transverse engines and Macpherson struts and fuel injection. "Get out of academia," Brodsky repeated over and over. "It will suck the life out of you."

I took him to see a new movie, Woody Allen's satire, "Love and Death." Brodsky hated it. I could sense him tightening up and shutting down in the first few minutes of the film. I could see his frown turning into a scowl. Why did he hate it so much? After all, it was a satire of Russian literature, and, of course, he knew the subject well.

I think Brodsky hated the film because it mocked and made light of what he loved passionately. There was another reason too, I believe. On a second viewing of the movie, I saw that it was not <u>really</u> a satire of Russian literature; it was a satire of <u>American</u> views of Russian literature, which is something quite different. Further, there were so many references to an American context that a Russian might not understand.

He steered me onto the works of Nikolai Zabolotsky, the same nearly-unknown Soviet poet whom Professor Fillipov in Leningrad had recommended to me four years earlier.

"An interesting poet!" Brodsky said. "And not over-studied, like Mandelstam, Akhmatova, Pasternak, and Tsvetaeva. You can plough new ground with him, rather than work in the over-tilled fields of the other poets."

He helped me by explicating lines that to me, as a foreigner, were confusing. I loved the crazy poem, "The signs of the zodiac are twinkling," for instance. It combined Zabolotsky's early surrealism with his love of nature and animals, combined with his dark view of civilization and an idiosyncratic pagan 'religion,' of sorts – all done in a captivating rhythm not unlike that of a fairy tale or a children's nursery rhyme. Brodksy showed me how images from the Russian circus were vital to the work. He did the same of explications for me with various other Zabolotsky poems, including "The Celebration of Agriculture," a long poem that helped lead to Zabolotsky's arrest in the 1930s.

I note that in Brodsky's explication of Zabolotsky's poems, he was doing the same kind of 'dissecting' for which he criticized the academics, but I didn't say anything. I think the whole purpose, and perhaps the only purpose, of literary criticism is to make the work more understandable, more easily appreciated and much more appreciated.

I spent a lot of my time working with the long poems of Zabolotsky's 'middle period,' which had hardly been studied, if even mentioned. They were difficult nuts to crack. One student from Denmark had written a thesis that was close enough to mine to merit attention, but these were the days before the JSTOR electronic database and the Internet in general. It took months to get a copy, but by then I had completed my thesis and had received my PhD. Reading it later, I found that it worked pretty well along with my thesis, and did not really contradict it. Some day I would like to meet this student, who is probably now a renowned Russian professor and specialist.

In the 1990's, some fifteen years hence, Soviet files were opened, and Soviet writers were 'rediscovered' and their long-suppressed works were published.

In retrospect, after several biographies and many scholarly articles had appeared in the fifteen years after I wrote my dissertation, I was able to judge the guesses I had made about Zabolotsky in the mid-1980s. With all the new data now available, it seems that I was dead-on right some of the time and dead-wrong other times. I think that overall, I broke even.

Money was tight for Julie and me, and that generated a good share of our arguments. It got to the point that every chance we had, we returned to Minnesota, where I would sneak in waitering shifts at The Lexington Restaurant and make enough money in tips to finance the trip and we would return to Ann Arbor with more dough than two months of a graduate school teaching assistantship provided.

So we drove to Minnesota often for the money. The more 'charming' I was at work, the more in tips I received. I taught myself to be charming around people whom I didn't know. It is a mixed blessing. Many people find me insincere. Maybe it's because I don't know how to turn off this 'charm button.' I am better around crowds of strangers than I am around a couple of friends.

Julie wanted to return to Minnesota because she missed family and friends and she didn't like Ann Arbor. I soon knew by heart all of I-94's exits. We traveled that road so many times and sometimes in winter, we managed to check out its ditches and culverts too. Kids, it is ironic that your trip to your adoptive Mother's parents follows the same freeway.

Julie and I often had car breakdowns on the way there or back. I was driving junkers – a couple of old Volkswagen beetles, one of which had its driver's door attached to the frame by a rope. A Renault 16. This car was great idea, far ahead of its time, but the French didn't know how to manufacture a front-wheel drive car with transverse engines. For one thing, they hadn't counter-sunk the engine bolts and screws. A front-wheel car's torque will cause everything to loosen, I saw. As we drove, then, little and inconsequential things, such as water pumps, liked to fall off. Today, most cars are built the way this Renault was – transverse engine, front-wheel drive, MacPherson struts, but they are built much better now. The 1965 Ford station

wagon that we drove across country on our 'honeymoon' with Gretta –
it was a dinosaur that soon died.

With each trip, I felt Julie drifting away from me. Our
relationship was as broken-down as the clunkers I drove. I tried to
deny it, but we slipped further and further apart. I grew more tense,
more insecure, more desperate.

So I choose to think about cars rather than relationships and
feelings and my graduate studies and my thesis, that loomed like a
black cloud on an already-dark horizon. What a male thing to do.
Shame on me.

My first new car, a 1974 Audi Fox, was about the worst car
I've ever owned. "Road and Track" and "Car and Driver" had raved
about its innovations. But, Audi still hadn't gotten used to the idea of
front-wheel drive and fuel injection. This Audi was a true lemon. It
was lucky we ever made it back and forth at all. I recall the countless
times I had visited the Ann Arbor dealership, checking out the car and
its features before deciding to buy. The sales people got to know me
and greeted me like an old friend and like to show off the Audi Fox's
features. On the day I took possession of it, however, I drove to the
driveway leading out of the dealership, and the front hubcap fell off. I
walked back to the dealership office with the hubcap in hand. The
sales people acted as if they had never seen me before.

The car wouldn't start in winter, even when my boss'
Chevrolet Vega (one of the worst cars ever made) started. He, a World
War Two Marine, hated foreign cars and gloated over me and my
lousy German Audi. To show how much he hated German cars or
German anything, he pasted a picture of Adolph Hitler over the car's
windshield. I soon got rid of the Audi Fox (I pronounced the word
'fox' in a slightly different way, I confess). I traded it in for a
Plymouth Volare, a car that was much maligned later, but which
served me well.

Enough about cars. Back to feelings. Back to life. Julie started
staying home longer, between, say, Thanksgiving and Christmas. This
hurt. I was desperate, didn't know what to do. I found it hard to
concentrate. My grades showed it. So did my insomnia. Then her
Father had a second heart attack and she stayed pretty much in
Minnesota all the time. When she returned to Ann Arbor with me in
1976, things were so bad between us that I decided to move back to

Minneapolis with her.

I had finished with my PhD classes and was writing my thesis, or, rather, supposed to be writing my thesis. I could do that, or not do that, in Minnesota just as easily as in Ann Arbor, I decided. I could work at the Lexington as a waiter four nights a week. We'd be far better off financially -- Graduate teaching assistants don't thrive on the salaries they receive. The move would improve our relationship, I was convinced, but something quite the opposite occurred.

Each moment was tense, it seemed. I felt like I was in an ever-tightening vice. I recalled a serial movie that terrified me when I was a kid: A man was locked into a small room, and all four walls started moving in on him. The bulk of my thesis weighed down on me, so that I ended up with a marriage that was falling apart, and a dissertation that refused to write itself, and a bank account that was often overdrawn. I was being yanked back and forth. I was desperate as I saw Julie slipping further away, and finding it more difficult to conceal her anger and frustration. It was something like watching someone whom you love carried away by an ocean's undertow, until they disappear into the distance.

In Minneapolis, we lived with Julie's Mother and younger Brother, just two blocks from where Sonya and I decades later bought our home. Writing my thesis, in this age before computers, I had written notes on various kinds of paper, and I stacked them into logical piles in the basement, thus organizing, or failing to organize properly, things.

Julie, I think, resented the time I couldn't spend with her. She didn't like the hours I 'stole' from her, locked up in the back room with my typewriter or in the basement with my notes and books, or at work at the Lexington. She didn't like that I spent two hundred dollars for a new typewriter, an IBM Selectric, state-of-the-art back then. I tried to explain how it had print 'wheels' you could change so that you could change the font, and one of the fonts was Cyrillic, and unless you bought a Russian typewriter, this was the only way to type in Cyrillic, and parts of my dissertation needed to be in Cyrillic. She was not at all convinced.

She didn't like my working nights while in Minnesota, or sleeping in late, so she started to go out at night. Soon, she was arriving home later than I. That was the beginning of the end, I could see, without further denying it or looking the other way. She was having affairs. I slipped into a deep depression. I felt myself being pulled by that ocean's undertow. I knew I had to get out of the marriage, but I was a coward as well as an optimist, and the two can often be the same. Eventually I did move out and I filed for divorce. I was hoping that filing for divorce might somehow bring her back. The opposite happened, of course.

Had I overlooked her affairs, had I been more sympathetic, would the relation have survived? The questions gnawed at me for a long time, even though I felt that the answer was an unequivocal 'no.' It took a year or two to climb out of my black hole.

Romantic love, particularly passionate romantic love, can come and go, but a Father's love for his children is a constant that never diminishes.

Kids, I could write a book about my relations with women. It would be depressing.

A real downer.

Dear Kids:

Hang in there. My adventures in graduate school draw to a close.

I had gone from department golden boy in 1971 to department outcast in 1975. Having a French woman come and go and then having a wife come and go probably didn't help. Neither did hanging around Joseph Brodsky, because he had alienated a number of professors and because I probably somehow affected his willingness to tolerate the pressures to 'go on the road' and earn points for America and for the University of Michigan. Worse, I was a leader in a graduate students' strike in 1974.

For revenge, I suppose, I got nailed at my preliminary examinations in 1975.

"Who wrote <u>Anna KareElena</u>?" they asked.

It was too easy. "Count Leo Tolstoy."

"What is the full name of her lover?"

"Count Alexey Kirilich Vronsky," I answered.

"Who were the other main characters?" It was still too easy. I went down the list that was burnt into my head, along with a thousand or so other facts, names, dates, poets, authors, works. "Well, there's Anna and her husband and Vronsky, we already mentioned him, and there's her Brother and Sisters and-"

"What was the name of Vronsky's horse?" they asked.

"Who?"

"Vronsky's horse! The one he rode during his race. Surely you remember the name of Vronsky's horse!"

"I don't remember." Stupid question. How much time were they going to waste?

"It was Fru-Fru!" one professor shouted.

I failed my prelims. I was so pissed that I hung up some sarcastic notices on the department walls. Another student, who, I am sure, knew less than I did, passed. It was rumored that she had been sleeping with her dissertation committee chair. I sulked for a couple of months and then I took the exams a second time. I passed. I wrote my thesis on Zabolotsky.

My problems were not with the thesis per se, but with my dissertation committee. Brodsky refused to be on my committee. "College professors are petty and vengeful," he said. "If you offend one, he or she will remember it forever. Remember, they have only their ideas. Carpenters and plumbers are much better off – they have their own tools, physical things. As for your dissertation, you will have to go through it without me. Good luck."

Good luck indeed. Brodsky moved out East, where he belonged. I forged together a committee of people who, it turned out, did not like one-another. This is not a good tactic, should you ever be required to set up a dissertation committee. My specialization was literature, but I was using a linguistics-based approach (Semiotics and Structuralism just coming into vogue). I was using ideas and techniques that were still too new, that had not seeped down through the appropriate thick graduate school strata.

The linguists on my committee didn't like the literature people, the literature people didn't like the linguists, and nobody liked my cognate member, a German professor of Hungarian origin who rambled on for hours on subjects no one cared about. Mark Kirkonen, my chairman, didn't have the clout to hold any of it together. I was pretty much ignored by Professor Danilova, what with my committee meetings preempted by her unscheduled visions of Jesus Christ, and not even during office hours.

She had no time for me, of course. I couldn't compete with Jesus, but when it came time for the last review right before typing up the final copy, and in town to attend my dissertation defense, the tongue-swallowing Professor Danilova finally managed to right herself, read my thesis, and tell me how much she disliked my approach, and that I had to re-write the whole thing, and why didn't I try to sound more scholarly anyway?

Not owning a shotgun, I did the requisite re-write, trying to synthesize the various opinions of various committee members (e.g., "Section Five is too long" …"Section Five needs some 'fleshing-out'"). This time I hired a hungry graduate student to type the thesis because I couldn't bring myself to plow through it yet another time. Professor Danilova frowned and shook her head. It was not scholarly-sounding enough. The cognate professor said my syntax was too twisted. I had prepared myself for this one. I pulled out a copy of an article written by this elegant cognate member, and I read aloud one of his sentences that went on for seven lines and that said absolutely nothing, the way a snake coils and swallows itself.

This was not good politics, but I had gotten my fill of my committee and of the department in general, and then the university was asking for a thousand dollars more because I hadn't taken enough dissertation-writing credits, and they wanted cash.

Despite all that, I somehow kept my mouth shut and I got my PhD, and I was happy to get the hell out of town.

I remember pounding on my steering wheel with joy, and honking my horn on I-94 when I looked through my rear-view mirror and saw the green sign with white letters that said 'Ann Arbor. Next Exit.' That sign disappeared from my rear-view mirror. I breathed more easily.

My dissertation sucks. I checked the Library of Congress catalog recently, and I was pleased to discover that not one person had checked. I could argue, if I wanted, that the reason no one checked it out is because they weren't able to find it. The committee had forced me to use their then-current darling transliteration style, against my own judgment and desires – the style that soon went out of style. Nikolai Zabolotsky had become Nikolaj Zabolockij or something like that.

Who? It doesn't matter. I don't want anyone to read my lousy thesis anyway.

Dear Anna, Katya, and Alex:

Okay, so I got a Masters Degree and a Doctorate in Slavic Languages and Literatures, with a specialization in Russian poetry -- in particular, the works of the 1930's Russian Expressionists. Look for those qualifications in the 'Help Wanted' section of any newspaper.

What were my connections with Russia, or with the Soviet Union, then?

In 1977 I had finished up my thesis, and I was working full-time at 'The Lexington,' Saint Paul's idea of a fancy-schmantsy supper club, while I searched for a teaching job.

Funny, but that year working as a waiter was the financial high point of my life. I had a three-bedroom apartment on Summit Avenue, Saint Paul's best-known fancy-dandy mansion-filled street that F.Scott Fitzgerald, before heading the hell out of there, called "a museum of American architectural failures." I drove a new sporty Fiat, and I recall waking up some mornings and muttering, "Damn! There's too much cash lying around this place again. I need to go to the bank!"

Compare that, kids, with my life now, after working for over fifty years. I live in a mobile home that's thirty-three years old and has sheds made out of Masonite that is rotting away not slowly enough. Only you, kids, keep me going at times.

Teaching jobs were hard to come by back then, but I finally got lucky. Adele Dubrovicha, my professor at the University of Minnesota, had worked in a Displaced Persons' Camp in Europe after the war, and she had met a super-enterprising Russian from Latvia named Ilya Ivanov. Ilya, a geologist by profession, had become head of the Russian Department at Southern Methodist University in Dallas at the time in the early 1960s, when colleges were dragging Russian immigrants off the street. He was looking to hire a young American professor – one who could take student groups to the Soviet Union.

Why the emphasis on travel to the Soviet Union? The Soviets had just published an article in "Pravda" about how Ivanov had used his time there, as a supposed leader of American students, to do bad, un-Soviet things, such as spending nights with a Soviet female comrade, and smuggling out forbidden books.

"Pravda" published a picture of Ivanov, as a college student in Riga, standing under a swastika and smiling.

The Soviets kicked him out and wouldn't let him back in.

Ivanov liked me, especially when he found out that I wasn't Jewish ("They are backstabbers and cannot be trusted, and watch out for the Jew who teaches Russian history.") Oh. Okay.

I flew down to Dallas for interviews with administrators and other professors, who seemed to like me too, although not extraordinarily so.

It is the truth that generally and almost without exception, I do not impress people at first interviews or at first meetings. I have slid into nearly every job I've ever had, whether it's waitering or teaching or practicing law or working as a law librarian. There has always been, it seems, considerable resistance to hiring me that must be overcome. Usually, I am 'reluctantly' hired. But soon thereafter I become a 'star.' I could come up with a long list, beginning with Navy Language School and ending with my second-to-last job, as a law firm librarian and instructor. (My last job, at the College of Law, didn't count because they had already heard I was a star.)

So in 1978 I was hired as an Assistant Professor of Russian at Southern Methodist University, and I celebrated that in Saint Paul. I had a PhD. I had a job. I was over my divorce. Life was good.

I had a super crush on darling, sweet, beautiful Mary, a grad student working at the Lexington. She was Irish and smart and pretty and from a good family. My job was to train her as a waitress and I had a hard time working with her and not dropping things. I was too afraid to 'make any moves' on her, however. I was shell-shocked perhaps. Later, when it was too late, I found out that she had been attracted to me too and had a hard time following me around without dropping plates. The Lexington must have lost a lot of china that year.

Then I decided to become infatuated with another red-haired Saint Paul Irish woman, but it seemed that she liked me only when she was intoxicated. I will write no more on the subject, and I probably should have written less. I don't want anybody suing my butt or any other part of my anatomy.

Ilya wrote from Dallas that he and his wife were visiting Saint Paul in early July for a Latvian convention or something, and he would like to see me. I invited them to stay with me in that gigantic apartment on that street of architectural failures, and they accepted. We had dinner with Mary, and they loved her. Mrs. Ivanova, a stern-sounding sort who was not all stern, was indeed stern one morning at breakfast in my apartment. Later, Ilya whispered to me that she had come across some 'personal reading materials' in his luggage. The materials had nothing to do with the Russian language or literature.

Then there was silence from Dallas. I had been hired, but no contract came. "You must be patient," Ilya wrote in late July. "All will be fine. Just some administrative problems. No need to worry."

No contract came in the mail within the next three weeks, so I called Ilya. "Is no problem," he said. "You will sign when you get here."

"What about my moving expenses?" I asked.

"They will all be paid. Save receipts. Please not to worry!"

So I drove down to Dallas in a rented Ryder truck without air-conditioning – an accessory that was mandatory for good health. This I discovered while driving a large circle all around the city of Dallas. Dear Sean Ryan, rest his soul, the son of the manager (rest his soul too, as you rest the soul of most people whom I knew) of the Lexington, following me in my car. We got lost, missing the turn to Central Expressway and we had to circle the city during rush hour when it was over one hundred degrees and there was no air-conditioning in the truck and Dallas freeways and highways were horribly under-built, considering the volume of trucks, busses, cars, and rented trucks.

We finally found Ivanov's place, late in the evening. There was a note on the door. 'Ilya in hospital.'

We met him and his wife in the hospital and then we slept two nights at their house and visited Ilya during the day. "All will be fine, all will be fine," he kept repeating, as if it wouldn't at all be fine. "You can live with me and Sandra – We have big house, two bathrooms. I will tell you how to maneuver this administration. There is a Jew or two you must watch out for."

Funny how prejudiced people often display the very traits they find so hateful in their targeted group. Carl Jung would have a thing or two to say about that. Nobody could connive like Ilya.

I decided it best not to move in with him, and Sean and I drove to an apartment rental office and we found a third-floor, one-bedroom apartment on Park Lane, which was then the northern edge of Dallas, where new apartment complexes were popping up daily, spreading over the parched landscape like kudzu. These were the hot days of Dallas' expansion. There are now miles of apartments and town houses beyond Park Lane.

Sean and I drove the Ryder truck to SMU and we dropped off at the curb all my books and teaching materials. They were stored in liquor boxes I'd taken from the Lex. People stared. Teachers looked the other way when we passed. I concluded that it probably was because of the liquor boxes on the street or in the halls of a strict Methodist campus. But why were all the people so cold and rude? What was all this crap about 'warm Texas personalities?'

But there was yet another facet.

Someone at SMU had decided that the school didn't need a Russian Department at all, and they had cancelled my position. Apparently, Ilya the geologist had done a lot of conniving to get the department started in the first place, and now someone had called his bluff and had over-run him.

The reason no contract came to me in Minneapolis was, simply, because there was no contract. And there would not be a contract, kids. I was up that proverbial creek, without means of proper propulsion, as they say, usually more crudely but equally as accurate.

Ilya had tried to force the administration into a squeeze play, you see. He figured that if I showed up on the SMU doorstep with liquor boxes filled with books, they'd have to accept me and give me a contract. Much later, I learned that they had decided to cancel the second position in Russian, the one I thought that I was assuming, and that instead, I would take Ilya's position a year later, when he retired.

Thus, I would end up being the single professor in the Russian Department, with my job commencing a year later than promised, and then this position would be cancelled eventually too, because one-person departments cannot survive no matter how hard that one professor works. (I know this from experience.).

The life expectancy of one-person departments is not very long. There are too many classes to teach, too much 'marketing' that needs to be done, too much effort to create and maintain a high profile, too much clerical work, and too much research and writing to maintain scholarly standards. There were not enough hours in the day or in the days of the year for me to receive tenure, years down the pike. Also, there was not enough energy in me.

But no one had told me about the year's delay of my full-time job, or I could have decided to forget all about driving down I-35 one thousand miles to the outskirts of Dallas for the first year or for the second year or forever. For that first year, it turned out, I'd teach one course each semester, for which I'd receive one thousand dollars. I think that my first check was for one hundred and eighty dollars, not enough to cover my rent, which was the cheapest rent I could find. I told Ilya I was going to file bankruptcy.

"You must not do that at a <u>Methodist</u> university," he said. He scrambled and came up with a five thousand dollar grant for me, which, he said, I would receive at the end of the school year. It turned out that he had approached one of the university's major donors, a renowned oil man, which infuriated the University administrators greatly. "Professor Ivanov is begging for peanuts from people who we want to give us elephants."

I put in a request for my moving expenses. "No. You can't get that until your contract begins, which is next August," the Dean wrote back.

I was broke. I requested an advance on my next check. I got it. I was able to pay some of my bills, and at least the power company hadn't shut off my electricity, which I needed badly for air-conditioning -- my Minnesota blood didn't like 116 degrees. Even with the air-conditioning running at full blast, I could feel the oppressive heat seeping through the apartment's cheap, paper-mache walls.

Credit card companies and banks sent me nasty letters. Hell, I should have stayed at 'The Lexington' and complain about having to make too many trips to the bank. In Dallas, I couldn't afford the next month's rent, or non-essentials such as food. I requested another advance.

The Dean sent me a memo about how I should learn to manage my finances better.

I was pissed.

"What finances?" I wrote back. "I was supposed to be making twelve thousand dollars a year, and you people are paying me seven thousand, it seems -- five thousand of which is supposed to come at the end of the school year. I can't live on it. And you won't pay me my moving expenses."

I wrote carefully this detailed memorandum, with colons in all the right places, and I worked hard to keep it as polite as I could. After all, Russian studies was a small world, so If I blew up at SMU, within months everyone in the world of American, Academic Russiandom would know about it.

The Department Secretary, a lovely and charming woman, and a student as well as a writer – She told me that I was called to the Dean's office at two that afternoon. I was supposed to be scared, I suppose. But I wasn't, children. I was pissed, and, figuring I was going to be given my walking papers anyway, I intended to give Mr. Dean a piece of my mind before heading back up I-35, holding myself back just enough to keep my professional reputation intact elsewhere.

I was surprised the first moment I walked into his office and sat down in a classy but uncomfortable upholstered chair. The Dean was entirely apologetic. He said that he had no idea Ilya hadn't told me about the one-year delay, and, in fact, that absolutely no one expected me to show up that year, except for a certain conniving ex-geologist. The Dean apologized profusely, called me a gentleman for the relatively restrained way I was handling it all, and he got me another course to teach the next semester, for fifteen hundred dollars.

But I was still way in debt, so I got a job in, where else, a restaurant. Ilya was shocked. "This is Christian university. We cannot have a professor working in restaurant, in one that serves liquor especially. It would not look good for the department. Your enemies will find out, and those Jews will use it against you."

To hell with him, as well as his disgusting anti-Semitism. I worked in a hotel restaurant anyway, making more money on weekends than I did during the week. I had worked hard find a restaurant that was out of the way. It would be somewhat embarrassing to wait on one of my students or a faculty member, no?

My job was at the Dunphey Royal Coach Hotel, which I called 'The Dumpy Hotel' or 'The Royal Roach.' It was a dive, and it was torn down soon thereafter. Dunphey had tried to grow too fast, from a single Massachusetts hotel to a giant chain, after getting money from Aer Lingus Irish Airlines and buying the Royal Coach chain and a bunch of Sheraton hotels. It was a typical case where management of a successful establishment is seduced into going national, can't manage multiple locations, and flounders and then dies.

I wore black pants and black shoes and a horrid shirt, not tucked in, decorated in orange, black, and green stripes.

Some nights we had no customers and some nights we had a few customers, so it was an easy place to work, and the employees were a most interesting group. In some respects, I had chosen well. No students or professors dropped by. The actors and crew for the "Dallas" TV show stayed at the hotel, although they usually ate elsewhere, except for Keenan Wynne. You'd go into the kitchen to pick up his food that he had ordered an hour ago, and the chef was nowhere to be seen, nor the assistant chef, nor the sous chef, not anyone.

Some days, an INS van pulled up to the front of the hotel, and the entire staff disappeared, either shoved into the truck or running from the premises. I was hoping that all of them could get the hell off the truck and run.

I cooked my customers' meals one evening when the kitchen was empty. The dish-washer was out back, smoking a long joint. The customers that evening complained about the lousy service, but not about the food.

I loved teaching, and it was good that I did. If the program was to build, I needed to teach five or six courses a semester because we were short one person. I also taught summer school and conducted student study trips to Russia twice a year and taught in the Master of Arts program in the evening. There was no time for research, and without books and scholarly articles, there would be no tenure, I knew. I saw the writing on the wall.

I think I did a better job than they expected. I quadrupled Russian enrollments, mostly by aligning with the Russian history professor, the Jew about whom I was continually warned. We became good friends. We enjoyed making fun of Ilya behind his back.

Together this history professor and I, along with Mary Vernon, an art historian, created a bang-up introductory course on Russian Culture, from which I mined language majors and from which he mined history majors and from which Mary mined art history students.

The problem was, according to Ilya, that I had 'given' half of this course to the enemy, the History Department, and to a Jewish professor besides.

At least I got to visit the Soviet Union once or twice a year, conducting the student study tours, which were really just tourist tours about which the students were later required to write a paper. I had an especially wonderful time when SMU art historian Mary Vernon came along as a co-leader.

Kids, we visited her in Dallas in the summer of 2008. You loved her, as I always. Besides, she had a great swimming pool. She designed the cover for this book. Bless her.

She could captivate anyone on any subject. Every palace, every museum, every church became a giant repository of fascinating information. I remember that in big museums, such as the Russian Museum in Leningrad, other tourist groups gathered around her as she guided our SMU students through the rooms. Even people who apparently knew no English followed us. Even the little old ladies who guarded each room while wearing felt boots, shivering, and dozing off – even they perked up and paid attention.

One time, it appeared that she had gotten too close to one of the paintings that she was discussing. A guard who knew no English tried to convey to her the proper distance for viewing a painting. Mary Vernon showed him her pointer, marked in centimeters, and she measured off the distance between her and the painting. The guard nodded, in awe. Mary was keeping the proper distance, exactly and instinctively. The guard bowed. It was a meeting of professional minds, a respected accord between two dedicated professionals.

The first year, we took students to Zagorsk, the museum and monastery complex a bit out from Moscow. As we went through the various churches and visited the grave of Boris Godunov, Mary and I noted that four people always remained directly behind us, keeping a 'comfortable' distance. "KGB, undoubtedly," said Mary, and I agreed. In my life, I have had enough encounters with KGB people and FBI people. Although, enemies, they resemble one-another. I can't put my finger on it, but I can often tell. Ask me later about the time a Soviet exchange student moved to SMU, and the FBI offered me a free liquor cabinet and all the women I wanted, in exchange for keeping track of this Soviet student.

Back to Zagorsk. It was a frigid winter day, and while we were inside, the temperature had dropped and the parking lot had become one giant skating rink. As we led our students to our bus, sliding much of the way and falling a few times too, we saw the four KGB people spinning the wheels of their Volga sedan, unable to move on the ice. Mary and I and a few students pushed the back of their car until it slid onto better ground and its tires gripped the pavement.

We waved at the car's passengers, and they waved back at us.

Teaching is a great ride, just like writing, as long as you don't do it to show off what you know. My students read Russian novels in translation and wrote marvelous, insightful things about them, as good as I have read in professional journals.

I wonder how many dried-up teachers harvest their students' fresh ideas. I recall one professor at the University of Michigan (whom I will not name because I don't like anybody suing me)who announced on the first day of our seminar on twentieth century poetry, that he was writing a book on proletarian poetry (a super-boring topic, to me and to others, and hardly worth examining), and he didn't want one word uttered in class or written in papers, that didn't touch on that subject.

At SMU, I smoked too many cigarettes and didn't eat enough, but classes were going well. One student was a problem. For my Russian Culture class, he turned in a geography paper that started out something like, "As the wide Amur River flows by, it is pleasurable to sit on its banks and sip native tea and sample the local cuisine."

Huh? This was not the writing of an SMU undergraduate, to be sure. But where did he get it? I thought "Readers Digest," but, no, that magazine was too anti-Soviet for such a benevolent tone. It had to be another publication with a similar narrative voice but not as anti-Soviet. Of course! "National Geographic!" I went to the undergraduate library and in fewer than five minutes, I had the 'Amur' article in my hands. The cheater hadn't changed a word. Lazy bastard.

I checked out the issue and stuck it in my desk drawer, then called in the student. I gave him many chances to back down on his claim that he had written the paper. He didn't admit to anything, "No, professor, I wrote <u>every</u> word of that!" He then decided to look offended.

I pulled the issue out of my drawer. He was silent.

I didn't turn him in, although I should have, according to the school's honor code, I think. He assured me that he had learned from this horrible occurrence, the <u>single</u> mistake in his otherwise pristine life, and he would never do anything like it again, even if his Grandmother continued dying. A month later, he ran for student council and won.

I think I should have turned the guy in.

Dear Young Adults:

The writing on the 'tenure wall' grew clearer and clearer. Without the time to conduct research or write scholarly papers and books, I would never get tenure, meaning I'd have to leave SMU in five years and find another teaching job for the next six years, or probably for fewer years, if I was lucky, and then it then would be time to move again. There are 'itinerant' Russian professors who bounce from school to school every year or so, earning wages that are embarrassing. I didn't want to become one of them.

I quit teaching in 1980 and started law school, law being the 'default' second choice of a career for many people. I got a job working as a bartender at S&D Oyster Company on McKinney Street, just south of SMU. I was able to eat dozens of raw oysters every shift because I slipped beer to the oyster shuckers next to me. It helped ease the tedium of their awful jobs. What they say about oysters is true, I think.

Then I got a clerking job at the law firm of Jones and Knight downtown in the First Bank Building.

Now, there are two types of clerking jobs in law. One is the 'courtship' job. They give you an office and a leather briefcase with your initials on it, right next to the handle, and they treat you like a real lawyer and give you research assignments and watch how you perform, with an eye to hiring you when you finish law school.

Then there's the second type of clerking job, where you just do what needs to be done and you get paid okay for it (fifteen dollars an hour then, a most respectable wage – about three times more than teaching Russian, for instance).

My job belonged to that second category of clerkships. I made copies and filled the Coke canisters and put together dreadfully long and complicated closing books and updated the loose-leaf research books and treatises and the firm's collections of statutes and regulations.

They liked me more than they thought they would (I told you already how that often happened), and I liked them, and by my second year of law school there was talk of having me do a 'real clerkship,' with embossed leather briefcase, office, and all.

But some of the attorneys were opposed to it. "It would be too uncomfortable," said one. "Making the transition from staff to attorney – it would not work out." This was the attorney who spent hours dictating every one-page letter, signing off on each one by dictating his invariable closing even, "Erik with a K space T period space Bennett with a double N and a double T." He had the same secretary for six years, but he didn't trust her, or anyone, to get anything right. He's now a law professor, which is right where he belongs, according to my way of thinking.

I quit that Erik with a K law firm, and I got another clerking job, this time for a crazy attorney named Wordy Jack Jones. He claimed it was his given name. If so, how could he <u>not</u> have become a lawyer? His office stood in a garish and failing, nearly-empty complex called 'European Village' that had nothing at all European about it, although it tried with its false towers and plywood balconies and rounded windows with plastic inserts. The only genuine European thing about it was a German restaurant that served no German food, but that closed a week or so after I started working for Wordy. The complex was deserted. Fine. There was no trouble parking. Ironically, the complex was not far from the Dumpy Hotel, on 'Northworst' Highway.

Wordy's secretary drove around the bad parts of Dallas on weekends, collecting cash in paper sacks from Wordy's criminal law clients.

Wordy was drowning in work. He could charm the pants off anybody but he was so busy charming people out of their pants or skirts that he had no time to do the work that he promised, which he didn't like doing anyway. One law clerk couldn't make that much difference, but I did an awful lot of law there, before graduating, balancing myself precariously all the time, right at the edge of malpractice.

Then Wordy got tied up with his own real estate investments which, two years later, would get him disbarred. Luckily, I had quit before that. And anyway, I was graduating from law school and would have a full-time attorney job soon. I would be a hot property, what with my Russian language and my law degree, and I would be rich too, no doubt living in one of Dallas' many gated communities, or perhaps I'd move to New York or Washington, D.C. I had heard that New York had lovely co-op housing in Manhattan.

One of Wordy's clients was a travel office owner. He needed someone to accompany a group of tourists to Hong Kong. People didn't want to fly Korean Airlines there because the Soviets had shot down a Korean Airlines passenger jet just months before. I was in Hong Kong only about sixteen hours, but I was much intrigued.

I did a series of short interview programs for Dallas public television, to go along with a documentary series about World War Two, and 'the second front,' where the Nazis and Russians fought, and which turned out to be the determining factor in the ending of the war. I made the mistake of saying on the air that the city of Leningrad had lost seven hundred thousand civilians during the siege, and, to give a sense of the scope of that loss, I mentioned that fifty thousand American soldiers were killed in World Wars I and II combined.

I received hate mail about not appreciating the losses of American soldiers, and threats about burning crosses on my lawn, but I had no lawn then. I also had no money.

I graduated from Law School in May of 1984, having worked most of the time at two-or three jobs simultaneously. I was lost in the ends of an extremely tangled and passionate relationship, and my grades were awful. I had the single distinction that I could do a passable imitation of the dean during student presentations.

My career timing had never been good, and it hadn't improved. For example, I had received my PhD in Russian the very year that federal government funding fell through for Russian language training, so the number of students decreased greatly. I had received a free ride through graduate school, but by 1977, the USSR was not so much of a threat anymore, and funding was cut and teaching jobs were scarce. Many of my fellow graduate students ended up driving cabs, selling aluminum siding, or waiting on tables in bars and restaurants.

And it was the beginning of the 'third wave' of emigration from the Soviet Union, the first being after the revolution, people like Olga and Elena and my other Russian professors in Monterey, the second being after World War II and the massive shifting around of people and nations. Now, with the Jackson-Vanick Amendment allowing emigration for hordes of Soviet citizens, I was no longer a hot property but cold property and out-dated and unwanted. I had been lucky to get my teaching job at SMU.

Having finished law school, I was ready for a high-paying job in the law, but the world was not ready for me, or else, my time had passed. I sent resumes to all the Dallas firms and to firms in New York and foreign cities and Minnesota, including the Soviet Union and American law firms that did business in the Soviet Union. Nobody wanted a new lawyer with mediocre grades and with a PhD in Russian literature. No one wanted an aging, recycled academic.

Whenever fellow law students, even those with grades as mediocre as mine, went to an interview, the hiring partners asked which law school classes had interested them the most, and what they saw themselves doing in five years, etc. With me (when I did manage to get an actual interview, that is), they demanded, "Why did you go to law school?" or "Why do you have a PhD?" or "Why did you quit teaching?" We never got around to discussing the subject at hand.

This was 1984, not a good year for looking for a law job. Oil prices had dropped, and the Dallas economy was going south. People living in four hundred thousand dollar homes with three hundred thousand dollar mortgages all of a sudden discovered they were living in two hundred thousand dollar homes with three hundred thousand dollar mortgages.

As for doing business with the Soviet Union, the shooting down of Korean Airlines Flight 007 a year earlier had killed that. Americans were smashing bottles of Stolychnaya Vodka in the streets. It was not a popular time for being a Russophile. Few people went to Russia, and no new joint enterprises were formed between the two countries. I lay low, presuming the storm would eventually pass.

I stuck it out that summer, studying for the Texas Bar exam and going to any interview offered. There were hardly any of those.

One came from a different part of Texas, an interesting part. I emptied my checking account that was nearly empty anyway, and I drove to Austin for an interview with the Texas State Department of Waste Management. How low would I have to stoop, I wondered, just to make a living? Waste management? After the bumpy career road I had traveled, that would have been a fitting conclusion.

But, I had been asked for an interview, it turned out, because the interviewer had been a Russian major before she got smart and got out of the field, and she thought it would be fun to talk about Russia during her day in the offices of solid waste management.

Me?

I went broke.

I wasn't even good enough for the sewers of Texas.

Dear Alex, Katya, Anna:

The earth circles the sun, the sun circles something else, and sometimes our lives make circles.

When I was teaching Russian at SMU, I conducted two study tours to the Soviet Union per year – one during the semester break following Christmas, and the other in early summer.

In the winter of 1978, dear Friend Mary Vernon and I led a group of twenty SMU students to the Soviet Union. They would choose a topic, observe it in the Soviet Union, research it back home, and then write a paper if they wanted to get credit for the course.

Our train took us to Leningrad. 1970 seemed so distant. Wounds had healed and their scars even had disappeared. As was so typical for such study trips, the American students were frustrated, if not angry, that their time in the Soviet Union consisted of visiting palaces in order to hear from a tour guide speaking broken English, who built the palace, who lived there, who died or was murdered there, how many pieces of china were contained in the buffets. In churches, they learned how many icons rested on the iconostasis, how tall was the onion dome, how many workers had died of lead poisoning while applying gold to the exterior of those onion-shaped domes.

This sort of thing can grow old for all but the most stalwart of scholars. It grew especially old, and rapidly so, for those young Americans who had put down a great deal of cash with the hopes that they would meet their Soviet counterparts.

Whole divisions of the KGB existed just to keep such meetings to an absolute minimum but sometimes there were chinks in this Russian stone wall. Maybe those young Soviet citizens worked for the KGB, maybe they were members of prominent families who feared nothing, or maybe they were simply brave or foolhardy.

Our fourth night in Leningrad, four students caught me at dinner. "Some Russians have invited us to a party. They are young even, not like the old Russians who are the only ones we've been allowed to meet."

I gave them permission to go, offered them a whole cache of warnings, and told them to be sure to get back to the hotel by eleven o'clock, long before the bridges would go up.

"There's one problem," said Dan, the apparent leader of the Americans. "We don't speak <u>any</u> Russian, and these Russians hardly speak any English."

"So?"

"Um, we'd like you to come with us. The other students are going to the Leningrad Philharmonic, right?"

"Right," I had to admit.

"Then you are free. Mary Vernon is going along to the concert." Dan was making a good case, and I could see already how this all would conclude. "You can come with us, Professor Jack!"

So I agreed, against my better judgment. A block from the hotel (a safe distance), a group of young Russians stood in a lazy circle, heads lowered, hands in pockets, faces nearly totally concealed by Russian fur hats whose flaps were allowed to flap.

Dan introduced me to the young Russians, who lowered their heads even further and glowered at me. Then they looked at one-another, then at the Americans, then at me. No doubt they considered me the American counterpart of a KGB 'goon.'

We took a trolley, on a route with which I had been familiar long ago. It passed right by Natalya's parents' apartment. The trolley, one of the sleek metal ones, was nearly empty. We chatted along the way, so that by the time we climbed the typically grimy steps of an old apartment building, the Russians seemed to have let down their guard a bit. They might have even begun to trust me a little.

It was a big apartment, so no doubt the parents of the young person throwing this party were Soviets of importance. No wonder these young Russians were not afraid of meeting Americans, although I did recall that they had remained two blocks from the Americans' hotel.

In the apartment, someone or two someone's, with great muscles no doubt, had pushed all the furniture to one side of the giant front room, and the pieces were all draped in white.

I interpreted. American guy with Soviet girl. Soviet guy with American guy. They lined up in front of me, the way a priest might give out communion. Sometimes the Russians helped me by explaining some of the new Leningrad patois. I got a headache, as I worked the bifurcated sides of my brain – American English (not much of a problem then) on one side, and Russian, ever-weakening, on the other side.

Soon, one of the Russians walked up to a side wall, and pulled down a wooden door half the size of the room. Inside it rested a giant reel-to-reel tape player of German make, and six or seven shelves containing rows of tapes in their cases, each case with English and Russian titles.

The music blared. It hurt my ears and gave my headache new meaning; yet, it had a positive side as well. The music was so loud that the young ones no longer wanted to talk – they wanted to dance. I noticed some of the Russian males and females studying carefully the moves of the Americans, and trying to imitate them.

The single exception to all this was a stout Russian young man with a square, red face. He stood in the middle of the room, doing things to the 'Twist' that Chubby Checker could have never imagined or he would have kept the dance to himself.

As if to separate themselves from this gyrating individual whose shirt had wet marks under its arms, the Russians danced off to the side. Some of the Americans looked on in horror as they too removed themselves from this Russian, who was now out of control, like a satellite that had lost its gyroscope and all communication with the earth. Others – both Russians and Americans, I could see, stifled laughs. The sweat marks under the square-headed guy's arms grew in circumference as he continued executing his version of how one should dance the 'Twist.' The other Russians and the Americans, off to the sides of the room, danced in the way that was then fashionable – the world of music and dancing having progressed far from the days of Chubby Checker and his 'Tveest,' as it was called in Russian. Square-Head was oblivious to all this, proving that one could easily lose oneself in the captivating rhythms of Chubby Checker's dance, and not notice what was going on nearby -- not even derisive laughter and the caustic remarks, in two languages, that increased in volume, keeping time with the dancer's sweat marks.

One of the Russians danced his way over to the tape player, and he doubled the volume. The walls shuddered. I could hear something pounding on the ceiling, I could hear that someone was outside the door, using words I hadn't heard since the week in language school nearly fifteen years earlier, when we had to study Soviet profanity. My ears ached.

Luckily, I stood alone, off in a corner, as far as possible from the tape player, and I was no doubt a left-over from a time long-passed. I took advantage of my freedom, and I slipped into a side room, opposite the tape player – a room separated from the big room by French doors, about half-way open or closed, depending on a person's viewpoint.

I was looking out at the dancers, but I sensed some kind of soft rustling behind me. A young woman stepped out of the shadows, stood alongside me, and rested her fingers on one of the panes of the French doors, about even with the pane upon which I had rested my fingers. I looked at her.

It was Elena.

She was now a full-grown woman in a woman's body, but her eyes were the same eyes that I had seen eight years ago, when she was about fifteen. This was the Elena, the star-struck young lady whom I could never understand, who had followed me whenever she could. She was the younger sister of Vera, at whose party I had met Natalya, eight years earlier. She was Elena who in 1971 explained to me why my dreams had all fallen apart, like a shattered Faberge egg, like my father's burnt out wreck of a truck.

Elena turned to me. Her eyes glowed as if there was candlelight, but there was no candle. Then traced her window pane and then looking through the glass into the room.

"That man out there? The one in the center of the room who is making a fool of himself?"

I was just about ready to say something caustic, but she cut me off.

"That man is my husband-to-be."

"Oh," I said, or tried to say, but it was more like deflating than uttering a monosyllabic word.

My head shook, in a direction that would have suggested a 'no.' I couldn't help it, couldn't stop it. I tried to stop it, but failed. I said "Oh!" one more time. There was no use even trying to think about smiling politely, there being no chance that I could carry it off.

Her slim fingers slid down the pane that she had been touching, and on the pane beneath it, she made circles, as if drawing something. Her eyes watered, I could tell. "He is very well-connected – rich, from a well-positioned family. He can travel abroad, to engineering conferences and such things. I will be able to go with, probably, although the KGB sometimes hold spouses as 'hostages,' making sure the other spouse returns."

She said all this, as if reciting it by rote. Then she turned to me, looked at me, her eyes now red. "I have no respect, much less love for my husband-to-be." Her voice was as quiet as a whisper but it was not a whisper.

"Then – then, why marry him?"

She turned back into the window, as if looking off into something distant. She drew a figure with gentle taps of her finger nail on the window pane. "It is the best I can do in order to create a life that is tolerable for me."

Then she turned, and looked at me without blinking. "I always hoped that, when I grew up a little, you would come back for me. You see, I have always loved you. That time in 1971, when we were in the record booth and I held you at the waist and you held me? We didn't have to hug," she said, almost with a laugh that made her eyes glisten more. "I made that part up."

This time, she spoke slowly enough and clearly enough.

I grasped every word of hers, and each word cut into me.

Elena, dear Elena, may you have found that which you needed.

My Dear Children:

You have seen me write and re-write these letters many times. In the earlier versions, I left out one story because I thought it would make me look boastful. I don't want these letters to become just one more arrogant memoir (e.g. 'Read on! I am a very important person; too bad you are not') .

But I think this story wants to be told.

I led SMU study tours to the Soviet Union during Christmas breaks in the late 1970's and in the early 1980's. What I am going to write about is something that happened around 1981 or so.

That winter, our group had a really fun Soviet guide. Many of them had been super-serious, suspicious, and not fun. But Maria was different.

The Taganka Theater is a more-or-less experimental theater that's located in an old part of Moscow where tourists hardly go. They were putting on a stage version of Mikhail Bulgakov's Master and Margarita. The censors for decades had locked up the novel on which this play was based, but now it was available – if you could find a copy, which was doubtful. Master and Margarita is my favorite book of all time, from all countries. I wanted to see that play, but we were leaving Moscow in two days.

Maria, it turned out, was also a big fan of Bulgakov. She was the one who suggested that we (Maria, I, and Maria's sister) should try to get into the play, as impossible as that might be.

The American females in our group lent Maria and her Sister American clothes, and I gave them a pack of super-long 'More' cigarettes, something that Soviets could never get. I am sorry that I don't remember the name of Maria's Sister.

The theater lobby was jammed, more jammed even than the insides of the Cathedral of Saints Peter and Paul. The square outside the theater was also jammed, and everyone was begging for 'spare' tickets, also looking for a scalper or two. There were no scalpers, no spare tickets.

I recall one man standing on the pavement. "I will pay 100 rubles for a ticket!" No luck. "I will pay 100 rubles for a ticket, and I will give you the suitcase where the rubles lie." No luck. "I will pay 100 rubles for a ticket, and I will give you my grandmother's antique, French suitcase!" No luck. "I will pay 100 rubles for a ticket, and I will give you my grandmother's antique, French suitcase, plus my Grandmother!" No luck.

I felt sorry for him.

Somehow we managed to push through the crowd and get into the lobby. There was much screaming, entreating, begging. One woman leaned back and looked at me. "You are a professor."

"How do you know?" I asked.

"Your tweed coat and the suede patches on your elbows. Where are you from?"

"America."

"America? And you know Bulgakov?"

"I have read his book so many times that I know parts of it by heart. I would be anxious, for instance, to see how this play handles the enigmatic figure, Affranius."

Without uttering a word, this woman grabbed my arm tight, and she pushed me, like Sisyphus' rock, up to the administrator's door, which was about three steps above the rest of the lobby floor. Maria and her sister followed.

Of course, the door said "Do not disturb."

She pounded on the door so hard that its frame rattled, and I was afraid she might crack the marble on the wall. Finally a thin man in a white frock stepped out. "What is the meaning of this disruption? This is right before a performance. I am busy!"

"Here is an American professor!" she said. "He is leaving Moscow tomorrow. He is an expert on Bulgakov, and it is absolutely necessary that he sees your play this evening! This is absolutely necessary!"

The man shrugged and then walked back into his room and shut the door. A few moments later, he came back out, holding a slip of paper high in the air. "I have one ticket, one ticket only, for the American professor."

"Thank you, sir," I said. "But I came with two friends, and I don't want to leave them. We all can't get in and so we will all go together to find something else to do this evening. Thank you anyway."

"Are you crazy? Are you out of your mind" screamed people. "Get in there! Don't be a fool!" They pushed me towards the theater's entrance.

Consider, for a moment, that the administrator's giving away one ticket meant that the others in the lobby, who had hardly any chance at all to see the play, were now losing practically all chances. Still, they commanded me to accept the ticket. Bless those Russians.

Meanwhile, Maria and her Sister leaned against a wall, vamp style, and they were holding two unlit 'More' cigarettes.

But 'More' cigarettes and American clothes cannot hide a Russian. There was something about their eyes perhaps, or something about their expressions that a foreigner might take as haughtiness, although it wasn't at all. I am sure that the people jammed into that lobby knew the real nationality of those two young ladies. I am sure that the administrator knew as well.

The administrator came out of his office again, and this time he was holding up three pieces of paper. "You, sir!" he shouted. "You are a genuine gentleman. I have never, ever seen anyone like you."

The people in the lobby clapped.

"Three tickets for you!" said the administrator. "One for you, sir, and two for your, ahem, American friends!"

People in the lobby cheered. I could not imagine people in such a situation in any other country cheering. Perhaps I am wrong.

How can you not respect and love those Russians?

My two American friends and I sat to the right of the stage, in the third or fourth row. Actors who were not then on stage sat next to us or, if they didn't have a seat, leaned against our chair backs. I stood up and offered my chair, but they refused.

"Shut up, Sir Gentleman," Pontius Pilate commanded. "And watch the damned play!" Somehow the actors had found out about the events in the lobby.

I have written, read, and edited this section carefully. I want to make sure I have it all down, just as it happened.

I was not the 'hero' in that story. The heroes were the Russians who insisted that I take tickets that could otherwise have gone to them. People who had few chances for top-quality entertainment. People who no doubt had difficulty getting to the theater. People for whom nearly everything was hard to obtain.

Who cannot be proud of such selfless heroes?

Dear Anna, Katya, Alex:

Had Elena returned with me to America, she no doubt would not have imagined the lousy life she would have encountered. No gold lined my streets.

In 1984, I was jobless. I was broke. It was hopeless. I had no future.

I put my stuff in a storage place on wrong side of Dallas, and I drove back to Saint Paul and moved into that corner of my parents' unfinished basement that wasn't occupied by another under-employed Brother.

It was not a fun time for me. I was a total failure and loser at age thirty-nine. I had no job, no mate, no future. For money, I went back to 'The Lexington Restaurant,' where I had first started twenty-three years earlier. I went through my days mechanically, wondering how long I could keep up this or any other charade before giving up on it all and cashing in the chips that I didn't have, and never had. Maybe I would hitch-hike around the world without a dime in my pocket. Maybe I could have written a book about it and that would have given me money.

At this time, at least, on the nights when the real manager of 'The Lexington' was off work or on vacation, I was the manager on duty. This was my single success in those days, my lone advancement.

I applied for a job with the just-opening Saint Paul World Trade Center. The director was impressed, but suspicious. "Your resume looks like a train wreck from the air," he said, and he was correct.

Luckily for me, I didn't get the job, because the Trade Center idea soon 'went south,' as they say when something like that sours. It had been built through the efforts of Saint Paul Mayor George Latimer, who used to practice law with a lawyer friend of mine from the Eugene McCarthy campaign days in 1964, and through the efforts of Governor 'Goofy,' Rudy Perpich.

In 1986, Latimer decided to run for governor, which didn't sit well with Governor Goofy, who had earlier tried to open a chopsticks factory on the iron range and then tried to create an industry to sell

Minnesota peat to European countries even though, it turned out, that Minnesota peat doesn't burn very well at all. He tried creating a vast amusement park/museum in a big hole in the ground near his birthplace, the hole made by iron miners.

The director of the World Trade Center resigned to head Latimer's campaign.

Governor Goofy, known for his vindictiveness, made sure the Trade Center in Saint Paul died on the vine, even though it was one of the few things that Saint Paul had ever won, whereas Minneapolis or Bloomington, Minneapolis' booming suburb, won things like baseball stadiums and hockey stadiums

Today the 'Saint Paul World Trade Center' is a half-empty office building with retail space on the lower floors that can't hold tenants. The closest they ever got to being international was opening an "Au Bon Pain" pseudo-French restaurant chain on the first floor, but it closed too after a few months.

They have a lot of plywood over shop windows in downtown Saint Paul. The city, from necessity and for appearances, had found a lot of clever things to do with empty storefronts. Large, plastic, tacky casts of 'Peanuts' cartoon characters were popular because Charles Schultz was born in Saint Paul, although he left it as soon as he could.

In 1985, I started working by the hour for my attorney friend from back in the Eugene McCarthy days. His firm had two other attorneys, and I got to work on their backlog of cases.

Many people don't realize it, but many struggling law firms actually have plenty of work -- too much of it, in fact. It's just that the low likelihood of some of those cases or transactions paying off puts them and their crumbling bank boxes and their faded legal pad pages and their carbon copies of correspondence or their machine copies of correspondence, into window-less back rooms.

I spent most of my time putting together a zoning case for trial, representing a real estate developer who could talk out of multiple sides of his mouth simultaneously, and who had a wooden leg that he took off during trials sometimes, no doubt, to win the jury's sympathy. During one trial, his technique backfired. He had bilked a fellow amputee he'd met during physical therapy sessions, promising a triple return on the guy's workers compensation settlement check. The plaintiff took off his wooden leg at trial too. The real estate dealer lost.

The poor plaintiff, an unemployed and unemployable painter, never collected a penny.

When my lawyer friend decided it would be cheaper to hire me on salary rather than pay me by the hour, he hired me on salary. I passed the Minnesota Bar Exam in 1985. I was now a Texas attorney and a Minnesota attorney.

But I didn't like practicing law and working too many hours and spending weekends in law libraries and wondering how many bad turns I had made in my life and why I didn't have enough money to pay rent anywhere. That's when I started writing novels.

Children:

Remember Olga and her Mother, Nina, from 1966, in Language School? We wrote each-other sporadically, for years. Remember the photo of mathematician Chebyshow that I mailed to them?

Olga was touched and she wrote me. Blessed old Nina managed to scratch a few lines of greeting too, reminding me of my 'promise' that I would become a writer.

Then, a few years later, I received a brief note from Olga. I could hardly read the scrambled lines that I never would have recognized as Olga's delicate Russian cursive. But it was indeed a note from Olga. Mama Nina had died, Olga wrote. Her lines of blue ink were blurred in places. I sent flowers and a card and didn't hear back. I sent Christmas and Easter and Name Day cards, but didn't hear back.

Ten years later, I found out what had happened. Olga retired from teaching the same year that her Mother had died, and Olga became a recluse. They found her in her house in 1984 after she had been dead over a week. No one had seen her in a long time and no one cared that they hadn't seen her. She had lost touch with the tiny Russian community in Monterey Peninsula, alienating those who hadn't already alienated her.

Trash and junk were the most valuable things that crammed her tiny Pacific Grove cottage. Stacks of egg cartons, neatly piled, stood in the living room. In the dining room, several years' worth of newspapers were stacked neatly and in chronological order. Ice cream cartons, washed and flattened and stacked, filled the kitchen. Styrofoam meat trays had been cleaned and stacked, yes, in the oven. Bags and boxes and containers and magazines and newspapers, in chronological order, took over whatever free space remained.

Michael Albertov, an attorney and the son of one of my language school professors, told me the story when I visited him in Monterey in 1992. He knew that Olga and Nina had money, but the coroner's office had done an inventory and had found no money, no safe deposit box keys, no strong boxes, no Will.

Michael had a hunch and started checking into things, and he requested the coroner's files. He looked at the photo of Olga's corpse, seated on the sofa, next to the giant television and stereo set that I remembered.

The proverbial 'light bulb' went off in his head. 'Where are the television set and the stereo?' He checked. They didn't show up in the coroner's inventory. It was time for more checking. It turned out that one night the coroner had pulled a couple of truckloads of stuff out of the tiny cottage in Pacific Grove.

There was an investigation and an indictment, and further searching of Olga's belongings. They found a will. The results changed my life. Read on, kids.

Dearest Children:

Olga, at Nina's urging too, had left me a hefty chunk of solid American stock. Bless them. I quit waitering and started writing, as Nina and Olga had commanded. In 1988, Jeremy Beale, of London's Robin Clark Ltd., accepted my Cold War satire, To the Devil, for publication, and I was now a published author.

I believe that To the Devil made sense only if a reader was familiar with the most famous Russian novel of the twentieth century, Bulgakov's Master and Margarita. Someone reading my story, without knowing the Bulgakov context, might have been mildly amused but hardly more than that, I believe.

Still, they wrote articles about me in the local papers. It looked like my life had taken a turn for the better. I started writing a second and a third novel. I couldn't get them published. I used to brag that I had earned a 'ton' of money on To the Devil because my advance was 2000 British pounds, and 2,000 pounds equaled a ton, right? Ha Ha.

Few got the joke, even me. When my money ran out and nothing else got published, I sold my car. Then I got a job at Tulips Restaurant on Selby Avenue, Saint Paul's lonely once-commercial but now nearly empty street that tried hard to be like trendy Grand Avenue, half a mile or so to the south and one-half block away from the wealthy inhabitants of Summit Avenue's mansions. But Selby Avenue was situated too close to people whose skin color varied.

A Saint Paul food critic wrote a scathing review of Tulips. This was right before I was hired, and right before the restaurant's clientele shrunk by about eighty percent.

In 1989, I was asked to give a talk at the annual meeting of a local writers' group. The subject was how to get published, how to establish oneself as a writer. Strange. They had picked the wrong person to talk about that.

I noticed one woman at the meeting. There was something about her – I could sense in her an intense love of writing. Given my failures in romantic relationships, I decided to ignore her. During the seminar's lunch period, I caught her staring at me. She was sitting with another man. This was all the more reason for not approaching her.

But she pursued me. I received cards in the mail. Then late one night, I was working as a manager at the Lexington while the real manager was away on vacation. In walked this woman from the seminar, with two friends, whom I later found out had decided to come visit me at work. This woman had overheard them, and she more or less invited herself to ride along with them.

We met. We talked. Her name was Sonya. The proverbial sparks flew. Soon we were in love. With a published novel and with a new love in my life, I was happy. I looked forward to the future. Although my publishing 'career' ended with the appearance of my first book, it turned out that eight years of utter happiness was mine nonetheless.

On January 29, 1989, I gave my book reading at Tulips Restaurant. About one hundred and fifty people showed up, thanks to some nice publicity in "The Saint Paul Pioneer Press," "Minnesota Monthly," and "Mpls-Saint Paul Magazine." My story made good copy. "Local waiter with four college degrees makes good. Holds out for the dream and wins."

It was a surreal book-signing event because there were no books to sign. The London publisher had sent them to 'Odegaard Books' on Grand Avenue in Minneapolis, not Saint Paul, and there was no Odegaard Books on Grand Avenue in Minneapolis, and the person in the Minneapolis Post Office was perhaps new, or else had a headache. There is no longer an Odegaard Books in Saint Paul either. It's an upscale hair salon now. Odd that Robin Clark Limited was located on the second floor of a building in London that stood on a street that once, long ago, had been fashionable. Downstairs, there was a hair salon.

The reading was televised on local cable. There was one child in the audience, and, of course, she was sitting right next to the microphone. She sniffled.

Rob Meyers' paintings covered the restaurant's purple walls. Rob was a dentist who fancied himself a painter, and his subjects included bleak Montana landscapes and dead animals and rusted-out cars and chicken coops falling apart in the weather. One night a couple asked to be moved to a different table because they didn't want to sit under an upside-down dead bird with an arrow sticking out of its stomach.

Rob wasn't a 'real' painter, it turned out. He had a projector and he blew up photographs on a wall and traced them on canvas and filled them in with paint. But he had a Toyota Landcruiser that went 'beep-beep' when he backed up, just like garbage trucks do, and a compressor over the back bumper, and he had lent crazy Bob, the owner of Tulips, a ladder that said "Meyerwerk AG" on the side, whatever that was.

He died two years later when he crashed his experimental airplane north of Saint Paul. Rest his soul. He was a character worth getting to know.

To the Devil, my Cold War satire, did not sell well. Once again, my timing was off. The Cold War was just ending when Robin Clark Ltd. published my book, and the book was never released for sale in the United States. The publisher was bought out by another publisher whom another publisher, a Japanese company, bought out.

Once again, I had failed.

Speaking of failures, why haven't I written anything about my 'love life' since going to law school in 1980 and until my marriage to Sonya in 1990, a period of ten years?

There is not much to write about, and the memories are painful and thus hard to dig down and reach them. Romantic love, particularly passionate love, can come and go, but a Father's love for his children is a constant.

It was clear that I had been attracted to 'femme fatales,' as they are often called. I had known a number of them, on more than one continent, and in Hawaii also. In Dallas, I was engaged to one for a few years, One of the main reasons why I resigned from teaching at SMU, in fact, was that she was a graduating student there, and it was not good for professors to date students – a truly good rule which I selfishly broke, but at least I got out of there as soon as I could, and she had graduated too. Nonetheless, my transgression was shameful. I still regret it, as I should regret it.

She was taking Russian literature in translation from me, and she wrote genuine 'A+' papers – no doubt about it. During class, she stared at me without blinking. She had big, dark, and beautiful eyes, as if inviting you in.

But she was from money, and I wasn't. One time I drove her and her Mother to Santa Fe from Dallas in my new Buick Century. Again, my timing was off. Buying a General Motors car in precisely that year when the quality of American cars was at its lowest? Not good timing at all.

I had as much luck buying cars as I did deciding with whom to fall in love.

It is easier to talk about cars than it is about love. It hurts less, and you don't have to dig down too far, into scabs that cover scars that lie over deep wounds wanting badly to bleed once again.

I own a book that was published in the 1990's, and it's called The World's Worst Cars. Let's count how many of those cars I bought. A Plymouth Volare, an Audi Fox (nearly identical twin of the Volkswagen Rabbit, which really won the honor of being included in the book, an award so well-deserved), a Chevrolet Corvair (whose cabin tended to fill with smoke and whose handling guaranteed accidents that somehow I avoided), a Fiat (fun to drive, whenever it started, which was not very often), a Buick (It came with 27 things wrong with it). I made countless trips to Buick dealers in Minnesota and Texas. I swear my list of things wrong with the damned car never dropped below 27. One of its irritating problems was that in order to get from reverse gear into forward gear, you needed to crawl under the car with a crescent wrench). Adding to the list of the world's worst cars, I had an MG 1100 (You know you have a bad car when it won't start in 'cold' weather, in Honolulu), and a Karmann Ghia (I knew I shouldn't have bought it when I found out I didn't fit in it – too tall, which produced neck aches). Gasoline leaked into the passenger cabin. It wouldn't shift, which wasn't much of a problem actually, because the car hardly ever started.

In the above-mentioned Buick Century, I blew a tire in Mule Shoe Texas, of all places, when my girl friend and her Mother sat in the rear seat. I needed to buy two new tires, not just one, so that the car would be balanced, and there were no bargains in tires in this single gas station in Mule Shoe or anywhere two hundred miles around it. I bought two new tires for an outrageous price, putting the purchase on the single credit card I had left, and I was broke. My passengers were my Dallas femme fatale and her rich Mother. As the car rose like a black angel on the hoist, and as I worried that the credit card bank might not allow the charge, my thoughts about law school gelled.

I quit teaching.

I started law school in 1980 and, of course, my relationship with this particular femme fatale blew up soon thereafter. She was driving me crazy, always pointing out to me which males at which bar were 'giving her the eye,' which man at the reception couldn't take his eyes off her, what it was like at the mechanics' place yesterday, or at tennis practice, or on the street, or off the street, or far from a street.

I suppose I am a rather insecure person, and I need much confirmation of my worth. I think all men, as well as all women, are essentially insecure. It's just that a male won't tell you and won't talk about it. And, I believe, maybe femme fatales act the way they do because of their own insecurities – they might need continual confirmation of their beauty as well as the worth of their minds -- at times they will think that men are only after their bodies.

This femme fatale didn't give me any confirmation of my worth. Quite the opposite. Was I the sucker who picked up the tab while she was sitting at another table with three guys she didn't know and I didn't know? Yes, and it got worse. How about us going to a hotel room after a rock concert, to visit with the band? We both knew the female vocalist. Three male band members were sprawled out on a bed. Guess who dived into the middle of them, leaving me alone at the door, surrounded by people I didn't know?

Her flirtations got more blatant than that, often shocking or at least surprising even her targeted males, as well as me. I decided to back out.

I tried to explain to her that I didn't <u>want</u> to leave but felt that I <u>had</u> to leave, in order to <u>not</u> go crazy, etc., etc. The more I tried to convince her, the more I sounded like a wimp, I believe.

If I should ever design a car, I would call it a 'Femme Fatale.'

I am sure this particular femme fatale had no idea whatsoever why I left. She insisted that she <u>knew</u> I had met someone else and that was why I was dumping her. I wish that had been true.

It took me a long, long time to 'get over' this particular femme fatale. Let's say eight years or longer, believe it or not. I got so tired of destroying my self-respect by looking for her car everywhere in Dallas, by asking everyone we knew about her, indirectly or cleverly (or so I thought). Sometimes I asked directly, or sometimes I 'accidentally' drove on a side street close to her Mother's house, etc. It was time to 'get out of Dodge,' as the saying down South puts it – how strange that this saying includes a word that also was the brand name of a truly bad Chrysler Corporation automobile, one, luckily, that I never owned although the Plymouth Volare was close.

I moved back to Minnesota. There were other reasons for the move too, such as my inability to find a law job in the Texas economy that, because of falling oil prices, was going down the toilet.

During those eight years, both in Dallas and in Saint Paul, I did not have a 'girlfriend.' I hate that word, but there seems to be no suitable synonym. I had no relationships, no relations with any woman, physical or otherwise. I spent my time and money writing novels nobody wanted to read, and seeing psychiatrists and counselors who didn't help much but who charged a lot for their visits anyway. When I lost hope and ran out of money, I pretended to get well, thanked them, and walked out.

Shrinks, like many car companies, don't give extended warranties.

I always expected that my femme fatale would wake up some morning in New Mexico, where she had moved, would see the light of day, and would come rushing to Minnesota in the dead of winter, even though she hated the cold and never used air-conditioning in her car, even when the Dallas temperature was above 100 degrees.

It took me a few years, but I was over her and I could get on with my life. Romantic love, particularly passionate love, can come and go, but, oh, it is fortunate that a father's love for his children is a constant.

I have known other femme fatales in my life, and I have avoided getting emotionally involved with them. It is easier to back out in the beginning than it is later on.

I believe that femme fatales are hardly ever happy. They jump from man to man, looking for that one thing they will never find – a love that makes them feel secure. Sadly, they usually pick the kind of man that will abandon them later. People try, but they cannot 're-wind' their lives and start anew, albeit this time with no 'issues', and this time, turning out a happy ending.'

"Good times and noodle salad." That's how Jack Nicholson characterizes it in "As Good As It Gets," which I command you to watch once you reach the age of fifteen, if not before.

Going back and re-playing our childhood dramas, this time with a happy ending? It can't be done. In the words of John Prine, one of my favorite singers, "You are what you are, and you ain't what you ain't."

May I help keep you children safe from my mistakes.

Dear Anna, Katya, and Alex:

I didn't go to Russia during the tumultuous 1990's. I was too busy failing at things at home. Nothing really appealed to me. I was living on the surface, a slippery and thin one at that. The Soviet Union fell apart in the 1990's.

One interesting (at least to me) phenomenon then was the great number of Russian marriage-matching bureaus that appeared on the Web, when the Web became popular, in the last half of the decade. Hundreds of those marriage bureaus extolled the virtues of Russian women, displaying photos of gorgeous women anxious to marry American men, and allegedly 'under contract' with these clubs that guaranteed success and satisfaction.

A work colleague asked if the wife of one of her husband's clients could call me. The wife lived in Toronto and she had no one to talk to in Russian, and she didn't know any English. She hadn't even tried to learn English, although she'd been in Canada for over three years. I wonder how their 'marriage' could have survived. Was he gay maybe? Was this marriage just a cover? I do not mean to sound homophobic, it's just that this is just one of a few scenarios that seem to fit. She was one of those Russian brides that came out of those friendship clubs. I don't know how her marriage had lasted for three years. She spoke no English; he spoke no Russian. Maybe that's why the marriage did last.

So she called me. And she called. And she called. I finally stopped picking up the phone when she called – I had acquired a new thing called "Caller ID," and although it generally did not work when telemarketers called, it did work when CRWFT (Crazed Russian Woman From Toronto) called.

One night the phone rang and then it rang and then it rang some more. It was time for me to practice some assertiveness, an under-used trait for me, a coward when it comes to being firm with people. I picked up the phone. I urged her, for a final time, to find some Russian émigrés in her city – I knew there were some, if not many. "Akh, I will have nothing to do with them!" she said. "Too many of them are Jews."

End of telephone conversations with CRWFT. I will not tolerate intolerance or prejudice.

These Russian wedding places, from which CRWFT and perhaps hundreds or thousands other Russian women came, were ostensibly 'friendship clubs,' thereby bypassing several Russian statutes. Everything was well-ordered, like your adoption, kids, and this marriage system worked smoothly. Lonely American males paid a couple thousand dollars to the agency. Then they landed by the plane-load in Peterburg or Moscow or several other cities and republics.

These companies knew how to exploit stereotypes on both sides of the Atlantic (or Pacific, if you were a lonely bachelor living in California). Russian women often thought of American males as being un-lazy like Russian males, un-chauvinistic by comparison (often true), and kind to their wives, even listening to them sometimes. American males sometimes thought of Russian women as easy-to-please, very feminine, and very submissive (hence, non-threatening) and ever-grateful for getting an exit visa from crumbling (or so it seemed then) Russia.

How did this system work? It worked very well.

These lonely American males were given a floor or two in a hotel. That evening, with the men still horribly jetlagged, there would be a 'party' in the hotel ballroom. The men filed in on one side, and the women filed in from the other side. The agency staff carefully pushed things along – no long engagements here, not even long dances – I read that the in-house DJs played only short pieces. Matches were generally made that evening, and by the next day, all the emigration paperwork was complete. Wow. Such efficiency.

I met one such woman, in Saint Paul, when I was working at Tulips, whose staff consisted of failed actors and failed painters and failed writers, like me.

At one table sat a lovely young lady facing a sort of nerdy-type guy. He was not too bad-looking, and he had a voice that wasn't altogether grating. I bet he could have found an American bride some day, especially if he spoke in low tones and spent most of his time in the dark.

In this tiny restaurant with its bad acoustics (brick walls and no sound-deadening materials, such as drapes), this male was doing what many people do when they are trying to communicate with someone who doesn't know their language – he was shouting. And then he pantomimed. Yuck. I felt sick. "This is a very romantic restaurant!" he declared, slowly and loudly, his arms pointing out the scope of the place. "There are many good restaurants in this city, Darling. Do you know what 'good' means? How about 'restaurant?' I must work tomorrow. In the morning. Do you know what 'morning' means?" He pantomimed the way the sun rises in the morning. Good grief. I wanted to run away, but I was fixed to my spot, the way a spectator can't help but look at a gory automobile accident.

The woman sat there, quietly but politely. Had I been she, I think I would have run to the exit and taken off in any direction, except going back into Tulips.

It was torture for me to witness all this. As they were leaving, I had a moment with <u>just</u> her by the cloakroom. "I arrived one week ago," she told me in Russian. She was scared and lonely, knew no English, knew no other Russians in the area, knew not what was in store for her.

I gave her husband the address of a Russian market, where his new wife could surely meet other Russian speakers. He didn't look so pleased. What, I was trying to put the make on his wife? Or was it that her gaining Russian-speaking friends would reduce her utter dependence on him, his indentured servant and bed-mate?

Dear Katya –

You are the lover of animals. In Minnesota, the first week in April is the time when you can dare think of thaws and planting, and you roll the garden hose out from the garage.

You found a water sprayer that was shaped like a bunny and weighed about seven pounds – it was made of copper turned green, probably deliberately made green during the manufacture process, just as most garden-related things are loaded with artificiality of one kind or another, Grecian gods pouring forth water from bent, long-necked jugs being no exception.

The bunny had belonged to my late Brother, Tom.

You were drawn to Bunny. You made a bed out of a cardboard box and you used towel scraps as sheets and blankets. You gave Bunny a bubble bath and we dried her with a towel that we had tossed into the dryer so it would be warm for Bunny. She indeed looked like a bunny, except for the hose attachment sticking out of her butt, Katya, which you couldn't quite explain except that you said it was because of a surgery after a car hit Bunny.

Dropping you off at school the next morning, you gave me explicit instructions on how to feed bunny, when to give bunny a nap, and when she needed to be held.

Dear Kids:

Careers. Not my strong point – perhaps worse than my luck with romantic relationships. For me, jobs often happen accidentally.

Take, for an example, the winding road that took me to law librarianship and legal research instruction, a career I finally liked well enough and that paid almost enough. It was to be my last job, after forty years of getting degrees and trying to find a career that lasted.

Like what happened in almost every aspect of my life, I didn't get things 'right' until I was in my late forties, or older. (For instance, I was in my late fifties when I became the Father of three unbelievably wonderful Russian children.)

Children, please don't get dizzy as I provide the barest of outlines of my job trail. Remember how, after I received my PhD, I worked in restaurants? Well, after <u>To the Devil</u> was published and didn't sell but my Nissan Sentra did (even though its inside door panels had melted in Dallas' heat), I gave myself one more chance to write a bang-up best-seller. No, I wouldn't give up writing novels – I loved it too much. I'd just give up on the idea of supporting myself by my novel-writing. I would become one of those thousands of American artists who work at their art, in secret often, but who figure out a kind of job that will sustain them without intruding too badly, on their artistic endeavors.

I am one of them. I don't write good best-sellers. I have a stack of manuscripts to prove it. Sadly, with novels, you either make it or you don't. Other artistic endeavors seem to offer tiers of participation. At the worst, musicians can play on street corners, right?. Or they can join some kind of struggling band or group. Similarly, painters can show their works at craft shows. Writers? You don't read out, especially in that Russian declamatory manner, your novels in bars or on street corners, at least after the police have questioned you and perhaps even thrown you into a drunk tank for a night or two.

When my money ran out, I went back to my old standby in a pinch, waitering. But the Lexington was changing hands, and so I needed to find a new place to work. No one seemed to want me, of course. I had too many college degrees; sometimes they found out about them even though I didn't put them on my resume. <u>Not</u> putting my years of graduate school on a resume meant, of course, that there were too many blank spaces that often were years in length. But putting in the education scared people off, and, besides, I'd never been too successful with <u>not</u> telling the truth.

The potential employers would think, 'How could this aging, wandering academic left-over (like brown or slimy-green lettuce at a buffet bar) be satisfied with <u>this</u> little job, given his academic background? Forget that I needed to eat. I would become the American equivalent of a Russian 'Holy Fool,' wandering from town to town, babbling and asking for coins.

I finally landed a job at Tulips Restaurant on Selby Avenue. I told you about it already, kids, but in a different context. I worked there for a couple of years, and I watched the restaurant go downhill in a neighborhood that likewise seemed to be going downhill, despite the city's hopes (that appeared to remain hopes long after it was clear that the neighborhood was going nowhere vertically, except the opposite of 'up,' and the city's investments were not at all paying off and probably would never pay off, and white people kept out of this neighborhood. After al….

I became friends with Bob Piper, the owner. You, kids, have met him and you like him a lot. Bob is another refugee from the world of changing careers and employment, failing in careers and reduced to unemployment.

But as I aged, waitering was taking its toll on my back (perhaps that has something to do with my three subsequent back surgeries). Those dinner trays were heavy, and you had to carry them high over your head sometimes. I was tall, and so sometimes during evenings when customers jammed the 'The Lexington Restaurant,' the servers asked me to carry their trays over the heads of the crowds. I was known to carry two oval trays, one over each shoulder, arms extended to their full reach, each tray holding as many as ten dinners.

So I needed a job, one easier on my body, and I knew I'd better get a job with medical benefits and other unnecessary things that no Americans really need.

I applied for lawyer jobs all over the world. No luck, of course. Not even a nibble. Then I tried for clerical jobs, and still nothing came my way. I took a civil service test for the City of Minneapolis. This <u>should</u> have made me eligible for a number of clerical jobs. I am <u>convinced</u> that I aced all their damned tests. No job offer. No job. Too bad. Lots of writers and artists and actors work at civil service jobs during the day, collecting great benefits and good salaries, while practicing their craft in the evening, right?

I tried Saint Paul. I tried the counties. I tried the State. No nibbles. I was over-qualified, I suppose, and here was this other applicant who clearly would treasure the job and feel oh-so-fortunate to have it.

So then I tried for a job as a paralegal or legal secretary. Nope. Too over-qualified.

Then, in desperation, an idea came to me. Work somewhere as a temporary -- as someone hired from one of the big temporary agencies around town. So I signed up with the Dolphin Employment Agency as a legal secretary. No one grilled me about my resume. It was great. I took a typing test and a general knowledge test, and I did well at both. The head of the company invited me in to her office and told me how happy she was to have me on her staff. She assigned me to Dorsey & Whitney, then the biggest law firm in town. I got rave reviews – typing 130 words per minute, etc.

As has sometimes happened in my past, I have started somewhere with a not-so-hot impression, but then things improve. Well, Dorsey loved me and they gave me very high marks so that Dolphin loved me too. Dorsey offered me a job that was substantially higher in pay than Dolphin, and with benefits.

So I started working at Dorsey as a secretary, and I became sort of 'in demand,' even though I literally had to teach myself how to use a computer mouse overnight. I worked as a 'floater,' in the Litigation Department one day, in Banking the next day, and then Corporate Law after that. Then I settled down to a few permanent jobs in the firm, jumping to a better position whenever one opened. There is a hierarchy, where they assign new secretaries to the worst attorneys, those who scream or who throw telephones at their secretaries (true!), thereby assuring the Human Resources Department (I hate that term – it sounds like people are chunks of iron ore or something) that they have hired the sturdiest of secretaries, and they have concurrently given an awful attorney a few weeks or even months of secretarial support.

The years went by. I didn't hate my job, and I was paid well, nearly three times more (adjusted for inflation, the GNP, etc.) than I earned as an SMU professor.

A few years later, my wrists started to bother me, particularly after the firm had remodeled its spaces and the computer keyboards were now quite high. The amateur architect wanted the working spaces to look more uniform by having all the counters at the same level, the fool.

Soon my wrists burned at night and my shoulders tingled. Then I couldn't sleep at all because of pains shooting up from my wrists to my shoulder. Yes, Carpal Tunnel Syndrome. I went to the Workers Comp person at the firm. She advised me to use my regular health insurance. "The benefits will be better," she said.

I was wary. Workers Compensation would come in handy if I had to change jobs or careers, for instance, and couldn't, for instance, type anymore.

The firm's workers' comp insurance company denied me coverage. Why? Was it because my novel-writing had also involved a lot of typing? No. In order to blame a company, it wasn't necessary to prove that it was the only cause of the illness, only that it contributed to the illness. There was no way, then, that a forty-hour-a-week job with heavy typing was not related to my carpal tunnel problems.

So I sued the bastards – the firm and the insurance company. I won. Not much, but I won.

The problem was, the firm didn't want to put me back in a secretary's cubicle, even though they looked so nice because things were at an even level, and the firm had spent thousands of dollars to create for each cubicle a little round chunk of marble where the attorney could sign documents, even though attorneys usually signed their documents in the offices, at their desks.

No, they denied me those impressive surroundings. I needed a different kind of job. They mentioned the library and I agreed. After all, one of my first jobs was working in my high school library (for a penny a minute back then, applied directly to tuition).

I did typical library clerical-type things – shelving books, creating lists, etc. Then one day I was sitting at a table near the reference desk, and a harried reference librarian asked if I could download a document for her from the Web. I had never been on the Internet before, but I didn't let it show. Finding and then learning about them and using the 'bookmarks' feature on Internet Explorer Version 2, on the Mac computer with its tall and ungainly monitor, I got the document for her.

Soon other librarians asked me to help them on the Internet. A couple of months later I had become the "Internet Wonder Boy," as it was termed. I started working with CD-ROM towers then too. I had become the 'techie' in the library.

Knowing that I had a law degree, they soon made me a more-or-less genuine librarian. But they couldn't call me a librarian because I lacked the requisite degree – this bothered the head reference librarian greatly, and when introducing me, she was always sure to point out how I wasn't a real librarian, but had been discovered in the firm and trained by her, as he started from nothing and ended up, thanks to all her efforts, with someone who could almost pass as a real librarian. I didn't understand all this. Others told me that I somehow 'threatened' her. I don't believe I did – I have never tried to be boastful or bragging in my jobs, but I couldn't think of any other reason. I became a 'Library Generalist,' and various other terms she invented for non-librarian librarians.

Rest her soul now. This brave woman who never smoked and never drank alcohol and never did illegal drugs or abused legal drugs and never ate unhealthful food –the poor woman died of breast cancer. I went to the hospital to visit her, but she didn't remember me.

Soon the head of the library started contacting me first. I edited all her memos – she was having big fights with the firm's managing partner, and I learned all kinds of juicy secrets about the firm that I couldn't tell anyone about unless I stuck them deep into a work of fiction. I tried, but it was a lousy novel.

She started asking me for advice. She liked me, I think, which, I think, made the head reference librarian like me even less and to remind more people of how she had discovered me and I wasn't a real librarian anyway, before the poor woman passed on to that big head of reference office in the sky.

I began training lawyers on how to use the CD programs that I installed and tested, and I taught them about that fairly new thing in the legal world called 'The Web.' Law firms tended to be about five years behind the business world when it comes to things like that.

I began speaking to groups, first inside the firm and then outside too. Even at conferences. Even in New York. Now the head reference librarian really didn't like me. Whenever she was assigned to speak somewhere, she sat in her office with a stop watch and practiced. I looked over my materials and more or less winged it all. I think she knew this and it did not please her. Rest her soul.

I was making a name for myself. That was cool. And I liked the people I worked with, particularly Polly, my office mate. (You have met her many times, kids. Katya, this is whom you called 'Loppy' when you were first learning English). Her husband, John, is the one who married me and your Mother. It was to him that Anna uttered an early sentence in English. She was asked to call people to the table. She walked up to the minister. "Sit down, please, John" she said in her incredibly low, resonating, and highly authoritative voice. Polly and John still talk about it and they still tease Anna about it and they still use her line until she blushes, which is soon.

This was a glorious time for librarians all over the country. People forget now, but in those 'early' days, when you wanted to see something on the Internet, you went to a search engine such as Magellan, HotBot, Lycos, or Northern Lights – nearly all of them gone now, in the bottom of the 'ashcan of history,' as Leon Trotsky might have put it if Stalin hadn't put a hatchet into the back of poor Leon's head in Mexico.

These search engine 'hits' were more-or-less secretly manipulated by the companies on the Web. It is a long story, and I could bore you for hours about relevance and the exploitation of hidden metatags, but I have bored you enough already and so I will drop this topic.

Anyway, the thing on the Web that you probably wanted in the first place might not show up at all, or it might be item number 3,422 on your hit endless hit list, where you could shake your head for hours and wonder how in hell how certain web sites had ended up at all, in any way or fashion, on your hit list.

Then Google came out. It knew how to overlook those manipulated metatags hiding behind each page. Its algorhythms took you directly to what it was that you wanted. It was magic. For a while, only we librarians knew about the powers of Google, and so attorneys marveled at the way we could find things for them, and they gave us great praise and raises in salaries too. We librarians and library generalists were uber-researchers. The attorneys and the firm administrators sat at our feet and gave us great praise.

Then the head of reference services at William Mitchell College of Law button-holed me at an AALL (American Association of Law Librarians) conference, and she told me how much I'd enjoy a position with the College. They'd help pay my tuition so that I could get a degree and become a real librarian, and cease being a law firm 'Library Generalist.'

I jumped ship. I was scared, turning my back on a position that I truly liked around people whom I really liked, and jumping into unknown waters. What I did know, however, is that the College sported an incredibly long list of employer-employee lawsuits.

I jumped anyway. What the hell, right?

It turned out to be an excellent move. I did interesting reference work, much of it for professors. I helped students and taught classes to some of them. I worked the Internet. I helped people who came in off the streets, desperate when, say, they were trying to get workers compensation coverage for a work-related injury, but the employer had hired dozens of attorneys and they were filling up the court docket file with a great number of motions and other papers.

Some of these cases bothered the hell out of me, but I had to be careful about crossing the line between pointing a person towards materials they need and not giving them legal advice. I couldn't tell someone, for instance, what the statute of limitations (for how long could you sue someone?) was for a certain claim, but I could go to the statute books and put my finger on the answer. I think some of my off-the-street 'patrons' were really hired goons checking up on my not giving legal advice.

After fifty-five years, I had finally found a career niche that I liked and that liked me. I was finishing off my library science degree, kids, when you came to me. You'll recall my evening and weekend classes.

Then my lungs, that part of the body that sustains life, intervened. My hiatus of career happiness ended, and I became what they call 'disability retired.' I was so grateful then to have three children who would keep my motors running and would push me on.

Dear Alex --

You are a lover. You can barely find fault anywhere or with anything. The van won't start? It can't help it – the weather is too cold. Lulu the dachshund messing on the floor? She can't help it. She's old.

Your room is a mess? You can't help it – you love toys and I love taking you to the used things stores and to garage sales. I can't help it because I love buying toys. The poor people can't help selling the toys – they need money. The factories can't stop making toys or people would lose their jobs and....

And so the trailer is a mess, jammed with too many things? It can't help it. The trailer is too small for four people, but we all manage just the same.

I hope that trait stays with you, Alex, so that some day soon you will say something such as, "My Dad is not playing football with the other Dads? He can't help it. He's old."

I hope you will say that with a some sort and with some quantity of pride.

Dear Kids:

Finally, after too many detours, we go back to Sonya and 1991 or so.

Even with all the career things going on in my life, I was happy. My relationship with Sonya was something quite apart. We respected one-another and maintained a deep love for one-another

We went to London on our honeymoon. We had a great time and we met my publisher, a shy man named Jeremy Beale, whose office on Goodge Street stood above a hair salon. The publisher and I took turns apologizing to one-another – I for writing a book that didn't sell, he for failing to reach a wide audience.

Nonetheless, I was happy. A year later, Sonya and I took a trip to San Francisco, a city I hadn't seen since my Navy days. We drove to the wine country, and then we drove down to Monterey. We went to the local cemetery there. Even though I nearly always avoid visiting cemeteries, for some reason I wanted to find the graves of my Russian teachers – They were all gone by now -- Nina Chebyshowa and her daughter Olga, the ones who left me money in their will, Shaky Andrei Govorov, my other professors. I remember that we stood in the cemetery manager's office, trying to figure out the cemetery map so we could determine where my Russian teachers were buried. Then I looked out the window of the office and I spotted a section of the cemetery where a number of tall Russian Orthodox crosses stood.

We walked there. I found all the graves. Thirty years had passed, but I remembered all these people. Sad. My memories had kept them alive in me for nearly three decades, but here they were, dead. My memories? Yes, they were only memories. They didn't perpetuate anything, except themselves.

In 1991, Sonya and I bought a house in Northeast Minneapolis, only a block away from where Julie's parents had lived.

Sonya worked as a legal secretary right across the street from the law firm where I worked as a librarian. She kept on writing. She almost sold the manuscript she'd been working on for years, a story set during the time of Queen Elizabeth the First. She got one of the best agents in New York.

But the book didn't sell. One editor said that even though she liked the story, she wouldn't be able to sell it because it didn't fall into any easy category. It was too mainstream to be a romance, and too romantic to be mainstream. (Years later, I tried to get Sonya's manuscript published again, when the genre lines seemed to have become more flexible, but I failed to find a publisher too.)

In 1996, Sonya began weakening. Once-lively, she was now tired. She turned pale. She lost weight. She had been born with some heart defects. For one thing, she had something called 'transposition of the great arteries.' Her heart was literally operating backwards, imagine! Thus, valves designed to open one way instead had to open the other way. Surgeries a decade ago had repaired her heart, but now it was giving her trouble again. By 1998, joy had gone out of her life. Everything was a drag. She pushed herself and her exhausted, blood-starved body through each day. I tried to find ways to help her. Sometimes I even tried playing the jester. It didn't help.

I recalled how for several years she had been engrossed in gardening, planting perennials and hundreds of annuals each spring. The amount diminished over the years. In 1997, she was sitting in the living room but watching me plant the pansies. Sometimes she waved. Sometimes she slept. In the spring of 1998, I did all the gardening, with no one looking on – she, the only person who could tell me that I had planted one plant too far to the left as well as too far to the right, too close to the house and too far from the house, too deep, too shallow.

Her doctors in the Heart Clinic at the University of Minnesota Hospital decided it was time for another surgery. They would repair her heart again, and all would be well for decades to come.

The Sunday before the surgery, Sonya asked me to cut her hair in back – she wanted to look as good as possible after the surgery. She recalled how awful she had looked after her previous heart surgeries, her face and entire body swollen beyond recognition – I had seen some of the photographs.

I drove her to the hospital very early in the morning, before the July sun rose. She lay in a hospital room, waiting for her turn at surgery – her surgeon, who had done her previous two surgeries, was going to do this one, but he was still in an emergency surgery that could not wait.

Sonya lay there, and the monitoring machines and all the other machines with their various gauges and buzzes and rings showed that she was slipping away. They elevated her bed so that her head was down, nearly touching the floor, and her feet were up in the air. This was a way to improve her blood pressure, they said. The hospital machinery showed she was diminishing fast.

She slipped into unconsciousness, and now the machines commenced calling out their various alarm signals louder and more frequently. Then the buzzes and ringing became even louder and they would not stop. If a machine can register and reflect events, these machines were doing just that. Three nurses and a doctor rushed in. Soon, over the hospital public address system, I heard them calling out her surgeon's name. There was no doubt for me that the announcing woman' voice was edged by panic.

I heard something then I'd never heard before in a hospital. I heard "Stat! Stat! stat!" called out three times in a row. I have heard 'stat!' uttered once over other hospital speakers, and on TV medical shows. I had heard 'stat!' shouted out twice even, but never three times. My high school Latin teacher, the one my Father criticized, had prepared me for what was going on. 'Stat' in medical parlance is actually not an acronym; it's short for 'statim', the Latin word for 'immediately.'

Her poor, harried surgeon rushed into Sonya's room as soon as he had finished up his emergency surgery and left his assistants to finish up things. In Sonya's room, he studied the screen of one machine that showed the pressures in various parts of her heart, and he couldn't figure out why there was such a difference. He grabbed the foot of Sonya's bed, and he ran, along with two orderlies and several nurses, all of them rushing Sonya and Sonya's bed, down the halls, to surgery. We had to run to keep up.

There were a few moments in the pre-surgery area as doctors quickly applied antiseptic liquids to her chest and as the two anesthesiologists stuck needles in both of Sonya's arms. They worked fast, super-fast, but I never saw one tremble or one twitch. Professionals. Bless them.

They gave me and Sonya's Mother and Father one moment before they whisked Sonya away, with great speed, into the surgery room. Through the small windows of the steel doors, I spotted four physicians and a number of nurses. I even spotted the nurse standing off to the side with a clipboard in her hands. I knew that she was the person who would record each sponge used, each device used, so that we could be billed later for them, and so that all could be comforted that nothing had been left accidentally inside the patient. There were a few seconds before they pushed Sonya through those doors, the ones sometimes leading to the River Styx.

All those specialists waiting in the surgery room gave me comfort. I leaned down and kissed Sonya lightly on her right cheek, as her head still remained just inches from the floor. She had slipped deep into unconsciousness, but I noticed that the gauges on the machines wiggled. A nurse confirmed that I was not merely hallucinating. I whispered to Sonya, "You are going to look great after this surgery! You'll see how well I had cut your hair in the back. I love you."

They pushed Sonya, now on a gurney, into the surgery room. Those automatic steel doors wheezed shut. The nurse said we should go to the waiting room, on the same floor and right outside the surgery area – they would give us updates every half hour. So we walked to the waiting room.

Hours passed. There were no reports. The volunteer at the visiting room desk stared into her computer. We asked. The computer showed nothing. We cornered nurses and doctors and orderlies who came out from those metal double doors. No one knew anything, or at least that's what they said.

We had arrived at the hospital early in the morning. It was now dark. Evening had come, a July evening, when days are long in Minnesota.

The waiting room had emptied. Still no news about Sonya, no reports as promised. Then we cornered a nurse who told us at around eight o'clock that Sonya was still in surgery. "There were some complications," she said. "But all will be fine. You can be confident, and you can relax. I will be back in a half hour to give you an update."

We didn't see that nurse again. Two hours later, there was no news about Sonya. Two hours after that, the waiting room volunteer was long gone, and the waiting room was empty, except for us and a janitor. I was able to break into the waiting room's computer terminal, and I saw that Sonya was still in surgery. I cornered a nurse in the deserted hallway and I demanded to know what was going on.

A physician with blood on his scrubs came out to talk to us. He was still wearing those funny, paper overshoes that physicians wear during surgery. "There have been complications," he said. "But I assure you that all is well. It will be a few hours yet, but then you will see your Sonya."

He had a Russian name on his badge, he had a Russian accent, and so I asked him in Russian, "Can you tell me, honestly, what is going on in there?"

He repeated what he had just said.

Sonya's parents were there. As were her sister and husband. So was my Brother Frank, who would die just a few years later. I decided that I'd better dash home to feed the cats, whom Sonya loved so much, and who had been alone for nearly a day. It took about ten minutes to drive home, especially at 3:00 in the morning when there were no cars or trucks or busses on the streets – it was either too early or too late for traffic.

I fed the cats and rushed back to the hospital, ignoring speed limits and even driving two blocks the wrong way of a one-way street. The elevator was too slow. I took the stairs.

There was no reason to hurry.

Sonya was gone.

She had died in the hallway outside the surgery room.

Her surgeon came out to us. His eyes were red, and a white paper mask still covered the rest of his face. He lowered his head. I am so very sorry this happened. Things were supposed to come out differently."

There was water in his eyes. Sonya had been his patient for over twenty-five years.

Dearest children:

Love life. Treasure life. Cherish it. Life can slip away so fast, so unexpectedly. Sometimes, when death is possible or even probable, you tend to ignore the signs. Sometimes the brain works in strange ways. Things, seemingly forgotten, pop up at the most unexpected times.

Out of somewhere, at that moment when I stood in the empty hospital waiting room, I recalled the words of Woland, the benign devil, in the Russian novel, <u>The Master and Margarita</u>. "The terrifying thing about a person's life is that it will end. But that is only half the misfortune. Not only will it end, but sometimes it ends when no one expects it."

It took many days for the reality to reach me, even partially. Sonya's funeral was a blur. I recall only that I read a eulogy and asked a lawyer friend to stand by, in case I couldn't finish it. I finished it, although I recall that my voice got weaker and weaker as I read. Later, many people said this was the best memorial ceremony they had ever attended. This gave me little comfort although I thanked those people for their well-intended remarks.

A few days after the funeral, her family and I scattered Sonya's ashes onto Nine-Mile Creek, not far from her parents' home.

My grieving? My way of grieving (or perhaps of not grieving) was to become extraordinarily busy. I answered sympathy cards, accepted visits from friends offering condolences, went out with them to eat or to visit them at the houses or in their apartments.

I continued to work at the law firm. I re-arranged the house, my house and Sonya's house, at least a dozen times. My 'office' or 'writing area' moved upstairs to one room and then another and finally to a third room, the room that had been Sonya's and my bedroom. I carted, by myself, too impatient to wait for help from anyone, my desk and file cabinets and computers up one floor or down to the basement, then back up one or two floors. I had moved my writing area to the basement, but it was moldy and damp down there. Besides, the floor was slanted so that as I typed, my chair rolled away from the desk. I moved my writing area up to the dining room, which came to resemble a disorganized office, but it worked. A friend who was a seamstress made me a set of heavily insulated drapes that closed off all corners of the house. I now lived in a shell, an hermetically sealed shell. Daytime or nighttime? You wouldn't know why would you need to know anyway?

Weeks later, while still incredibly busy, I was insisting that I was okay – I had passed through the first few stages of grieving that they talk about, and I was arriving at acceptance, but then one day at the law firm I looked down and saw that I was wearing one brown shoe and one black shoe. I clearly had failed in my attempt at running away from the recent past or at trying to forget it.

Except for work, I stayed to myself for nearly two years. The solitude and all that moving of furniture did not help, did not diminish pain, did not help me forget. I fell into a deep depression, my on-again, off-again friend, known well by me, and known better each time that we visited one-another.

My life was over. I was fifty-three and a widower.

Then I met your mother, two years later, and a new life began.

Then you arrived, and a new life really began.

Dear Kids:

So you see that there was one an extended period of happiness in my life, even though it ended unexpectedly and poorly.

In 2000, Patricia Hampl, a writer who had been one year behind me in grade school, contacted me and told me that I should attend a writers' seminar in, guess where, Peterburg. I hadn't been to Russia since 1987. Russophilia? It was dead in me, or at least buried alive.

Going back to Russia? I feared it, yet I had a 'feeling' about it that I could not ignore. I signed up and went, as if commanded to do it.

Classes were interesting. They were held daily. The students critiqued one-another's writing, and then the professor would intervene. I was lucky. My professor was Josip Novakovich, a fine bit of luck for me. Each evening, we had to revise the things we had written for classes the next day. Still, I made time to wander around the city.

What was that about hogwash I mentioned earlier about today's Russian critics, you ask? At one seminar, two young Russian literary 'experts' were discussing the cultural life of Peterburg in the 1970's. "Akhmatova and Tsvetiava and Pasternak and Zabolotsky and, in particular, Mandelstam were all passé by then," they said. "No one read them in the 1970s and no one cared about them or their writings."

Bull shit. In the 1970's and even in the 1980's. I saw Russians engaged in samizdat (self-publishing), secretly passing around, at great risk, hand-written copies of pages composed by those writers and poets, and typed on thin paper. It worked this way: If you wanted to receive the beginning pages of a certain work, you promised to make one copy of those pages and of the pages you would receive later. This system came to be known as 'Samizdat' ('self-published').

Soon, some of these works found their way to the West, where they were gladly published in countries that didn't like the Soviet Union. The works published in the West and smuggled back into Russia? They came to be known as 'Tamizdat' ('published over there').

So all these poets were passé? Hello! Russians risked much just to get a few pages of those poets' works. They didn't even <u>know</u> about some writers or works (e.g., <u>Master and Margarita</u>) until decades later, when a more lenient government allowed them to be published.

The seminar went on for a month. Then as now, Russian mosquitoes seemed as big as military helicopters and they left giant welts. You didn't dare close the window in the dorm or you'd suffocate. And screens? Never heard of them!

The city was dirty, buildings were crumbling, trash blew everywhere. The stores were loaded with articles for sale (that was good), but no one could afford them (that was not good.) The ruble was low, the dollar high, so for foreigners there were big bargains; for natives, barely anything.

Before, when the city was under a different name, shops were empty, except, perhaps, for occasional jars of cucumbers, as I mentioned earlier when talking about the jammed stores, inefficiencies, and surly workers in 1970 shops. In those years, everybody had a tiny amount of money, but things like living spaces and medical care and education were free. People seemed to get by and, I felt (perhaps wrongly and so I shouldn't write it and look like a fool) that people were more or less satisfied with their lot – pretty much everyone was on the same level. Who cared if you had only one skirt if everyone else had one skirt. The only people to envy was that quiet covey of the elite who drove around in big cars with drapes along the windows and shopped in stores whose windows were obscured and whose entry required a permit.

But now, in 2000, there were plenty of private cars, and they choked the roads, which, clearly, had not been built to handle such traffic. (I believe that Russian drivers are the most reckless of all drivers – they aim for pedestrians.)

Trash was all over the place; the winds blew paper and other junk up against buildings and curbs. Poor Saint Peterburg – she looked like an aging lady, down on her luck – you know, the old actress who smears lipstick all over her face and wears too much rouge and keeps expecting people to rush up to her and praise her for her beauty, and for producers to rush up and offer her roles.

Yet, the people on the streets looked generally healthy, and they seemed to be at least a foot taller than their parents. So something must have been going right, at least in Peterburg. In 1970, at six feet and four inches, I had felt like a giant – I couldn't even stand up in some of the busses unless I managed to put myself under one of the roof vents.

But no more. Young Russians were surprisingly tall, particularly the women, and I had never seen so many young people there. This, truly, was a new generation, and they were not about to accept the lives lived by their parents.

Some of those people, kids, could have been your birth parents or relatives.

I blended in with crowds on the streets. Neither my height or my clothes would mark me as a foreigner. What a change! I could be anonymous. No one would stare at me, and what, by the way, had happened to that old Soviet practice of staring at people, unblinking, unmoving, stone-faced, for long periods of time?

Who would have thought that a few decades could bring about such improvement? Devastation can occur fast, but improvement, I believe, takes lots of time.

But here, in your city, I witnessed an unbelievable transformation.

People wore brighter and more varied clothes, sometimes breaking all the rules of fashion, but who cared? They talked loudly on the street. Couples fondled one-another along the banks of the Neva, across from the Winter Palace. People drank beer, right out in the open. There were beer gardens right on Nevsky Prospect, for heaven's sake! Some bars were open all night. You couldn't tell, looking at a crowd of young people, whether they were Russian or tourists from the West. What a mighty change since 1970, my first visit!

Volvos and Mercedes raced down the streets or parked on sidewalks; at night, their burglar alarms made for a discordant symphony.

This was all wonderful, but I must admit that sometimes I missed the old Russia.

Dear Adults Concealed in Children's Bodies:

It was during this writers' conference in Peterburg in 2000 that my Russophilia revived. It was as if I was awakening, fresh, from a long rest. It was like running into old friends and realizing how much you had missed them.

I had been to your city so many times – at least twenty in the past twenty years. It became hard to tell what was a scrambled remembrance of past events and what was a 'new' dream. Or, what had been real and what had been a dream.

Whatever. After decades of stagnation, or decades of my spirit being stifled and ignored and undernourished or unnourished at all, I was back in a place where I felt I needed to be. That was such a great and wonderful feeling, after a decade and a half of wondering where I should be and what I should be doing, and with whom.

I was not Russian. I never kidded myself, nor did I try to change my behavior or attempt to look 'Russian.'

There was one exception. One time I tried to smoke like a Russian. I practiced at home, on Laurel Avenue in 1988, after my book was published. I looked into a big mirror that hung over the fireplace, just to make sure I was doing it correctly. I held my cigarette between my left thumb and my first to left fingers. I burnt myself. It hurt for days. I learned my lesson.

Yet, even though I was not Russian and didn't try to look Russian and didn't want to be a Russian, something tugged at me. Something. In English, you say, "I am drawn to Russia," for instance. In Russian, you utter the phrase that perhaps is best translated as, "Something pulls me to Russia."

Well, that 'something' was still pulling at me, as it had been pulling for over thirty years.

I don't know what it is.

Dear Alex, Katya, Anna-

Isn't it coincidental that I 'met' your Mother in Peterburg, in a way. I had seen her sometimes at the law firm, where she worked part-time as a receptionist while attending cooking school. I was a Library Generalist then and I passed her many times during the work day because I drank a lot of coffee and because I had to pass her to get to the men's room. I don't think we ever spoke to one-another, not even a 'hello.' I knew her by face, but not by name. Her voice intrigued me – as a receptionist, she often had to page lawyers and staff.

Right before I left for Peterburg, Rebecca, a mutual friend, (whom you met, kids, at a picnic at Saint Paul's Como Park), recommended that I write your Mother, since she was bright and sharp and literate and quick-minded (all of which was true).

I sent your Mother an e-mail on the first day I was in Peterburg, I think, or soon thereafter. She wrote back. Soon we were writing one-another daily, and the messages got longer and longer and more personal, and, at least for me, more significant.

It was that chain of e-mails that pulled her and me together, I believe, such that a year later, we decided to hell with the age difference and what people said, we were going to become a couple.

All this started in your city, kids – a relationship between an American and another American who worked near one-another back in Minneapolis.

Imagine.

Dear Children:

Your city, Peterburg, wasn't doing all that well around 2000, the time of my writers' seminar and about the time that all of you all were born. It wasn't as if the fall of the Soviet Empire had brought a new gilded age for the city or had spiffed-up and returned the earlier gilded age, the way you pick up your once-dirty laundry, now sparkling and clean, at a dry cleaners.

There was work to be done, minds to be changed, policies to be updated.

This is about the time that your birth Father and Mother disappeared on you. Do not judge them harshly, do not hate them by any means. This was a difficult time for all in Russia.

Beggars were everywhere – old people with fixed pension incomes that could scarcely pay for one loaf of bread, and myriad others whom this particular 'revolution' had overlooked.

"Howsoever you treat the least of these…."

There was an old beggar who sat on the sidewalk near the side of the Cathedral of Our Lady of Kazan. He seemed about five feet tall. He had thick gray hair and a bushy moustache and reddish skin with nary a wrinkle (drunks are blessed with that), and he played a small accordion, poorly. He probably hadn't changed clothes since Gorbachev. He probably didn't have any other clothes.

I wondered where he lived, what he'd done in his life, where he was during the siege, when the Nazis had cut off Leningrad for 900 days. Did he live alone?

I gave him money whenever I passed. And why not? I stopped in a grocery store off Nevsky Prospekt a few days later, and I bought four giant bananas and a bag of Russian crackers. I gave them to the accordion player. It was a bargain for me (less than two dollars), but it was a good chunk of the accordionist's monthly pension, I bet. (Maybe my calculations are all wrong and I will be criticized for this.)

When I studied there in 1970, the crackers would have cost me about five dollars American. The bananas could not have been bought at any price. Same goes for any other fruit, during the long winters.

But what about all the other beggars who lined Nevsky? What about the gypsies with their multiple layers of drab clothing? "Ignore the gypsy boys!" one Russian university administrator said. "It is a pose."

But the Gypsy boys stole the camera and its case right off the shoulder of one of the workshop professors, at a crowded Nevsky intersection. The boys ran off at top speed, said the professor. Chase them? Try to apprehend them? Try to recover the camera and case? No way. The boys were gone, replaced by other boys, clearly innocent of this particular crime. The camera and case? No doubt they had passed rapidly down street after street, from one fast-fingered gypsy kid to another fast-fingered gypsy kid, never to be traced. Notifying the police would have done no good, I am sure.

In front of the Cathedral of Our Lady of Kazan, a heavy-set old woman in peasant clothes lay crouched on the pavement, head to the ground, heaving her body as if sobbing (you couldn't see her face). Her beggars' plate lay on the cracked pavement nearby. She rocked and heaved like that for hours on end, days at a time. A fake? Possibly.

But the guy in military fatigues with no legs, sitting in a rickety wheelchair -- was he a fake too? Or those missing legs -- was that Afghanistan? Or an industrial accident?

There was a tall, thin man, about forty years old, who wore the simple black robe of a Russian Orthodox priest. He stood erect, with head bowed, holding a small brass plate for coins, at the Kazan Cathedral's entrance. The script of the beggars' plea on a small card hanging from his neck had a curious Church Slavonic look to it, even though it was in contemporary Russian. Was he really a priest or monk or deacon or whatever? Did he have any connection with the cathedral in front of which he stood? How did he manage to groom his beard so well? Perhaps he imitated photos of Rasputin. What a strange, yet fitting and gentile bow he perpetually made. Was he a beggar or a real priest? I don't know, but I suspect that he was a creative beggar.

Was there a business to begging? Who got the choice spots? Which poses worked the best? Using puppies and kittens must have been effective -- so many beggars used them. These beggars got the money.

What is there about people that they show more pity for animals than for people? What is there about me? Maybe it's knowing that although the crouching, heaving old lady might have been faking, and maybe the old guy with the accordion lived pretty well from his begging and his pension, the misery of those kittens in tiny boxes was real.

I hesitated to take pictures of people. Part of it was a holdover from Communist days. People hated having their pictures taken then. Some said it was because they were ashamed of their bodies, their shabby clothes, the living conditions that their faces and bodies and clothing revealed. Soviet citizens, drowning in Communist propaganda posters and slanted radio programs and anti-Western TV programs and newspapers and magazines? They knew that their standard of living was far lower than those in the West, and they knew that their bodies and clothes revealed all that, screamed out all that. Others said there was something Eastern about not taking pictures. Taking your picture steals your soul.

So, I have lots of photos of palaces and churches and vistas, but woefully few pictures of people. Next time, I want a giant telescoping camera lens, one that picks out people far away and makes it look as if they are nearby. That way, I could catch people, their natural selves, rather than poses But a telephoto lens sticking out like the neck of a crane? On which street would a Gypsy boy steal it?

Another reason for the Russian hatred of cameras? Lack of spontaneity, and loathing of it. In 1971, I asked a big, round-face woman selling oranges and potatoes if I could photograph her -- she looked so perfect, lording over her vegetable and fruit stand, inside the little park that runs behind the Admiralty Building. She agreed. But it took her a half hour to arrange her potatoes and turnips and carrots and herself, so that everything was 'just so' or 'tak nado' as they might say in Russian. The result was a photo so rigid and posed that it resembled a studio painting.

Spontaneity is not Russian. One evening during the 2000 writers' conference, I went with some of the young 'uns from the seminar at three in the morning to a bar where people dance naked or nearly so, day and night. (In Texas, they would call this 'nekked,' which is something nasty, whereas 'naked' is more matter-of-fact.)

The bodies of young Russian women (a great quantity of which I observed in the crowded nekked bar that night) did not appeal to me so much, I admit. I talked about this with the young American women in the bar.

"The Russian women are starving themselves to be thin," the American women concluded. "They don't exercise. There is no shape, no muscle to their backs or butts, no tone at all. Any bits of 'excess' flesh appear as unhealthy blobs here and there."

As for Russian men -- well, these American women would have advised you not to rush right over.

There was nothing spontaneous about that all-night dance bar. A woman with a grating voice and a scratchy mike went on for hours, commandeering the show. "If you are wearing a white shirt, raise your left hand. Pick a dancing partner who is wearing a black shirt. If you are wearing black, raise your left hand and then pick out a partner who is wearing white. The process went on forever. The Russians smiled at it all.

And the cheap plastic bandstand right across from Kazan Cathedral? It was the same way. The band played half a song, and then the DJ took over, with a voice sounding just like those you hear on any commercial radio station in the States. The sound system was almost too good, so unlike the scratchy amplifiers that the vendors used down the street to sell rides on canal boats. "Esteemed guests, avail yourselves of a rare opportunity to enjoy a cruise along Sankt Peterburg's enchanting waterways, and view the city's many wonders!" Those people with their cheap, old, scratchy microphones, called the city 'Sankt Peterburg,' with the <u>Sankt</u> part included, it seemed, only when people, like those sellers of boat ride tickets, were being pretentious.

I wanted to get a picture along the side of the Cathedral of Our Lady of Kazan. I wanted a photo of that old man and his accordion with its blotchy, chipped keys. Maybe I'd slip him fifty rubles and then sit next to him, telling him he had an interesting face that told many stories. Perhaps he'd warm up to me and then I'd hit him with the request. It would be like <u>buying</u> a photo from him, but not <u>really</u> buying it. Him. His moustache. His brown, stained sports coat, his wrinkled pants. His short legs stretched out ahead of him, on the pavement.

But, while I was thinking through all of this, a fat female tourist waddled towards him with a camera at her face. I saw the horror in the old man's face. He sprung up, much faster than I would have thought he could, and he hobbled over to a parked taxi, faster than I would have imagined. He jumped inside and the cab took off. I saw him light a cigarette and pass one to the driver.

I did not take his picture, but I will remember him, the pose he had created for himself, the pose that shielded the real 'him.' A brain can work like a camera, if you tell it to.

Down the street a little, I came across a cardboard box perched on a small rickety table. Inside lay a puppy with four kittens curled around it. At the back of the box, wedged against the wall of a pharmacy, lay another motionless puppy and two motionless kittens who lay on the puppy's back. Why were the kittens not playful? Were they merely drowsy? Were they so accustomed to the passing crowds that they didn't care? No. Their eyes were watery. They were sick, as were the puppies. The box seemed unattended.

But nearby stood a rough-looking man with a blotchy face and a couple of bruises -- he'd been in fights, no doubt, or had fallen drunk, on the pavement. "Help give nourishment to God's little creatures!" said his placard. I bent down to the kittens. I saw the man move, waiting for me to reach for my wallet or coins.

A middle age Russian woman was there with her daughter or niece. "The kittens are not moving at all!" the woman remarked.

"They are probably sick," I said. "Look at their eyes."

The woman was almost crying, and the young girl looked on with horror. "Look at that man with them!" the woman said to me, shaking her head.

I wanted to take all those kittens home with me -- those and all the others down by the underpasses on Nevsky near Sadovaya, the tunnels that lead into the Metro. Maybe I should have stayed in Peterburg and started an organization for abused and abandoned animals.

I don't know whether I hated the man with the bruised face and the kittens, or whether I felt sorry for him. I think I felt both. Where did those kittens come from? Did these people breed them, or buy them, or did the people prowl the city's courtyards, snatching them from their feral mothers, the way flower vendors pick flowers for their stalls?

In those days, Peterburg was nowhere, nothing, everything. It was neither East nor West, neither North nor South, but all of them. I listened to a talk by Cultural Historian David Epstein. He told us that the problem with Saint Peterburg is that it's a city with a southern mentality that refuses to believe it is in the north.

I thought back over my thirty years. Yes, I loved that city, and I hated that city. Truly, I had Russophilia.

Dear Alex, Katya, and Anna:

On my last day in Peterburg, after the seminar concluded, I decided to make a lone, farewell stroll through the city. I was over fifty, after all, and I was involved in a career having nothing to do with Russian. What chance was there that I'd ever return to this city that I had known for so long? I realized that I needed to give this beautiful, captivating city an adequate farewell, the way you say good-bye to a lover, with a mixture of sadness and relief – a person with whom you pretend you are close and will remain in contact and always be friends, supporting one-another through hard times, but knowing you'll never see him or her again.

I walked my personal pilgrimage, all the way from the Alexander Nevsky Monastery to the tip of Vasilievsky Island, and then back to Herzen Pedagogical University, a short block or two behind the Kazan Cathedral. It was a heck of a walk, one that few make, I bet -- either Russian or Foreigners. My zigzag trip took the entire day.

I visited Dostoevsky's grave and worked with some confused Russians who were trying to figure out the Old Church Slavonic script on his headstone. One student in the crowd had a Russian dictionary, and so we sounded out, and eventually discovered, the writing etched into Dostoevsky's gravestone.

I stopped in the stores where I used to shop, when they were empty with goods but crammed with people, and then when they were full of goods but empty of people.

I visited the 'secret locations' where in the 1970s, we had exchanged literature and poetry back and forth between countries, with the KGB no doubt watching every move. Maybe it was the man waiting for a bus, maybe the woman walking from gravestone to gravestone.

I crossed over arching bridges and I came to the building where Natalya and her parents and her grandmother had lived. Where were they now? Where was she now? What had happened to me, to us, to them, that such youthful dreams and fantasies would die because living could not sustain them? Natalya's building was now a government office, void of apartments. I spotted through the window sparkling floors and painted walls. It all used to be dark and drab. What was it about me that I missed the dark and the drab?

I wondered if some agency of the government shunted Natalya and her parents out to one of the formless suburban concrete fortresses that, in true Russian fashion, looked like they were under construction as well as falling apart from age and neglect – all at the same time, and possible only in Russia. Natalya and her family had felt rooted in the old city, and they didn't at all like the blocks of new, tall apartment buildings sprouting up in the environs. Maybe they were living out there then, in 2000. Would a visit to Natalya in any way harm her or the life that she then led? I don't know, didn't find out, wouldn't know how to find out, even if I had wanted to.

I needed to fence in my sadness – let's stick to visiting places, not people, and saying farewell to those places, being the shells that once held me and those whom I had known there. I don't believe I could have withstood the sadness that would fill me if I had visited people from my past. I touched many of the places when I stopped – a piece of dirt, part of a full-grown linden tree, the stones at the entrance of a former apartment building.

As we get older, I think, that big part of the heart that once burned with passion becomes a giant repository for sadness, longing, and regret.

I walked lengthwise through the middle of Vasilievsky Island, almost to its end, passing pharmacies whose empty shelves thirty years ago had nothing that I or anyone else needed, for relief from bed bug bites or from other, more serious maladies.

I walked to my old dorm from the 1970's, out towards the far end of the island, very near the Gulf of Finland. Our four-person cells were now sensible two-person dormitory rooms for graduate students from the former Soviet republics. I talked with a few of the residents as we sat on a bench near the building entrance. One of the males was filleting a big smoked fish, most of which was shrouded by newspaper pages.

Another male was writing his thesis on international law, in English. He asked me to read his paper. He brought down a stack of onion skin paper, the kind I hadn't seen in decades, and I read his paper while he looked on, as if trying to read my expressions. The paper was nearly perfect, except that he had confused 'per se' with 'pro se.'

Lucky for him, the error was at the end of a short paragraph that stood on a page all its own. He wouldn't have to re-type much at all.

He and the others invited me to dinner, but I knew it would turn into an all-night affair with much reminiscing and drinking and hugging and toasting one-another and our countries and peace among all peoples and nations. I declined, as delicately as I could. It is not good manners in that city, in that country, to decline anything offered.

As I turned to walk away from the dormitory, I realized how long it had been since that 1970 exchange program. Tall linden trees nearly filled the courtyard. They had been scraggly twigs, with hardly a chance of survival, when I had seen them each morning, thirty years earlier.

The oddest thing? Guess what, kids?

I had misread my plane ticket. I had arranged my trip so that I would fly out on Friday, right after the seminar's concluding ceremony, like so many other seminar people.

But I didn't remember that, and I didn't think to double-check my return ticket. I thought I was heading out on Sunday. Well, I was supposed to fly out that Friday.

So, then, it was as if that extra day, that Saturday, that pilgrimage day, was a gift.

A foreigner in Russia with an expired visa?

I knew I was done for. The customs people or the border guards would haul me away. Maybe they had a prison where you could work your way out. And even if no one hauled me off, how could I come up with the money to purchase airline tickets? It would cost about $3,000, no doubt, because one-way tickets are far more expensive than tourist round-trip tickets, since I had missed the flights for which my old tickets would have worked.

Surely, that extra day was meant to be.

Guess what? Well, guess what?

I went out to the airport Sunday morning. I had to lug my luggage up a long flight of stairs to get to the Northwest Airlines office. My suitcases and bags were weighted down with books – I don't know how I made it up that stairway, but I certainly owe several thank-you's to the doctors who diagnosed me, and the surgeon who did my heart surgery seven years earlier.

Guess what?

I managed to catch each identical flight for which I'd been booked on Friday – every one of them, even on a Sunday, and there were four. Incredible.

Perhaps I was meant to take that day of contemplation for myself. Perhaps I needed to see, and process, the inscription on Dostoevsky's headstone, a biblical quotation that Dostoevsky had chosen as the epigraph of his The Brothers Karamazov:

> Amen, Amen, I say unto you, except a kernel of wheat fall onto the ground and die, it abideth alone: but if it die, it bringeth forth much fruit.

That 2000 visit was my last. I was done with Saint Peterburg, I had concluded everything. We were now, by my proclamation, fully separated. I was all finished up with that enchanted, bedeviled place that had hounded me, beckoned to me, loved me, hated me, sung to me, screamed at me.

I was done with all of it.

But the city was not done with me.

My Dearest Children -

1999 – 2002: those were the years when you three were born.

Four years after my 'very last' visit to Peterburg, I went back two times, to get you three kids.

All my interest in things Russian? All my visits to the country in general and to your city in particular? All of them led me to you three kids, living in that white, two-story Peterburg orphanage, far from the city's center.

Dear Anna, Katya, Alex:

Are your Peterburg memories still there, somewhere deep inside you? Will you ever regain that which you lost? Try to bring them up to the sun and daylight, just like the way we dug up stones for our walkways, remember?

Discover the breadth and depth of Russian culture and of your city's culture and history. Please. You are Russians; you must. You are from Peterburg. You must.

I am losing my memory, as do many old people, and in this case, there is no reason for optimism. Powers of memory do not return for old people. Part of it is from aging, to be sure. Why shouldn't the brain have the same right to stop working so hard and so well? Bladders and bowels and hearts have such rights.

My memory may get worse, but I will never forget the details of your adoption, and of your childhood years spent in this country, with me.

Me? I will need to find a job when I reach age sixty-five and my disability insurance runs out. If I worked at anything before that date, the insurance company would merely take my money and subtract it from their monthly payments. I am no dummy. I am taking advantage of this two-year hiatus. I spend a large part of it with you three children.

When I reach age sixty-six and the insurance checks stop showing up in my checking account, then I will probably sell the house on wheels and the Honda Civic that remains faithful it its dotage. I will have filed bankruptcy, and I will give back to the bank the Ford conversion van that you kids love because of its captains' chairs and the comfortably-dim inside running lights.

We had a good time with it, but now it's time to part. After all, parting is a part of living, isn't it?

Lulu the dachshund will have joined Gretel in heaven by then, as will have Vivie, the cat, who saw me through two marriages and the ending of both.

The doctors are keeping an eye on the spots that line the balloon around my lungs. I remain hopeful. I need to be around for you.

I don't know what will happen. But, hell, I made it this far, right? Or how far have I gone, actually? I was born poor, when my parents had filed for bankruptcy. What do they say about apples and trees?

I am not being maudlin, but realistic. I have cardiac graphs that are now seventeen years old. I have a breathing problem that taxes my heart. I have legs that swell, and I am out of breath much of the time.

I, the agnostic, keep dropping religious terms. Is it just that they are so much a part of our culture and lie deep under its surface?

May God give you that which you need.

Dear Katya, Anna, Alex –

We use a fluorescent shop lamp for our main lighting in the living room. Last night, I needed to change a bulb, those fragile, four-foot long, glistening white tubes just begging boys to bust them.

I stood on a mattress to do it. I could have moved the mattress first, but that would have taken hours, right? Our living room is packed. Two mattresses on the floor make up our communal bed, although Anna, getting older, sleeps next to us on the sofa. Six bookcases and the TV shelf and a wire kennel and a recliner crowd the mobile home living room.

So there was no question of moving the mattresses. I would take my chances.

I lost.

I fell sideways, into one of the wooden book cases that I had made. I split one of the shelves.

I did not fall 'all the way down,' and I didn't want to express any pain. Still, the three of you were crying, and Katya, with her red face, was screaming.

I joked about my falling, offering to do it again, for a fee. You laughed, but there was something contrived about your laughter.

I have since fallen a number of times, in front of the children.

I laugh. You laugh, but it doesn't hide the fear appearing in your eyes.

Funny, but Katya says she will not miss me when I die, just like she won't miss Lulu the dachshund. Katya has video tape of both of us.

Katya mentions my dying every now and then. The others act as if they are trying to get her to shut up.

Maybe all of you have prepared yourself for the future better than I.

Dearest Anna, Katya, and Alex –

When there is a divorce involving children, especially young children, everyone hears the same rule: 'Never, <u>ever</u> say anything negative about your ex-spouse when there is any chance at all that the children might learn of it.'

That means divorced people must be extremely careful of what they say and write. Today, extra care is needed. There are no expiration dates on the web. If they write something in an e-mail or in Facebook or Twitter or other web sites, what they wrote might be floating out there, in the cosmos, forever.

Your Mother and I follow the rule. So do our families. My Sisters do not walk up to Anna, for example, and tell her that her Mother is a terrible person. Your Grandmother doesn't tell you that I am a terrible person.

No one benefits from doing such things.

Each of you children, at one time or another, has said something that shows you feel responsible for the divorce. This is not at all true, not in the least bit. The seeds were planted before we adopted you.

And, you all have asked me, at one time or another, why I live in an old, broken-down trailer and why I drive an old, broken-down car that I painted with a can of paint and a paint brush.

I believe I can explain some of this money stuff, without breaking the rule of not saying anything negative about your Mother or her family. And, my telling you this will help you understand that you are in <u>no</u> way responsible for the divorce.

Please remember that memory is a bad historian. Remember too that everyone has a life story in which they are the hero. So what I write will be different from what your Mother writes, and what she writes will not necessarily be what your Grandfather or Grandmother might write, and the same goes for all your aunts and uncles.

In my story, there are no villains. If we needed one, I would choose Wisconsin's community property laws and rules (but I really don't feel that they are villains either).

So let's talk about things in general terms. They might pertain to many people, not just to your Mother and me.

Imagine a married couple, Cindy and Robert, who live in Racine, Wisconsin. Robert tells Cindy that he wants to buy a Ferrari.

"You're crazy!" says Cindy. "In no way will you buy a Ferrari."

But Robert sneaks out to a dealership and he buys a Ferrari anyway, getting the bank to finance him so that he must make a monthly payment to the bank.

Cindy doesn't know a thing about any of this. She doesn't know that Robert bought a Ferrari after she told him not to. She somehow doesn't know that he's making monthly payments for the car.

Divorce time in Wisconsin?

Cindy is responsible for <u>one-half</u> of the debt on the Ferrari, a car that she didn't want him to buy, that she didn't know he had bought it and had financed it. Tough luck, Cindy. Hand over the money.

Okay, let's look at George and Martha, who live in Milwaukee, Wisconsin. Imagine that they bought a beautiful house in a very good neighborhood, but that buying the house left them really strapped for cash.

"I want an addition to the house," says Martha. "I want a new kitchen and a sitting room downstairs, and I want a master bedroom and a bath upstairs."

"That would be very nice," says George. "But we just bought this house. We can't afford an addition."

"Don't worry about it!" says Martha. "I'll get the money from my Father. He's rich. He knows I'll pay him back, a little each month. It's no concern of yours."

Divorce time?

Well, that new kitchen and sitting room and master bedroom and bath? It is a <u>big</u> concern for George.

Martha's Father sends George invoices for half of all the work that was done on the house.

So what do I do about such a situation? I laugh. What else can you do?

I get philosophical. Nature loves symmetry, right? If you see a butterfly whose right wing is about an inch long and whose left wing is about eight inches long? That's an accident of nature, or else perhaps it's the result of people tampering with nature (pesticides, fertilizer, etc.).

A frog with one right leg and two left legs? Again, an accident of nature, or else perhaps it's the result of people tampering with nature (pesticides, fertilizer, etc.).

Symmetry? When I was born, my parents were poor. They lived in a tiny basement apartment, and they took care of the building so that they could get a reduction in rent. They filed for bankruptcy.

Symmetry? I am poor. I live in an old trailer. I filed for bankruptcy.

Nature has a sense of humor. Nature likes irony. So do I. Nikolai Gogol called it 'laughter though invisible tears,' a saying worth considering.

Anna! Katya! Alex!

Hold my hand, and let us together walk to the heart of the heart of the heart of this matter and many other matters already experienced or to be experienced.

I am publishing this book, and I will work hard so that it will sell sell sell. The more copies, the better. A hundred copies. Five hundred copies. A thousand copies. I hope more.

Why?

Some will surely say that I am exploiting my children for my own gain.

Okay.

What gain?

Money? I would have to sell a couple thousand copies just to get enough money to put new siding and a bit of insulation on my trailer, not to mention repairing the wood rot that is working hard to convert this fairly big trailer into two smaller trailers, each rolling in an opposite direction.

What is the average shelf life of a mid-list book these days?

Fame? Why do I need fame? I'm not looking for a better job (or any job at all). I'm not looking for advancement. I believe adulation might soon become tedious, odious, and it no doubt would hinder my writing or at least take up hours that I could have spent writing. (I have four books in me that I must finish, and I go out of my way to buy green bananas.)

So why sell sell sell?

If I publish this and make a few copies and give it to you three children and to a couple of friends or relatives, that would be nice, and at various times during your lives you might actually pick up the book and look over a section or two and remember a bit of how things were when you were young and when you had a father, and you might smile and reminisce.

So why sell more copies?

Selling many copies serves as powerful validation and affirmation for each of you.

"Papa, do you really think someone would want to read about us?" You asked me that so many times, as we discussed earlier, and the answer is always the same: "You can be sure a lot of people would love to read about you." Or, as they say in some parts of Minnesota, 'You betcha!'"

But there is more, kids. It's difficult to articulate and some readers will glide over it without digging down into it.

That's fine.

You are three wonderful American kids. When not with me in my run-down trailer in this 'community,' you dwell in an upwardly mobile, upper middle class chunk of affluent Western Wisconsin, the cheese state. You fit in well. You are already masters of achievement of many things in that environment. No one would know you were adopted, or that you were born in Russia, in the captivating city that lets no one's memory forget.

Only a linguist would be capable of discerning traces of your Russian language.

But things are often not as easy as they first appear.

Behind each of you, or, rather, inside each of you, three characters stand, wondering if and when they will be acknowledged, when they can breathe fresh air, when they can see day and night.

Who?

These are your Russian selves.

Where are they now?

When will they come out?

I don't know, but I know some other things.

A person cannot live well after blocking out the first years of their lives. Anna, for you, this is over four years. For Katya, it is two years or so. For Alex, one or two years or so.

But these first years are absolutely critical. That's when each of you became a 'you.'

Some experts believe that personalities are formed while a child is still in the womb. All experts, I am sure, would agree that the first year or the first two years or for sure the first four years are seminal years in the formation of character and personality.

When a person blocks out years like that, it's often related, they say, to a thing called 'trauma.'

In your cases, perhaps you consciously chucked your Russian language, your Russian memories, your Russian selves, just so that you could adapt to life here more quickly, more fully. Maybe that is the reason for your grand successes that make everyone, especially me, so proud.

Fine.

But sometime, and who knows when, but sometime, each of you will be working to synthesize yourself, to make decisions about who you are and why you are you and what you will do.

You haven't finished off a giant jigsaw puzzle if you are left with a stack of pieces that don't seem to want to fit anywhere.

Some people ignore parts of their lives, and they shut down their memories. Perhaps they are burying a few traumatic events. They never work on it or through it. They get no help and ask for no help.

Sadly, so often these people end up in lousy relationships, or addicted to drugs, or caught in the jaws of any number of disorders, perhaps starving their bodies as if doing so will starve out the part they don't want to face. Or cutting, that act so symbolic and becoming so commonplace -- When a person feels they are boiling over with pain or gut-wrenching feelings and must create some kind of emergency relief valve that may be hardly bigger than a small slit on the forearm. Or mutilating yourself (a thing apart from cutting), running from something, hiding from something, punishing yourself for whatever it was you are holding down, whatever it is that demands so much of you, thereby sapping your energy and leaving little of you to do anything else or even to be you.

So, please, get to know those Russian people in you. Greet them. Talk with them. Show them around a bit. Introduce them to other people. Encourage them. Nurture them.

Find your roots, kids. Live through the pain so you can leave it behind, the way animals molt and leave an empty shell.

I don't mean that you must spend numberless hours talking to a shrink or hitting pillows with spongy bats or listening while a circle of hurt people whine their hurts and then everyone begins comparing – 'My pain is bigger than your pain!' 'No way! Your pain is like a little dot, and mine is the whole world.'

There are rewards for all of this work. Having a sense of self is not a bad thing at all. Going back to your 'roots' and re-learning your first language and examining your glorious country and your astoundingly important and graceful, pretentious and understated city of your birth – you will appreciate things that are wondrous and that are part of you.

I have taught college students and graduate students and law students. In those places, I have seen students struggling with their pasts, if they have been adopted or if they came here when young. They want, they need that part of their 'selves' that seems missing but is really there, hiding, that critical part about their first years in a different country, that part they have tried to snuff out, but it came out, enraged, all on its own.

I have seen students who come to resent their adoptive parents. 'Why did they take me away from the place where I was born, from the place where I belonged? What have you taken from me?'

Those questions linger, even as those students love their adoptive parents and appreciate all they have done for them, including, perhaps, taking them away, sheltering them from chaos or war or rebellion or the abrupt, painful shifting of courses that countries can take.

That's where I hope this book will come in. I don't know how old any of you will be when you first start this job of integrating, but I fear I won't be around.

So, selling this book?

The number of copies sold proves to you the importance of your mission. People will find out your real names when you let them know, and then they will acknowledge your Russianness, which in itself will induce you to find more things to acknowledge concerning your Russianness. It is hoped that Russian or 'almost Russian' readers of this book will serve as your guides, replacing what your Father would have done if he was still alive and trying to do a good job of it.

For such work, sometimes painful, you will be richly blessed. Not only will you end up with a whole and integrated person, you will now flow in a Russian river of beauty and meaning and substance and soul.

Damn. As un-religious as I am, I nonetheless find myself returning to the inscription on Dostoevsky's tomb:

> Amen, Amen, I say unto you, except a kernel of wheat fall onto the ground and die, it abideth alone: but if it die, it bringeth forth much fruit.

I am so happy for you -- envious actually -- that you are Russians.

Dearest Anna, Katya, and Alex:

It is time to finish off this massive tome and go 'off-line.' Or 'Cut!' as they say when they stop filming a scene for a movie.

This is not the kind of book that you are supposed to read from cover-to-cover, in order. Consider it more of a reference book. I wish I could make an index. I have a friend who is a master-indexer. She knows who she is and who I mean.

Look at things this way. Your Mother is in her early thirties now. She will be around for a very long time to answer your questions about her and her family, her early years, about your time in Russia, which are your early years, and about your adoption – all of it in bits and pieces, as she thinks best, and as you ask.

I will not have that chance to sit around you or walk with you and give you my memories of things, or to tell you things about myself that you probably would want to know then, when you are older, have grown more.

Instead I have written you these letters.

I hope I haven't left too many things out, or that I haven't written too much. Are there 'too many notes,' the words that Mozart heard, in 'Amadeus?'

The divorce is another matter. I did not write about it much here, even though it was a big event in your young lives, as well as in mine. I don't believe your Mother has discussed it with you either.

But you have an absolute right to know, when you are mature enough to process it. I am sure Your Mother will talk to you about it. I may not be alive then, so I will have written my version of things, and you will receive it, if and when the time is right, even if it's after I'm gone.

Your Mother's story about the divorce will do doubt vary from mine, but it will be equally as valid. Remember, when listening to your Mother talk about the divorce, or when reading my thoughts about the divorce – Memory is not a good historian.

Not my memory. Not your Mother's memory. Not your own memories even.

You will have to puzzle things out on your own. Such is the way, I think, whenever you children, or any children, try to discern the motives of their parents or try to remember events from their own early years.

When you read or hear about the details of the divorce, do not expect to encounter bombs, unexploded mines, grenades, guided missiles, explosions, earthquakes, bolts of lightning, or thunder claps that rattle your souls. The reason I don't write about it now is quite the opposite. The reasons behind the divorce are complex, and the nuances are subtle.

My Dearest Katya -

I remember one day after the separation, when I came by to pick up some of my things at your Mother's house.

You were standing at the top of the stairs, crying. "When will this divorce be over?" you asked.

Poor, poor kid. You had heard people talking about 'getting through the divorce,' or 'finishing up with the divorce.'

To you that meant one thing: Once the divorce was 'over,' I'd come back to live with you and your Mother, all the time.

Leaving you kids was the hardest thing I've done.

I can't read or proof-read or edit this letter, and other letters too, without my hands starting to shake.